ICELANDIC FOOD AND COOKERY

ICELANDIC FOOD AND COOKERY

Nanna Rögnvaldardóttir

HIPPOCRENE BOOKS
NEW YORK

Photographs by Brynjólfur Jónsson.

Book and jacket design by Acme Klong Design, Inc.

For more information, address:
HIPPOCRENE BOOKS, INC.
171 Madison Avenue
New York, NY 10016

ISBN 0-7818-0878-2
Cataloging-in-Publication Data available from the Library of Congress.
Printed in the United States of America.

For Jón Karlsson, who made a writer out of me,
and Alan Davidson, whose work inspired me to begin writing about food,
and who gave me the idea for this book.

CONTENTS

Foreword ix

A Short History of Icelandic Food and Cooking 1

Festive Food Traditions 9

Icelandic Ingredients. 17

Recipes. 27

Soups. 29

Starters, Spreads, and Dips 43

Fish and Shellfish Dishes 63

Meat Dishes 95

Game Birds. 117

Vegetables and Salads 127

Desserts 139

Cakes, Pastries, and Cookies 159

Breads 199

A Few Old Recipes. 213

Index 229

Icelandic Index. 239

FOREWORD

I grew up on a remote farm in northern Iceland in the 1960s. Icelandic society has changed so much since then that sometimes it seems to me this must have been the 1860s, not least in culinary matters. The food of my childhood was partly the old traditional Icelandic food, salted, smoked, whey-preserved, dried, and partly the Danish-influenced cuisine of the home academy my mother attended—heavy sauces, roasts, endless porridges, puddings, and soups.

Things were much simpler then. Apples were red by definition, haddock was almost the only fish worth eating, and a meal was not complete unless it included potatoes, invariably boiled. The spice drawer contained ground pepper and curry powder for savory dishes, cinnamon and cloves for sweet dishes and cakes, and not much else.

Electricity had not yet arrived but there was a huge coal stove in one corner of the kitchen. At least it looked huge to me, but the kitchen now seems very small, so it probably wasn't. And there was no refrigerator but a couple of barrels, filled with fermented whey, stood in the larder and the icy, tangy liquid drawn from them was the most refreshing drink imaginable on a hot summer day, when the sheep were being sheared.

Today's young Icelandic chefs win awards in international culinary competitions and can master any cooking trend and technique that comes their way. The shops are full of exotic ingredients and apples and oranges are no longer the only fruit, as I discovered when I tasted my first banana at the age of seven. But that is not what this book is about.

It is about the food I grew up on, the food Icelanders think about when they get a bit nostalgic, the food our mothers and grandmothers cooked. It is also partly about the food that has been slowly replacing it, as more vegetables, fruits, and spices gain a permanent place in the Icelandic kitchen. And it is about food traditions and the love of food.

Nanna Rögnvaldardóttir

A SHORT HISTORY OF ICELANDIC FOOD AND COOKING

For the contents of the first half of this summary, and for some of the historical information in other sections of the book, I'm heavily indebted to culinary historian Hallgerður Gísladóttir, head of the Department of Ethnology at the National Museum of Iceland, and her groundbreaking work *Íslensk matarhefð* (The Icelandic Culinary Tradition). Another valuable source is *Saga daganna* (High Days and Holidays) by Árni Björnsson, a well-known authority on Icelandic folklore and traditions. An abridged version of his book is available in English.

What Did the Settlers Eat?

Most of what can be said about the diet of the people who came to Iceland in the Settlement period (AD 874–930) is guesswork. There are no written documents dating from that period, no cookbooks, no traveler's descriptions, and no trade accounts. What we have is the evidence of the sagas, written centuries later and not really all that concerned with culinary matters, and some scant archaeological evidence.

Until very recently, it has been assumed that the great majority of the settlers came directly from Norway and other Scandinavian countries to Iceland and carried with them pure Norse customs and culture—including foodways. New genetic research has turned up some startling results: Although most of the men came from Scandinavia, it seems that a majority of the women who settled Iceland actually came from the British Isles. Either the Vikings who later came to Iceland settled for some time in Ireland and Scotland and married local women, or they raided the shores on their way to the new country in the west and took the women as slaves.

One might perhaps expect this to be evident in some way in the cooking, which was almost always women's work, but it isn't really so. The clearest evidence of Celtic influence in Icelandic cooking is probably the use of dulse (a seaweed), which seems to have begun during the Settlement period, at least in some regions. Dulse was frequently eaten in Ireland but almost unknown as a food in Norway.

That does not mean the first generations of Icelanders ate exactly the same food as their ancestors had done in Norway. The settlers needed to make some changes to their diet as soon as they arrived. They found a virgin country with rivers full of fish and with birds that had never had reason to fear human enemies, but no large game animals. No fruit-bearings trees grew there; no edible nuts, almonds, or acorns were to be found; there were only a few types of wild berries.

Barley could be grown after land had been cleared but the growing season was short and hazardous and yield was often low. Iceland was never self-sufficient as a grain producer, not even before the cold period that began in the fourteenth century. During the early part of the "Little Ice Age," as that period has been called, home-grown grain disappeared almost completely.

Even when grain was grown, it was probably used less for bread than for porridges, which were considered more economical to make. But bread was certainly not unknown; it is often mentioned in the sagas and in other contemporary sources and seems to have been more of an everyday food than it became later on.

Another thing that greatly affected Icelandic cooking was the lack of salt. This may seem surprising, considering that Iceland is surrounded by saltwater. Other maritime nations usually do not have trouble harvesting salt from the sea, either by natural evaporation or, in colder climates, by boiling seawater until only the salt crystals remain. This was done in Norway, where lack of salt rarely was a problem, and the settlers were initially able to use this method, but lack of firewood soon became a problem. A lot of fuel is needed for salt processing and the sparse Icelandic forests were soon overexploited, as demand for wood for cooking, heating, and other things was great. After a few centuries, Iceland could be considered a deforested country.

This lack of salt was probably felt very early on and Icelanders were forced to change their methods for preserving their food for winter. Almost all slaughtering was done in the autumn, as hay and other feed was expensive and it wasn't economical to feed animals that were going to be slaughtered anyway. The climate wasn't really suitable for air-drying meat, although fish was usually dried. Instead, the meat was smoked.

Preserving food by pickling in fermented whey was known in Norway in earlier times but never widely used there, as Norwegians used salt instead. In Iceland, whey preservation became common early on. Much of the cow's and ewe's summer milk was made into *skyr*, a soft cheese product, and huge amounts of whey accumulated as a by-product. The whey quickly fermented and the acidic liquid that resulted, called *sýra* in Icelandic, not only preserved food and its nutrients remarkably well, it even adds to the nutritional value of it, since vitamins from the whey seeped into the preserved food. It also tenderized and softened the meat and gradually dissolved bones. Fish and cattle bones were sometimes kept in the fermented whey until they softened and then they were boiled and eaten, although they seem to have been rather unpopular.

Food that is to be preserved, for example blood puddings, liver sausages, fatty meat, sheep's head and headcheese, whale blubber, seal flippers, etc., is usually boiled and cooled, then placed in barrels and submerged in fermented whey. It will keep for many months in this manner and will gradually acquire a more sour taste. It is sometimes said that all food will eventually taste the same if it is kept in whey for long enough and there is some truth in that.

The settlers brought livestock with them—sheep, cattle, pigs, horses, and goats, as well as chicken and geese, and maybe ducks as well. They probably tried at first to let the animals run wild and forage food in the woods but soon discovered how severe the Icelandic winters can be. Hay and other feed had to be provided. Beef was probably far more common during the first centuries of Iceland's history than later on, when the cattle were almost exclusively used for dairy production. Whale meat and blubber was eaten whenever available and a large whale stranded on the shore could provide meat for the whole surrounding region for a long time. Seals were hunted for their meat and hides.

Salmon, trout, and char was fished in the rivers and lakes from the earliest times and the rich fishing grounds close to the shore were utilized. The fishing boats were small, open rowing boats, never larger ships.

The Middle Ages and Onward

We do know a little more about food in the late Middle Ages from written sources: the sagas, law texts, and various documents. But these old authors were not writing about food or about cooking, which was usually a woman's job and not very noteworthy. If cooking is mentioned at all, it is usually as background, and rather vague; it may be mentioned that the women are in the kitchen cooking porridge, which is then served to the men, but there is no description of the porridge, or how it is served. And while a law text may mention the picking of berries, there is nothing to tell us how the berries were used.

There is one surviving fifteenth century cookbook manuscript written in Icelandic, but it isn't Icelandic in origin. This is a small manuscript, part of an old medical miscellany, translated into Icelandic from a Danish manuscript but probably Provençal by origin. It has recipes for sauces, dips, oils, desserts, and chicken dishes. Although some of the recipes may have been used in Iceland—after all, someone took the trouble to translate the manuscript—the recipes clearly cannot be used as examples of Icelandic Middle Age cuisine. So the oldest surviving Icelandic recipes really date from the eighteenth century.

As mentioned earlier, grain was never easy to grow in Iceland and its cultivation gradually disappeared in the late Middle Ages. From then on, all grain had to be imported and consequently became expensive. Most of the imported grain was used for porridges and soups. And what was imported was not whole grain but flour. It was not until the eighteenth century that Icelanders began to build small watermills and make their own querns. This meant that they got better-quality flour than when Danish monopoly merchants could ship any flour they could buy cheaply to Iceland.

Well-off people baked bread but the majority of Icelanders rarely made or ate bread; instead they would eat dried fish spread with butter or other fat. This would often amaze European travelers, who were used to bread being the "staff of life" and the mainstay of the diet of the poor. And the bread that was made was usually thin, unleavened flatbread, made from rye or barley. Due to lack of firewood, ovens were virtually unknown, except in a few very wealthy households, and there was no professional baker in the whole of the island until the early nineteenth century.

Iceland moss (a type of lichen) was frequently used to stretch the flour further. This may have been done from the earliest times, since these lichens grow in Norway and have been used there in a similar manner, although not to the extent that they were used in Iceland. The use of Iceland moss seems to have increased gradually, as grain cultivation diminished. In the vast wilderness of the north and northeast, the lichens grew in abundance, and groups of people would go into the mountains to gather them, sometimes sleeping in tents for a week or more, and return with dozens of large sacks stuffed full of their pickings. Another local plant that was often added to bread was dulse, which was gathered at low ebb in late August, especially in western and south-western Iceland.

Dried fish played an extremely important part in the diet. It was on the menu daily and replaced bread in some ways. It was dried completely, then beaten thoroughly to soften it, and eaten with butter or other fat, such as fish oil. Even the fish heads were dried and every edible scrap was consumed. In Icelandic, 109 different names are known for the various muscles in a single cod's head, and there are 156 names for bones and cartilage.

Fresh meat was usually only on the menu for a few weeks in the autumn, although well-off people sometimes slaughtered a lamb or gelded ram for Christmas and other special occasions. Almost all meat and offal was smoked or preserved in whey. In a cold, harsh climate, people need a lot of calories to survive, so fatty meat and pure fat were highly prized. Rent was usually paid or at least calculated in butter and rich landlords, churches, and bishop seats accumulated huge butter mountains. This butter probably would not suit modern tastes; it was unsalted but was often kept for a long time, so it tended to go sour or rancid.

Some beer had been brewed in Iceland in earlier times but after barley cultivation disappeared in the late Middle Ages, the local beverage was *sýra*, fermented whey, which was collected in large barrels in kitchens and larders. It was said that two-year-old whey was fully developed. By then, it was so sour that it was usually diluted generously with water, sometimes one part *sýra* to eleven parts water.

Icelandic foodways probably did not change all that much until the late eighteenth century, when educated men, influenced by the Age of Enlightenment, began to try to teach their countrymen to grow vegetables, and use the food they already had in new ways. They did not meet with much success at first. Icelanders generally distrusted this newfangled food.

Danish Influences

Traditional Icelandic food—the food most people over forty grew up on—is to a very large extent influenced by Danish cooking. Iceland had been under Danish rule since the Middle Ages but it wasn't until the nineteenth century that this began to be reflected in the cooking to any great extent.

Most of the traditional Icelandic cake and cookie recipes came from Denmark, and so did a great many dishes that are now considered extremely Icelandic in character. Danish cookbooks were in used in Iceland during the nineteenth century and the earliest Icelandic cookbooks are largely translations and adaptations of Danish and Norwegian cookbooks and recipe collections. The first of these, *Einfalt matreiðsluvasakver fyrir heldri manna húsfreyjur* (A Simple Cooking Notebook for Gentlewomen), was published in 1800. The authorship of this small book is very unclear, with conflicting evidence put forward by a man who certainly did contribute to it, a president of the High Court of Iceland.

Whoever the author or authors were, they came from the uppermost layers of Icelandic society and the recipes in the book clearly reflect that. This is not what Icelandic housewives were cooking at the time. This is upper-class Scandinavian cooking, described to enable well-off Icelandic housewives to entertain their families and guests, although two versions of many dishes are presented—one for the upper class, one for the workers. However, this book never became widely known, or much used.

The next cookbook, which is a much more substantial work, was not published until 1858. Although large parts of it are more or less translated from Danish cookbooks of the time, there are many unquestionably Icelandic recipes in the book. The author, born in Copenhagen of an Icelandic father and Danish mother, spent her childhood in both countries, was probably educated in Denmark, but married an Icelander and lived first on a farm, and later in the town of Akureyri, so she had gained a wide experience which clearly comes through in her book.

The first truly Icelandic cookbook was Elín Briem´s *Kvennafræðarinn* (The Women's Educator), first published in 1889 and sold 3000 copies in the first year. It became the first Icelandic-language cookbook to gain wide distribution. It was reprinted three times and became very influential.

At the beginning of the 20th century, most Icelandic rural homes were still largely self-sufficient regarding food, even though grains, sugar, coffee, and a few luxuries had to be bought in the village store. This was also true of many town homes; even in Reykjavík many still kept cows, sheep, or hens in a shed in their backyard.

But this was also the time of great changes in Icelandic kitchens: The open fireplace was giving way to the cooking stove, which was considered such a wonderful device that it was named *eldavél* (cooking machine) in Icelandic. And the stoves had ovens for baking. This opened up a new world and Icelandic hospitality underwent a big change. Now visitors were no longer offered dishes heaped with smoked lamb, dried fish, and whey-preserved food. Instead, they got served mountains of cakes and other baked goods; yet this was only the beginning of the Icelandic cake deluge.

Ovens had been virtually unknown in Iceland up to this time, except in a few wealthy homes. Cookies and pastries had mostly been fried in fat—pancakes, crêpes, crullers, and other goodies. These early ovens were not easy to operate, lacking any thermostats of course, and it was an art to arrange the hot coals and other fuel so the cakes and cookies baked evenly. Sometimes they had to be turned several times while baking. Still, Icelandic housewives managed to churn out vanilla wreaths, crescents, spice cookies, cones, almond macaroons, and innumerable other cookies and cakes in these ovens. And let's not forget the *vínarterta*, served at all coffee parties at the turn of the century.

Most dishes were fairly bland; few spices were used and then sparingly. Often salt and pepper were the only flavorings, but some housewives had in their cupboards cinnamon, ginger, cloves, allspice, and bay leaves, and sometimes nutmeg, dried lemon peel, and vanilla extract; only the very brave ones had a jar of curry powder to add to their fricassee sauce—but did so very timidly. A traditional Icelandic curry is very mild indeed. Some recipes mention "soy," not oriental soy sauce, but gravy browning, a homemade or store-bought caramelized coloring for brown sauces.

Onions were imported but other vegetables used were those that could be grown in Iceland: Potatoes, rutabagas, turnips, kale, and a few others. Fresh fruit was rare, with the exception of berries and rhubarb (treated as fruit in Iceland). Porridges and puddings were very popular and for special occasions, a grand many-layered dessert like trifle was made by those who could afford it, or maybe a custard flavored with vanilla, rum, almonds, lemon peel, chocolate, coffee, or even canned pineapple.

During the 1920s and 1930s, increasing influence of home economists and cooking teachers at the homemaker's academies (the so-called "porridge schools") can be noted and the cookbooks of the Depression era put greater emphasis on varied everyday food than most earlier books had done.

The most influential cookbooks of the twentieth century are without question Jóninna Sigurðardóttir's book, first published in 1915 as *Matreiðslubók fyrir fátæka og ríka* (A Cookbook for Poor and Rich; the four subsequent editions were just called *Matreiðslubók*) and Helga Sigurðardóttir's *Matur og drykkur* (Food and Drink), first published in 1947 and still widely in use. Both these ladies had been educated in Denmark and their cooking is sound middle-class Danish cooking, with an Icelandic twist.

Helga Sigurðardóttir can safely be called the grand lady of Icelandic cooking. She wrote several popular cookbooks before she published *Matur og drykkur*, which soon became the Icelandic kitchen bible and remained in that position for decades. This is the epitome of Icelandic-Danish cooking, the comfort food modern-day Icelanders feel nostalgic about but rarely cook themselves; flour-thickened sauces, the Sunday roast leg of lamb, pork roast with cracklings, lemon mousse, prune compote, fish salad with mayonnaise sauce, meatballs in brown sauce with jam, and Danish apple charlotte.

Most meals had two courses; the main course and a substantial dessert. The main course was usually fish or meat, simply cooked and served with potatoes in some form. Potatoes were an integral part of each meal and to this day, many still refuse to consider a meal complete without them. On weekdays, the dessert was usually a porridge, milk pudding, or a soup of some kind.

Vegetables were a bit more varied than they had been earlier and cultivation was increasing. Cabbage and cauliflower largely replaced kale, and carrots replaced turnips. Tomatoes and cucumbers were grown in greenhouses heated with water from hot springs but were still rare. Fresh fruit—apples, oranges, and sometimes bananas and pears—were mostly seen at Christmastime.

Elaborate cream-filled layer cakes and tortes made an entrance in Icelandic coffee parties during the war. Besides whipped cream, these grand creations were often decorated with jam, buttercream, custard, almond paste, canned fruit, and candy.

Many Icelanders used to view vegetables primarily as a supplement, something to make the "real food" last longer, and when they could afford to buy their fill of meat and fish, they saw no reason to add greens, often called "cabbage food." By the 1940s variety increased; for instance *Matur og drykkur* has some recipes using both fresh and canned mushrooms. Other canned vegetables, like string beans and asparagus, were also available by then. The use of tomatoes was increasing and the Icelanders also discovered tomato ketchup and mustard.

There was little increase in the use of spices but still a few newcomers like paprika made their appearance. On the other hand, spices like cinnamon, cloves, and allspice had virtually disappeared from savory recipes even though they were still used for sweet dishes and cakes. Dried herbs were almost unknown and fresh herbs were rare, with the exception of parsley, chives, and dill.

The Food of Today

It was in the 1960s that Icelanders began to travel abroad, and cooking trends from foreign, but not exotic, countries became more evident. These were the "shrimp cocktail years" of the western world and Iceland was no exception. The omnipresent Icelandic "cocktail sauce" was invented in the early years of this decade, without doubt influenced by European shrimp cocktail sauces, but the Icelandic version enjoys a much more versatile role.

At home, the Sunday roast leg and rack of lamb still held the throne but breaded and pan-fried lamb and pork cutlets and lamb Wiener schnitzel decorated with herring, capers, and lemon were also popular treats. Some were even more daring and made roast beef or T-bone steak on feast days. Poached or pan-fried haddock was still the most common everyday food and any meat or fish that was pan-fried was usually covered with bread crumbs and fried in lots of margarine or butter. Meat was usually well done or overdone and fish and vegetables were often overcooked as well. Dishes made from ground meat became increasingly popular and one of the dishes of this decade was beef patties with fried egg and onions.

Icelanders were slowly learning to eat vegetable salads and the most common was coleslaw made from grated or shredded cabbage, grated carrots, and chopped apples, often with lots of mayonnaise dressing. A salad made from grated carrots and raisins was also very common and both were frequently enriched with crushed canned pineapple. Other accompaniments mostly stayed the same: boiled potatoes, sometimes glazed, and boiled vegetables—such as "ORA green beans" (named for their canning factory; actually marrowfat peas)—but rice and spaghetti were beginning to be seen, largely as additions to, not replacements for, the ubiquitous potatoes. Spaghetti was mostly served in a so-called "Italian sauce," usually a béchamel sauce with some tomato paste or ketchup added.

Trade restrictions were beginning to ease a little and some types of vegetables and fruits were available year-round. Desserts made from fresh and canned fruit partly replaced the dried fruit compotes, sweet fruit soups, and gelatin desserts of earlier decades.

The first pizza parlor was opened in 1969 but did not survive long. Just a few years later, most people were familiar with pizzas and some even knew how to make them. These early homemade pizzas were usually covered with a thick layer of fried ground meat, ketchup, canned mushrooms, pineapple chunks, and grated cheese. Hamburgers invaded the roadside shops. They were fried to death, often served with a pineapple slice and a fried egg, and almost always eaten with a knife and fork.

Various kinds of seafood and vegetable gratins gained popularity during the1970s and 1980s, partly due to the influence of the Icelandic Dairy Produce Marketing Association. New types of cheese were now being manufactured and the Association's experimental kitchen was constantly churning out colorful leaflets with recipes to introduce people to these new cheeses. Dishes that combine fish and cheese are more often seen in Iceland than in most other countries, probably due to the influence of these leaflets. Icelanders also learned to appreciate langoustines and shrimp, formerly regarded with horror, and a shrimp dip with Ritz crackers became obligatory party food. Scallops also gained popularity, along with many types of fish not formerly eaten, like monkfish and ocean perch.

An everyday meal no longer had to have at least two courses but starters and soups became increasingly common at dinner parties. Everyday desserts were slowly disappearing and Icelandic housewives gradually moved away from the baking frenzy of earlier years. At the same time, more and more types of bread became available in bakeries, and some people baked their own. An increasing awareness of nutrition and a healthy diet could be noted.

The Icelandic restaurant scene underwent dramatic changes in the 1980s and new restaurants mushroomed. People began to dine out without a special reason, which had been almost unknown, and they found many unfamiliar tastes to savor, as Italian, Chinese, American, and Indian restaurants emerged.

At the beginning of a new millennium, Icelandic cooking, not least restaurant cooking, has become increasingly international in character. More ingredients have become available in Icelandic shops and it has become easier to cook authentic foreign dishes and follow every modern culinary trend. But at the same time interest in Icelandic resources has been on the increase. Local game has been popularized and flash-fried guillemot and puffin breasts have appeared on restaurant menus, to the horror of many experienced housewives, who had been taught to cook the birds for not less than three hours. Many recipes mix traditional Icelandic ingredients and exotic vegetables, fruits, and spices.

Now almost any type of spice can be found in specialty shops in addition to all kinds of vinegars and oils, oriental fish sauces, Mexican hot sauces and salsas, and so on. As elsewhere in the western world, extra-virgin olive oil, balsamic vinegar, sun-dried tomatoes, pine nuts, and black olives are among the key ingredients in innumerable trendy recipes. And then there is the garlic. Icelanders began a love affair with garlic in the 1980s and now it is sometimes said that they are the greatest garlic importers in the world; Icelanders use more garlic per person than any other people who do not grow their own. Ginger and chili peppers have also soared in popularity, along with fresh herbs.

At home, lamb no longer reigns supreme and people now eat less haddock—and that means less fish, because other types of fish have not really managed to replace it in the Icelandic heart. Pasta has to some extent replaced haddock and potatoes as everyday food. However, many Icelandic pasta dishes are awash in heavy cream and cheese sauces and sometimes the pasta seems merely an addition. Cooked pasta or rice has also become a common side dish to all kinds of meat and fish dishes; and boiled potatoes are no longer regulatory.

Desserts are not often seen now except at dinner parties or on festive occasions, but coffee parties are still popular—and most Icelandic housewives are still able to muster their old cake-baking skills when needed.

Interest in cooking has been on the increase in recent years, even though people cook less at home and more ready-made food is available in stores. It has never been so easy to cook good food.

Many food customs and dishes are connected to certain holidays, although perhaps not as many as in other European countries. Some of these customs can be traced back in time hundreds of years, others are fairly recent, and some have ancient roots but have been resurrected or reconstructed in recent years.

New Year

Áramót

There are no special food customs connected to New Year's Eve *(gamlárskvöld)* or New Year's Day *(nýársdagur)* in Iceland, although the New Year is enthusiastically celebrated, with grand displays of fireworks—in Iceland, everyone is allowed to shoot fireworks and as the clock nears midnight, the sky over Reykjavík and other towns is practically ablaze.

These two days are more or less a repeat of Christmas, with a large family meal on New Year's Eve, where roast lamb or pork is often served, or perhaps turkey or other poultry. On New Year's Day, the after-effects of the revelry of the night often means that nobody wants to do much cooking, so cold meat is frequently served—leftovers from the night before, or maybe cold smoked lamb.

Epiphany

þrettándinn

In Iceland, Christmas begins on Christmas Eve and lasts for thirteen days, and the last day is called "the thirteenth." Many people say goodbye to Christmas in some way—by taking down their Christmas tree and decorations, by shooting fireworks and holding bonfires to burn off Christmas, and some invite the family to finish off the remaining Christmas cookies and candy.

Thorri Feasts

þorrablót

According to the old Icelandic calendar, the month of Thorri *(þorri)* begins on a Friday between January 19 and 25. Thorri may be a distortion of the name of the old thunder god, Thor *(þór)*, but it has come to mean a personification of the Winter King—often portrayed as an old, harsh man that lays a blanket of snow and ice over the whole country and is very reluctant to let go of his "ice fetters."

Even though Thorri feasts were held at midwinter in pagan times, there is really nothing that connects them to the present day feasts of the same name. They are a twentieth century phenomenon, although there were a few instances in the nineteenth century when small groups of people gathered for a midwinter feast they called Thorrablót. The present-day catered Thorrablót is partly an invention of a Reykjavík restaurant owner in the 1950s—he thought there might be a market for traditional and disappearing Icelandic food that had never been served at restaurants before.

Thorrablót are now held in almost every town and community in Iceland and clubs, workplaces, and others arrange their own feast, so many people end up going to several of these during the month of Thorri. They may even reach into the next month, Góa, in which case they are usually called *Góugleði* (Góa's Feast). Most Thorrablóts are catered by restaurants but in a few locations, people still bring their own Thorri food in the customary specially made deep wooden trays.

The following are some of the traditional offerings at a Thorrablót:

Hákarl, fermented shark, usually buried for months to allow certain unhealthful substances to leak out, then air-dried. It is usually served in bite-size cubes and washed down with ice-cold *brennivín*. It is divided into two types, *glerhákarl* (glass shark), the part closest to the hide which is chewy and semi-opaque, and *skyrhákarl* (skyr shark), soft and tender inner parts. Both can have a pretty strong taste.

Harðfiskur is fish that has been dried, then beaten until soft. Many farms used to have a special stone ("the fish stone") for this. The fish was placed flat on the stone and beaten with a heavy mallet. This is something I recall having done in my childhood, although not regularly, as it was heavy work to thoroughly beat the fish. The fish is often eaten with butter. *Harðfiskur* is one of the old delicacies that has survived and is now sold in every shop, usually as a very popular travel snack.

Whey-preserved whale blubber used to be a staple at the Thorri feasts but it has disappeared now, as there is no whaling. One side of a piece of sour blubber is very stringy and tough, then the texture changes gradually, and the other side becomes so soft it can be cut with a fork. Whey-preserved seal flippers are occasionally seen at private feasts but rarely served by caterers.

Hangikjöt, smoked lamb, is one of the most popular offerings and almost the only thing some of the younger guests will eat. It is served cold and cut into thin slices. *Magáll* is a thin fat-streaked slab of meat off a sheep's belly. It is usually boiled, then smoked and cut into thin slices.

Lundabaggar used to be a piece of lamb meat, often the heart, rolled in a lamb's intestines and suet before being cooked. It was eaten fresh or whey-preserved, and sometimes smoked. Now the name seems to have been transferred to rolled, fatty flank of lamb, soured in whey. *Bringukollur* is fatty meat from the breast of the lamb, usually on the bone. The meat is cooked, then preserved in whey. *Hrútspungar*, lamb's testicles, are pressed and preserved in whey, with a mild, slightly sour taste and a peculiar texture, fairly similar to roe, but smoother.

Halved sheep's heads, *svið*, are sometimes served and *sviðasulta*, headcheese, both fresh and whey-preserved, is a must at a Thorri feast. The head is boiled until the bones fall out and the meat (with eyes, tongue, and everything else) is pressed into a mold to set, along with a little of the gelatinous cooking liquid. Lamb trotters used to be treated in a similar manner but are rarely seen now.

Blóðmör (blood pudding) and *lifrarpylsa* (liver sausage), both fresh and whey-preserved, are always to be found at these feasts. They are served cold in slices. Recipes for both are to be found in the last chapter of this book. There are also recipes for the traditional side dishes, which are mashed potatoes, mashed rutabagas, steamed rye bread, and rye flatbread.

There are other, less traditional offerings that have mostly been added in recent years to cater to the tastes of those who do not like the traditional food. Among these are pickled herring, salted lamb, and perhaps a stew.

Brennivín (caraway-flavored schnapps), vodka, and other alcoholic beverages are always served, along with beer and ale.

Beginning of Lent

Föstuinngangur

Lent is the forty days before Easter and although Icelanders no longer fast during this period, the days preceding Lent are feast days in Iceland, as in many other European countries. Ash Wednesday, the first Lenten day, is celebrated in some towns by children, who go around in fancy dresses, sing popular songs, and receive candy in return. They used to pin small bags containing ashes or stones on unsuspecting victims but that custom has mostly disappeared.

Monday and Tuesday, on the other hand, are associated with special foods or treats, when people used to indulge themselves before beginning the fast. Monday is *bolludagur*, Bun Day, and it is customary to eat a lot of cream-filled buns. That custom dates from the late nineteenth century and was probably introduced by Danish or Norwegian bakers, although some goodies would have been eaten on this day much earlier. Medieval Icelandic law texts say it is allowed to eat a double portion on Monday and Tuesday preceding Lent. Much of the bun-eating now takes place on Sunday, however, since Monday is a workday and there is less time for baking.

Monday used to be called *flengingardagur* (Spanking Day). In earlier times, Catholic people would often spank themselves to be reminded of the pain of Jesus. Later, this turned into a comical parody of sorts and people began spanking each other instead of themselves. It became a kind of sport to try to catch people in bed or still asleep and spank them, often using a special wand or decorated stick, and to escape the spanking, people would pay a forfeit of buns. Icelandic children often still make their own *bolluvöndur* (bun stick), or buy them in shops, and use them to spank their parents to get some buns.

Icelandic bakers estimate they sell one million of these buns on and around Bun Day every year, which means almost four buns for every Icelander. Many people also bake buns at home. The two most common types of buns now are yeast buns (which make up 70 to 80 percent of the bakery buns) and choux pastry buns (cream puffs), but other types are also baked. In the first half of the twentieth century, the buns were usually made from cake dough. Often a *jólakaka* recipe was used, perhaps with an extra egg or two added, and the raisins were left out. Deep-fried buns are also known and formerly *ástarpungar* (Love Balls) were served on Bun Day.

Immediately after this bun orgy comes Shrove Tuesday, which in Iceland is called *sprengidagur*, Bursting Day, when most people gorge themselves on split pea and salted lamb soup (page 40). Traditionally everybody would eat as much as they possibly could, to the point of bursting, to prepare themselves for the seven meatless Lenten weeks to follow. This would in earlier times usually mean smoked lamb or mutton but in the nineteenth century it was replaced by salted meat and a hearty pea soup was quite appropriate as an accompaniment.

Sun Coffee

Sólarkaffi

Sun Coffee is not a national holiday, nor is it celebrated on the same day in all the locations where it is held. The reason is that in many narrow valleys and fjords in Iceland, the sun does not rise above the mountains during the darkest winter days. This happens mostly in the Western Fjords and the Eastern Fjords and this period can last several weeks, even months. This does not mean these places will be engulfed in darkness twenty-four hours a day, though; daylight lasts a few hours but the light will be fairly dim. The Sun Coffee is held to celebrate the re-emergence of the sun from behind the mountains, if only for a few minutes.

In some towns and villages, people will get together in a community hall for their Sun Coffee. Others celebrate at home with family and friends. Cakes and cookies are served along with the coffee, sometimes elaborate creations, or perhaps more traditional treats like crepes, crullers, and Christmas cake. People who have moved away to a place where the sun does not disappear will sometimes celebrate on the day when the sun will be showing itself again in their old home.

Easter

Páskar

There aren't really any special food traditions connected with Easter in Iceland, unless one counts the chocolate Easter eggs given to every child and many grownups as well. These are a twentieth-century tradition, though. A few weeks before Easter, they appear in all shops, sometimes having a whole supermarket aisle devoted to them. The thin chocolate shell is filled with candy and there is always a small strip of paper inside with a printed proverb.

Although many people do serve lamb at Easter, that cannot be said to have any special significance, as it does in some other countries; after all, a leg of lamb is the traditional Sunday roast in Iceland. In earlier times, the first meat meal after the many weeks of fasting would have been smoked lamb or mutton. It used to be traditional to serve a thick rice or barley porridge, made with cream or milk, on Easter Sunday and sometimes also on Maundy Thursday, the week before Easter.

First Day of Summer

Sumardagurinn fyrsti

The old Icelandic calendar year had only two seasons, summer and winter, which is why we celebrate the first day of summer in late April, when it isn't even spring yet, or not so that you'd notice. But it is a very old holiday, dating back to pagan times, and the custom of giving presents on this day is mentioned in the fifteenth century. It never disappeared and has recently undergone a revival.

In the nineteenth century, the usual feast dish on the first day of summer was a thick, rich rice or barley porridge, slowly simmered for a long time and studded with raisins. No special dishes are connected to this day now, except in certain families. I, for instance, always make the thin, traditional crepes and serve them with jam and whipped cream on an old plate with a blue flower pattern—you can hardly get more Icelandic than that on this most Icelandic of all holidays.

Seamen's Day

Sjómannadagurinn

This occurs on the first Sunday in June, unless that happens to be Whitsunday (Pentecost, fifty days after Easter), in which case the holiday is moved to the next Sunday. This festival, held in all fishing towns and villages around the country, as well as in Reykjavík, celebrates the importance of fishers and other seamen in Icelandic culture and history. Coffee parties, often arranged by women's clubs and displaying a huge selection of baked goods, are usually held in community halls but the main festivities take place outdoors, usually around the harbor.

Independence Day

Þjóðhátíðardagurinn

Icelanders celebrate their independence on June 17. On that day in 1944, Iceland celebrated its independence from Danish rule at Thingvellir. No particular food customs connected to this day have emerged but some people will invite family and friends over for coffee and cakes. And if weather permits, the outdoor grills are put to use and grilling parties are held in many a backyard or balcony.

Harvest Celebration

Töðugjöld

The Icelandic harvest feast was a tame affair compared to some other countries. When the last bale of hay had been brought home in the autumn, it was usually celebrated with a meal. Sometimes a lamb or an adult sheep was slaughtered and cooked for the feast, and perhaps a thick and creamy porridge was made. Pancakes, crepes, crullers and other treats were served with the coffee. The harvest celebration has now disappeared almost completely.

St. Thorlak's Day

Þorláksmessa

Christmas begins on Christmas Eve in Iceland so December 23 is a hectic day for many, as there are so many last-minute preparations to do. The day is named for St. Thorlak, Þorlákur Þórhallsson, a bishop at Skálholt in the late twelfth century, who died on this day in 1193 and has been revered by Icelanders ever since, even though he was not formally canonized until 1985.

Icelanders do not have a tradition of eating fish at Christmas but fish is traditional on St. Thorlak's Day and in later years, the fish of the day has become putrefied skate (*kost skata*). This custom began in the Western Fjords and spread all over the country. The skate, which is left to ferment for several weeks, has an extremely strong and unpleasant smell that intensifies while it is being cooked. The man of the house (who is often responsible for the cooking of this particular item) is sometimes banished to the garage and has to cook the skate on a gas burner there, or else the whole house might stink of ammonia come Christmas. Instead, the smoked lamb is often cooked in the kitchen and produces a smell that almost everybody loves.

It has to be said, though, that the taste of the skate is not nearly as bad as the smell, although opinions may differ. Some prefer it so putrefied that it brings tears to their eyes and their breath smells of it for many hours afterward. An eighteenth-century poet praised skate of this kind to the skies and said it was "better than *brennivín*" (caraway-flavored schnapps), which is praise indeed, coming from an Icelander.

The skate is usually cut into chunks and poached, sometimes in the cooking water from the smoked lamb. It is served with *hamsatólg* (melted sheep's tallow with cracklings) and/or *hnoðmör* (sheep´s tallow that is kneaded and dried before it is melted), along with boiled potatoes. It usually gets washed down with several straight shots of *brennivín*.

Christmas

Jól

Many food-related traditions are knitted to Christmas and the preparations often begin with Christmas baking. Although most Icelandic housewives do not bake nearly as much as they used to, a lot of Christmas baking still gets done and for some, it is practically the only time of the year that they do any baking at all.

Many bake several types of cookies. Besides the recipes found in this book, some traditional Christmas cookies are vanilla wreaths, species, meringue cookies, chocolate cookies, spice cookies, coconut macaroons, serina cookies, farmer's cookies, and several others, and Sarah Bernhard cookies are a fairly recent tradition in many homes.

Cakes also get baked. Many have adopted the tradition of the English Christmas cake but the Icelandic Christmas Cake, as vínarterta is sometimes called in America, has more or less disappeared. Some still bake it for Christmas, though, and my mother always makes both the regular and the brown version. Meringues and layer cakes, filled with whipped cream and various kinds of sweet creams and mousses, are also made.

Many families or groups of friends come together for one evening in December to make leaf bread (page 200). Others meet for candymaking or other such activities, but this tends to involve only the women and children, not the whole family.

Restaurant Christmas buffets have become very popular in recent years and are usually attended by groups of people, often workmates. Another Scandinavian pre-Christmas tradition that enjoyed popularity for a while was *jólaglögg*, "Christmas glögg," where people drank lots of hot spiced red wine, usually generously fortified, and munched on spiced cookies.

In Iceland, Christmas begins on Christmas Eve. The shops close at noon or a little later and at 6 p.m., the church bells ring to signify the beginning of Christmas. By that time, dinner will be well on its way in most families and some sit down to eat as soon as Christmas arrives, because the children are eager to begin opening their presents.

There are many traditional Christmas main dishes: Smoked lamb, eaten in at least 90 percent of Icelandic households at least once during the Christmas holidays. It is served on Christmas Day in most homes, but some families still serve it on Christmas Eve. Ptarmigan, so closely knit to Christmas that some people would be willing to postpone the festivities rather than miss it. Roast goose with a fruit stuffing is a festive dish that can be really very good. Some feel roasted pork with cracklings is a bit old-fashioned but others say "yes, but that's exactly why we want it for Christmas." Smoked and salted pork rack is a safe bet, since it is difficult to turn into a failure and most people like it. Roasted leg of lamb is an old favorite which is all the more appreciated since it is no longer served every other Sunday in many homes.

There are recipes for most of these dishes in the book but not for turkey, which has recently become a very popular Christmas dish, because there aren't really any traditional or Icelandic recipes for it. The same goes for beef dishes.

Side dishes vary, of course, depending on what the main dish is, but not as much as could be expected. Glazed potatoes, for instance, can be served with almost everything except the smoked lamb. Red cabbage goes with most of these dishes too, as do boiled carrots and peas, and Waldorf salad or an apple salad is very popular. Leaf bread is very traditional with the smoked lamb in many families, but others never serve it. Dessert is often ice cream, store-bought or homemade, or a mousse (lemon and pineapple are popular flavors, and of course chocolate), but for many, rice pudding or *ris a l'amande* is absolutely essential. Evening coffee, with cakes and cookies, is often served after the presents have been opened.

Christmas Day can be lazy or hectic, depending on whether you stay at home or attend a large family party, but unless you should happen to host such a party, there usually isn't much cooking going on. Most people serve cold smoked lamb and only have to prepare a side dish or two. Boxing Day, the day after Christmas, is a holiday in Iceland and is usually leftover day. There tends to be lot of good food left over from the two preceding days and there is no need to cook anything new. And there are even more family parties to go to.

The traditional Christmas beverage, sometimes drunk with all Christmas meals, sometimes just with the smoked lamb, is a mixture of a fizzy orange flavored lemonade *(appelsín)* and a dark brown nonalcoholic ale *(malt)*. This is usually enjoyed by young and old alike but some adults may prefer Christmas ale or red wine.

"Sewing Clubs"

Saumaklúbbar

I feel that the Icelandic sewing clubs warrant a mention here for various reasons, even though they do not belong to any particular day or season. They are, however, culinary exercises and the sole Icelandic cooking magazine, *Gestgjafinn*, devotes a whole issue to them every year. But I'm not sure if I can describe them—I remember once asking a friend: "Have you ever tried to explain sewing clubs to a foreigner?" and she said: "Foreigner? I can't even explain them to my husband."

A sewing club is not a club, and hardy any sewing ever gets done. They are small groups of women—often old college mates, childhood friends, or otherwise connected—who meet at the home of one of the group, maybe once a month, to talk, gossip, share their joys and sorrows, and enjoy one another's hospitality. If the group is large—

ten or more—several members will sometimes bring cakes and other goodies but in most cases the host of the evening will provide all the refreshments.

Some of these gathering can turn into virtual calorie orgies, or showcases for the culinary skills of the hostess, but others are much more moderate. There is usually a layer cake or two (or three)—the Rice Krispies cake I've provided a recipe for (page 182) is quite typical. There is often a hot dish, usually involving bread, and a cold savory dish as well—for instance a party sandwich loaf (page 210). There may be crackers and dips, or a cheese platter, and a multitude of other things, both sweet and savory. This is washed down with lots of coffee and often a few glasses of sherry or wine. A sewing club meeting is almost always held in the evening and will frequently continue well past midnight.

ICELANDIC INGREDIENTS

The following is a brief discussion of some ingredients that are regularly used in Icelandic cooking and a few others that are less popular but are included in the recipes of this book, or are at least mentioned here. Some of these ingredients are probably unfamiliar to American readers, others may be well known but their role in Icelandic cooking requires some explanation.

Baker's Ammonia

Hjartarsalt

Baker's ammonia, ammonium carbonate, hartshorn—these are all terms for an ammonia compound that is used as a leavening agent in many traditional German and Scandinavian cookie recipes. It gives the cookies a texture that can't really be reached using other leaveners. It can usually be omitted or replaced with baking powder but the cookies will be different from the original. It can be hard to find in America but should be available in many pharmacies or by mail order.

Baker's ammonia is only activated by heat, not moisture, and your cookies will emit an odor of ammonia while they are baking, but the finished cookies will not carry any trace of ammonia smell or taste. Baker's ammonia keeps almost indefinitely in an airtight jar but may evaporate when exposed to air. Icelandic stores sell ready-to-use baker's ammonia but in some other countries, it may be necessary to dissolve the substance in liquid before using.

Bilberries

Bláber

The Icelandic *bláber* literally means "blueberries" but these berries are in fact bog bilberries, *Vaccininum uliginosum*, which grow wild all over Iceland. Regular bilberries, *Vaccininum myrtillus*, grow there too, in certain regions, and are called *aðalbláber* ("main blueberries," which is fitting, since they are generally thought to be superior to bog bilberries). Both species have been gathered since the Settlement and their arrival in late summer has always been eagerly awaited by young and old alike. They were generally eaten with skyr and even layered with skyr in large barrels and preserved for months in this manner. Soups and puddings were also made from the berries, or they were simply eaten with fresh cream.

Char

Bleikja

The Arctic char is found in rivers and lakes all over Iceland, even where little nourishment is to be found, but in that case the fish will grow slowly and be very small when reaching maturity. Some spend part of their life in the sea to feed. Then they return to spawn as *sjóbleikja* (sea char). Others are landlocked and spend their entire life in still water. There are several varieties, some of them confined to just one lake. In Lake Þingvallavatn, for instance, Iceland's largest natural lake, there are four distinct char varieties, in addition to a large trout native to the lake.

The char is popular and people have been fishing for it ever since the Settlement. It is treated the same as trout (both species are collectively known as *silungur*): poached, fried, made into soups, baked, grilled, salted, smoked—the possibilities are almost endless.

Crowberries

Krækiber

The lowly crowberries *(Empetrum nigrum)* are small, black berries that would probably not be considered a delicacy in any country where sweeter-tasting and more flavorful wild berries are abundant, but Iceland has only crowberries, bilberries, and bog bilberries (wild strawberries and stone brambles can also be found but they are rare), so there is little competition. Crowberries are picked in huge amounts in autumn. Most are probably eaten at once, plain or with skyr, but some of the berries are made into jam, or the juice is pressed out of them, sweetened, and preserved.

Dulse

Söl

Dulse *(Palmaria palmata)* is an edible seaweed that has been used in Iceland since the earliest times. The oldest Icelandic law texts deal with the right to collect dulse, which was an important economical concession; dulse was collected, transported to inland farms, and sold in exchange for other goods. This usually took place in late August, when the dulse is mature and at its best.

Dulse is rarely eaten fresh, as it tends to be very leathery. It is dried and compressed and will keep very well, since it is salty. The saltiness is part of what made it so appealing in salt-starved Iceland of earlier times, but even today, many appreciate dulse as a snack to chew on or as an addition to soups and bread. It was often served with dried fish, along with lots of butter, or added to stews, porridges, and blood sausages.

Dulse is available in many health food stores. It is very rich in vitamin A and some trace elements, so it was an important addition to the Icelandic diet.

Fish Cheeks and Tongues

Kinnar og gellur

Fish cheeks have recently become trendy in some American restaurants but Icelanders are among those who have always known them for the tender and delicious bits they are. Cod cheeks, fresh or salted, have long been popular and many consider them the best bit of the fish—or rather, since many Icelanders do not care much for cod, the cheeks and throats may be the only parts that are consumed locally; the rest of the fish is processed and exported to foreign markets.

What are commonly called cod tongues in English are actually throat muscles, *gellur* in Icelandic. These are tasty little titbits, well-known and loved in North Atlantic maritime regions like Newfoundland and Iceland, but are often regarded with suspicion and even disgust elsewhere.

Gravy Browning

Sósulitur

A small bottle of gravy browning is an indispensable item in most Icelandic households. Most traditional meat dishes are accompanied with a brown sauce and it should be medium or dark brown, not pale, so several drops of gravy browning are often applied to acquire the desired color. Gravy browning is really just caramelized sugar and water, so it doesn't add any discernible flavor to the sauce. Oriental soy sauce can be used instead but may have a slight effect on the flavor.

Guillemot

Langvía

The common guillemot, the very closely related Brünnich's guillemot, the razorbill, and a couple of other birds are commonly known in Icelandic as *svartfugl* (literally "blackbird"). Millions of these birds breed in Iceland, mostly in the large bird cliffs in the Western Fjords, in the Westmann Islands off Southern Iceland, and at a few other places, such as Drangey in Skagafjörður. *Drangeyjarfugl,* "Drangey Bird," was a spring treat when I was growing up. These birds were used much more in earlier times and in some regions, they and their eggs were a large part of the diet, especially in spring and early summer, when little else was to be had. People would come from far away to hunt the birds and gather their eggs. They were eaten fresh—usually boiled in a soup—or they were salted, smoked, or pickled in whey.

Iceland Moss

Fjallagrös

Iceland moss *(Cetaria islandica)* is not a moss at all, but a type of lichen. Actually, the Icelandic name is even more off botanically; it means literally "mountain grasses." Iceland moss doesn't look very edible. It is sold dried and is very hard and brittle, staghorn-shaped, and grayish in color. Nevertheless, it was vitally important for the grain- and vegetable-deprived Icelanders throughout the centuries. It was chopped and added to soups and porridges, bread, sausages, and several other types of food, especially in the north and east of Iceland, where it grows profusely in many regions. In many homes, it was eaten daily in some form.

Iceland moss almost disappeared from the Icelandic diet during the first half of the twentieth century, even though some people continued to use it occasionally, not least for health reasons. It is said to have some soothing and antibiotic effects and it is often used as a cure against a sore throat, cough, bronchitis, asthma, indigestion, and loss of appetite. It is now an ingredient in some health products, and rye flatbread containing some chopped Iceland moss is popular. In Iceland, it can be bought in some stores. It is used for soups, bread, and a few other things.

Horsemeat

Hrossakjöt

Icelanders love their horses and generally treat them well, but they do not share the aversion for the eating of horseflesh that most English-speaking people seem to have, despite the fact that consuming horsemeat was forbidden for many centuries. One of the conditions the Icelanders set for accepting Christianity in the year AD 1000 was that they should be allowed to continue to eat horsemeat in secret. This cannot have continued for long, however, and horsemeat was not eaten again until the nineteenth century, except perhaps during severe famines.

In the early part of the twentieth century, the use of horsemeat became very widespread but it has been slowly declining again. There are few specific horsemeat recipes, as almost any beef recipe can be used. Horseflesh is fairly similar to beef, although it has a sweetish taste that not everyone likes. The flesh of young horses is very lean and tender but it will spoil faster than other meat so it must be fresh.

Langoustines

Leturhumar

Foreign tourists in Iceland are sometimes in for a surprise when the lobster they ordered from the English version of the restaurant menu turns out to be not lobster at all, but langoustine, also known as scampi, Dublin Bay prawn, or Norway lobster. This small lobster relative is properly named *leturhumar* but since the real lobster, *humar*, is not to be found in Icelandic waters, its name has been more or less taken over by its lesser-known cousin. Whatever the creatures are called, in Icelandic or English, they are a treat, and Icelanders love them.

Lumpfish

Hrognkelsi

While neither the male nor the female lumpfish can be called particularly attractive, the sexes can easily be told apart, at least during the spawning season, because then the underside of the male *(rauðmagi)* becomes a brilliant red. The male is quite good to eat and is rather popular in Iceland. The female *(grásleppa)* does not change its appearance but its flesh turns into a glutinous mass and becomes absolutely inedible. The female is, however, a far more valuable catch, because it is often filled with roe which is sold at high price as lumpfish caviar.

Monkfish

Skötuselur

Monkfish is a firm, meaty fish. Icelanders discovered it in a big way in the 1980s. It is a very ugly creature, all head and tail with nothing in between, that may look like a mismatched joining of several species (the Icelandic name means "skate-seal") and most people used to think of it as inedible. Now it is the favorite of many and grilled monkfish is especially popular in summer, but it can also be sautéed, deep-fried, baked, broiled, or cooked in soups and stews. The tail flesh is white and firm and the texture and flavor is somewhat reminiscent of lobster.

Pearl Sugar

Perlusykur

Pearl sugar is a decorating sugar with very large, glossy crystals, used in several

Scandinavian cookie recipes. It is fairly heat resistant and does not caramelize easily when exposed to high heat during baking. It can be substituted with lump sugar, coarsely crushed with a rolling pin or mallet, or with coarse granulated sugar.

Potato Starch

Kartöflumjöl

Potato starch was much used as a thickener in puddings, compotes, and dessert soups but its role in Icelandic cooking diminished in later years, since these treats are not seen as often as they used to be. It is also used for certain cakes and cookies. Potato starch is a pure white, finely ground flour. It is dissolved in a little cold water and stirred into a hot mixture that has just been taken off the heat. The thickening effect is immediate and the mixture must not come to a boil again, after the potato starch has been stirred in. Cornstarch is a possible substitute but will have a slight effect on flavor and the soup will become opaque. Arrowroot is often a better choice.

Ptarmigan

Rjúpa

The rock ptarmigan is a small northern game bird, found both in Europe and America, where it is know as rock ptarmigan. Its usual habitat is mountainsides and high-lying, barren ground. Ptarmigan has been hunted in Iceland since ancient times but the bird seems not to have been highly prized here until the early twentieth century. Now braised or roasted ptarmigan is traditionally served on Christmas Eve in many families. The taste of the bird depends very much on its diet but red grouse is probably the closest substitute, if ptarmigan is unavailable.

Puffin

Lundi

The male puffin in its full splendor is an impressive bird despite its small size, with its many-colored beak and dignified look. The puffin is by far the most common bird in Iceland and the population is estimated at around 9 million. Is usually caught in a net, just as it flies out of its burrow; it is relatively easy to catch and an experienced catcher usually has no trouble netting several hundred birds per day. These days it is usually eaten fresh but smoked puffin is also a popular delicacy.

Rainbow Pepper

Regnbogapipar

In recipes that call for (roughly) crushed peppercorns, Icelanders often use a colorful peppercorn mixture that includes several types of pepper and sometimes other spices as well. The most popular mixture, called rainbow pepper, includes black, white, and green peppercorns, pink peppercorns and whole allspice. While not a pepper at all, allspice is treated as such in parts of Scandinavia, especially in Finland and Sweden, where it is called *kryddpeppar* (spice pepper); this is occasionally seen in Icelandic also. Some rainbow pepper mixtures omit the allspice.

Razorbill

Álka

The last great auk in the world was killed at Eldey Island, a small rock off the southwest coast of Iceland, in June 1844, after this huge, flightless seabird, sometimes called the penguin of the north, had been hunted to extinction in all other countries. Its smaller relatives, the guillemot and the razorbill, still thrive and are frequently on the menu in some regions. It is estimated that 60 percent of the current razorbill population of 380,000 pairs breed at Látrabjarg and this is believed to be the largest razorbill colony in the world. These birds can be quite good to eat but tend to have a fishy taste, which can be eliminated by soaking them overnight in milk or water mixed with a little vinegar or salt.

Reindeer

Hreindýr

Although reindeer are abundant in Norway and Greenland, Iceland's neighbors to the east and west, they are not native to Iceland and there were no reindeer here until the mid-eighteenth century, when a flock was imported from northern Norway. Those animals did not fare well but a later attempt was successful and flocks of reindeer have been running wild in the eastern part of Iceland for over two centuries. They are the only large game animals in Iceland. The stock is carefully monitored and hunting permits have now become so sought-after and expensive that the price of the meat has risen very high.

Rhubarb

Rabarbari

Rhubarb is, of course, not really a fruit at all but it is often used as such. It is a hardy plant that thrives well in a cold climate and it used to be the only "fruit" commonly available in Iceland. Rhubarb cultivation began to spread in Iceland in the latter half of the nineteenth century, which wasn't all that much later than in the rest of Europe. It became very widespread before long and by the mid-twentieth century, there was a small rhubarb garden at almost every farm and a rhubarb patch in most town and village backyards. Rhubarb was harvested all summer and preserved in various ways throughout the winter.

Roe

Hrogn

People treated roe—especially cod roe—in various ingenious ways in the old days. It was, of course, poached and eaten fresh, but it could also be preserved in whey, pan-fried, or smoked. Sometimes the roe was kneaded with rye flour and made into flatbread that was cooked on embers or on a griddle, or into dumplings that were cooked in a broth or soup and eaten with meat or fish. These days roe is usually poached and eaten with poached fish, served in salads, or sliced and fried.

Rutabaga

Gulrófa

Rutabagas became known in Iceland in the nineteenth century and for a century or so, they and potatoes were the only two vegetables commonly grown in Iceland. A few other vegetables were grown by keen gardeners but only those two were widely cultivated and rutabagas seem to have been even more popular than potatoes, although that changed later.

Rutabagas are boiled and served with fish or salted meat, or they are added to soups and stews, and sometimes they are mashed. There are other cooking methods as well; they can be very good when roasted, or they can be grated and made into patties which are then pan-fried.

Sago

Sagógrjón

Real pearl sago is an almost pure starch obtained from the stem of the sago palm and made into small pellets, which are white when dried but become transparent when cooked. It was much used in many European cuisines in the late nineteenth and early twentieth centuries, especially in puddings and soups, but is not often seen these days.

Sago used to be fairly common in Danish cooking and it occurs in several recipes in older Icelandic cookbooks. It was sometimes called *viðgrjón*, "wood pellets," which is pretty accurate considering the origin of the substance but hardly a fair description of the texture. It is still occasionally used and can be found in most supermarkets but what is sold as pearl sago today isn't real sago; it is potato starch, made to resemble sago. The texture and thickening effect is similar and both products are virtually tasteless, so the substitution doesn't matter much.

Salt Cod

Saltfiskur

"Lífið er saltfiskur" (life is salt fish) is a well-known Icelandic saying, originating in one of Nobel Laureate Halldór Laxness' novels. And salt fish—especially cod—has for two centuries been one of Iceland's main exports and a very important local food staple.

Now salt cod can be bought either dry or presoaked and most people opt for that version, but if the fish is bought dried, it needs soaking in cold water to remove the salt. The fish is either sold bone in, or boned and skinned. It is usually soaked for 24 to 48 hours and the water is changed several times, or it can be soaked in running water, which will shorten the soaking time somewhat. At my childhood home, the salt fish was soaked in a bucket placed in a small running brook a short distance from the farmhouse and a loose cover was placed on the bucket to prevent the farm ravens from nicking some of the fish.

Salmon

Lax

It is said that when the settlers first came to Iceland in the ninth century, every river was full of salmon, trout, and char. And they still are, to some extent at least. There are over 100 salmon rivers in Iceland and wealthy foreign sport fishers have been coming to catch salmon there for well over a century. One of the best salmon rivers, Elliðaár, runs through Reykjavík, the capital. The rivers are generally clean and free of industrial pollution and so is the sea around Iceland, where the salmon spends a year or two of its life to fatten up.

The salmon season usually runs from early June until the middle of September and in earlier times, salmon was so abundant in certain regions during the summer that people got thoroughly bored of it, so bored that they sometimes preferred to go hungry rather than eat salmon yet once again, after having had it for every meal, six or seven days a week, in every conceivable form—poached, fried, salted, smoked, mashed, in soups, and so on. Later, when Icelandic salmon rivers became popular with sport fishers, it was much more profitable for farmers to sell fishing permits than catch the salmon themselves, so for decades, salmon was a luxury that normally was served maybe once or twice a year. In recent years, this has changed again as Icelanders began salmon farming, and salmon is now almost an everyday dish, often less expensive than haddock.

Skyr

Skyr

Icelanders will tell you that they have no cheesemaking tradition that has survived since the Settlement, because they won't admit that skyr is actually a fresh cheese. No wonder, perhaps; skyr actually looks and tastes much more like thick, Greek-type yogurt. In Iceland, it is available in many forms, often mixed with fruit and flavorings, and usually sweetened, although natural skyr is available, too.

Unsweetened skyr, made from skim milk, is a very healthful product. It is almost fat-free and has a lot of calcium and vitamins. There is a recipe for making skyr on page 225.

Smoked Lamb

Hangikjöt

Hangikjöt, literally "hung meat," is an Icelandic delicacy loved by almost everybody. Smoking used to be the main preservation method for meat—salt was expensive, drying was not really an option because of the climate, but the (usually windowless) kitchen was more or less smoke-filled anyway, so it provided a ready-made smokehouse. Although most *hangikjöt* is made from lamb, mutton is preferred by many, as it is more flavorful.

The leg is the most common cut to be smoked but the shoulder is also good, even preferred by some, especially when served hot. These days the meat is often boned and tied into a roll before it is smoked but meat on the bone has more flavor. The meat should not be too heavily salted, and the fuel used for the smoking matters a great deal. I come from the north of the country so I'm partial to sheep dung–smoked meat, which may not sound appetizing but provides a very good flavor. Others may prefer birch or other fuel.

Smoked lamb is usually boiled. The tendency has been to overcook it, which makes it dry, but some people prefer it that way. The meat can be eaten hot or cold, and thin slices of smoked lamb are very popular for sandwiches and other bread.

Third Spice

þriðja kryddið

Although the "third spice," better known as monosodium glutamate or MSG, is not used anywhere in this book, it is not uncommon, especially in recipes from the 1970s and 1980s. I've often been asked about the term by English-speaking people who have come across Icelandic recipes using it and do not realize it is MSG, so I thought appropriate to explain it here, even though I never use it in my own recipes.

Trout

Urriði

Some of the salmon trout (sea trout, brown trout) of Iceland live in landlocked lakes, others spend the winters on feeding grounds in the ocean and return in spring and early summer to spawn in rivers and lakes. The latter are known as *sjóbirtingur* (sea-bright) and are generally considered superior to non-migratory trout. Trout and arctic char are collectively known as *silungur*. Most recipes for that call for *silungur* will work well with either species.

Whey

Mysa

Throughout the centuries, whey has played an extremely important part in Icelandic cooking. Brown cheese *(mysuostur)* was made from fresh whey and it was used in soups and porridges. But most of the whey that was produced during the summer, largely as a by-product of skyr-making, was gathered in large barrels, where it would soon ferment. Fermented whey, *sýra*, was extensively used to preserve food, and also served as a beverage.

Today, the role of whey has diminished dramatically but it is still used in cooking to some extent, especially in fish cookery, where it is often used as a substitute for white wine. Fish that is poached in whey or a mixture of whey and water will be whiter and firmer than if plain water is used. Whey adds a slightly sour tang to soups and stews. It can also be used in breadmaking.

Wild Goose

Villigæs

Two species of wild goose breed in Iceland, the greylag goose *(grágæs, Anser anser)*, which is mainly found in the lowlands, and the smaller pink-footed goose *(heiðagæs, Anser brachyrhynchus)*, which breeds in the central highlands. Both are hunted in the autumn and are usually roasted, or made into stews and soups if the bird is old. They are treated exactly alike in cooking.

Wild Sorrel

Hundasúra

Wild sorrel is one of the few salad herbs that grows widely in Iceland and was sometimes used for cooking, but more often eaten fresh, picked straight from the ground, mostly by children. In the fishing village where I lived as a teenager, there was a small wild sorrel patch at one corner of our house, and my younger sister and her neighborhood friends would sometimes gather there in summer, sit around the sorrel patch, and nibble the leaves while chatting among themselves. It is a nice salad herb, with a very mild, tangy taste.

Wild Thyme

Blóðberg

Wild Icelandic thyme *(Thymus praecox opiz),* grows profusely in many Icelandic regions but seems not to have been used much in cooking, although it was certainly used for herb teas and health remedies. It was also used to flavor whey. It is mentioned in nineteenth-century Icelandic cookbooks but it wasn't until the grilling craze of the late twentieth century that people began to use it to flavor their food—it is popular for grilled lamb, for instance. The wild Icelandic thyme, which should ideally be picked in spring or early summer before it flowers, isn't particularly potent, but the flavor is stronger if it is picked wet, in early morning or just after a rain shower.

RECIPES

Choosing recipes for a book such as this is not an easy task, although it would have been made much simpler if I had confined myself to traditional, pre-1970 Icelandic cooking. For that part of the project, I drew on my own and my mother's experience and recipe collections, and consulted a wide panel of friends and colleagues who contributed with suggestions, opinions, and recipes. I also went through almost every single Icelandic cookbook published in the first two thirds of the twentieth century—not a big feat, really, since there are so few of them.

Most of the selections were fairly obvious, as both the people and the books I consulted would mention the same dishes over and over again, with some slight variations between regions. In most cases, I've chosen either the most common version of a traditional recipe, or a version that has been used in my own family for a long time, and translated them without any significant alterations, although I've adapted and tested them using American measurements. I also cut down somewhat on the fat in a few recipes. If I've altered a traditional recipe in any way—usually because a particular ingredient may be difficult to find—I always mention the changes I've made.

The modern recipes were more difficult to pick. I wanted to show how ordinary people cook these days, especially when they want to treat themselves using Icelandic ingredients. I did not want recipes you could find in every other European or American cookbook or magazine, I wanted recipes with an Icelandic flavor. It is somewhat difficult to define this concept and opinions will vary, but to me it means fish (fresh, smoked, and salted), shellfish, lamb, and game birds; all kinds of dairy products; vegetables such as tomatoes and bell peppers; herbs, especially thyme, parsley, and chives; spices and flavorings such as garlic, curry powder, and paprika.

These newer recipes come from various sources. Several were published in my 1998 cookbook Matarást. Others are adapted from other recent cookbooks or recipe columns, which I've studied to try to discover what people are really cooking, as opposed to what is published in cookbooks. All the recipes have been chosen to show certain aspects of Icelandic cooking today.

SOUPS

If you ask an Icelander to name the traditional Icelandic soups—excluding the sweet ones—chances are most people will come up with the same 3 soups: meat soup, pea soup with salted lamb, and halibut soup. All are substantial soups, always served as a main course, never as a starter. The two meat soups share the same vegetables: potatoes, rutabagas, and carrots. The halibut soup is a bit more exotic—even faintly medieval, with its sweet-sour taste and dried fruit. Yet these soups are all simple, hearty, and wholesome, and can be very good indeed. All are still popular, even if they are not served as often as they used to be.

In addition to these traditional soups, I have chosen a mixture of older and modern soups that I feel are essentially Icelandic in character, even though some of them may not be unique to Icelandic cuisine. The vegetables used are grown in Iceland, either outdoors or in hothouses. The herbs and spices are traditional in Icelandic cuisine, even though some of them are imported. And the main ingredients are certainly Icelandic—lamb, fish, shellfish, and game.

CHERVIL SOUP

Kerfilsúpa
Serves 6 as a starter

Chervil is one of the few herbs that grows easily in Iceland, and grows wild. It can often be found growing profusely close to old, abandoned farmsteads, or in village gardens. It was commonly used to flavor soups and stews but most old cookbooks also have a recipe for chervil soup, basically a meat broth to which a liberal amount of chervil is added at the last moment, as the flavor is delicate and does not survive long cooking.

Soups based on the same recipe were made from several other herbs and leaf vegetables, including chives, cress, sorrel, and spinach, even scurvy grass. Meat stock is the traditional base for these soups but chicken or vegetable stock can easily be substituted.

2 tablespoons butter
2 tablespoons flour
4 cups good quality lamb or beef stock
1/2 cup thinly sliced carrots (optional)
Freshly ground pepper
Salt
1 cup packed chervil leaves, chopped
3 hard-boiled eggs, shelled

Melt the butter in a heavy saucepan. Stir in the flour and cook for a minute or two, then gradually stir in the stock. Bring to a boil, add carrots, and simmer at low heat for 8 to 10 minutes, or until carrots are just tender. Season to taste with pepper and salt. Stir in the chopped chervil and cook for 1 minute.

Serve on individual soup plates. Quarter the hard-boiled eggs and decorate each plate with 2 egg quarters and perhaps a chervil sprig or two.

POTATO KALE SOUP

Kartöflu-grænkálssúpa
Serves 6 as a starter

Potatoes and kale reached Iceland in the eighteenth century and were among the first vegetables to be grown here. Most people were slow to accept them, though; there were regions in Iceland where potatoes were still virtually unknown at the beginning of the twentieth century. They later became an inseparable part of any meal and still retain that position in many homes. Kale, however, has fallen somewhat out of favor and is not seen so often these days. This simple autumn soup, dating from the early part of the twentieth century, combines these vegetables very nicely.

6 cups lamb or beef stock
2 cups peeled and roughly grated potatoes
2 tablespoons grated onion
3 cups packed kale, washed and shredded
Freshly ground pepper
Salt
2 tablespoons butter

Bring the stock to a boil in a large saucepan. Add potatoes and onion and simmer for 15 minutes. Add kale, season with pepper and salt, and simmer for 3 to 5 minutes more. Stir in the butter and let it melt. Taste and adjust seasonings if needed. Serve with lots of freshly baked bread.

ICELAND MOSS SOUP

Fjallagrasamjólk
Serves 6 as a starter or dessert

You are not very likely to encounter this soup anywhere outside Iceland and even here, it is never seen on restaurant menus, though a few people still make it at home. Iceland moss, a type of lichen, can sometimes be found in health food stores outside Iceland. The natives have long known the health-giving qualities of the plant, and so have others as well; recipes for healthful restoratives made from it can be found in some old European cookbooks. For instance, *A Plain Cookery Book for the Working Classes* by Charles Elmé Francatelli, Queen Victoria's chief cook, has two recipes for Iceland Moss Jelly, and says that "Iceland moss is to be had of all chemists," adding that "The use of Iceland moss jelly is strongly recommended in cases of consumption, and in the treatment of severe colds, catrrhs, and all phlegmatic diseases of the chest." The following basic soup used to be a very common soup in Iceland.

1 cup loosely packed, dry Iceland moss
4 cups milk
1 teaspoon salt, or to taste
1 tablespoon brown sugar, or to taste

Briefly soak the Iceland moss in lukewarm water, then chop it roughly. Bring the milk to a boil in a saucepan. Add the Iceland moss and simmer for 5 minutes, stirring often. Remove from heat and season to taste with salt and sugar.

The soup can also be simmered for up to 2 hours, which will produce a jelly-like, slightly sweet pudding. There is also a sweet version, where the Iceland moss is initially cooked briefly in a thin syrup, and the soup is thickened with a couple of eggs.

JULIENNE SOUP

Júlíönusúpa
Serves 6 as a starter

The Icelandic name of this soup actually translates as "Juliana's Soup" and people often think it is named for some woman but it takes its name from the fact that all the vegetables are julienned (cut into matchsticks)—a cooking term unfamiliar to Icelanders and consequently misunderstood. It is one of many soups that were introduced to Iceland by cooks trained in Denmark during the nineteenth and early twentieth centuries.

Other vegetables that may be used include turnips, parsnips, celeriac, cabbage, and string beans. It is a bit time-consuming to cut up all the vegetables into matchsticks but they can also be grated coarsely. A food processor with a cutting or grating disk is a very handy tool when making this soup.

2 tablespoons butter
1 cup halved and thinly sliced onion
1 cup julienned leeks
1 cup julienned carrots
1 cup julienned potatoes
1/2 cup julienned celery
6 cups vegetable stock or meat stock
1 bay leaf
Pinch of dried thyme
Freshly ground pepper
Salt
1/4 cup chopped parsley

Melt the butter in a large saucepan. Add onion and sauté at medium heat until softened but not browned. Add leeks, carrots, potatoes, and celery, and stir-fry for a couple of minutes. Add stock, bay leaf, thyme, pepper and salt to taste, bring to a boil and simmer, partly covered, for 15 minutes.

Remove bay leaf, taste and adjust seasonings if needed, stir in parsley and serve with lots of crusty bread.

SALMON SOUP WITH WHEY

Laxasúpa með mysu
Serves 6 as a starter

Whey, the traditional preserving liquid and refreshing beverage of Iceland, is far less used now than in earlier times. However, its use in fish cookery has been increasing. In Iceland, it is sometimes used as a substitute for white wine in recipes, as it is much cheaper. If whey is hard or impossible to get, substitute equal quantities of dry white wine and water.

2 cups whey
1 salmon head (around 1 pound)
1 medium carrot, finely chopped
2 tablespoons grated onion
2 bay leaves
Freshly ground pepper
Salt
1/2 pound salmon, skinned and boned
2 egg yolks
1/2 cup cream
1 to 2 tablespoons chopped dill

Combine whey and 2 cups water in a pan, add the salmon head, carrot, onion, and bay leaves, heat to a boil and season with pepper and salt. Simmer for 20 minutes. Remove from the heat and let stand, covered, for 15 minutes.

Strain the stock through a fine sieve or cheesecloth and reheat it. Cut the salmon fillet into small cubes, add to the stock and simmer for 3 to 4 minutes. Whisk the egg yolks with the cream in a bowl, then gradually whisk in a couple of ladles of hot soup. Stir the egg mixture back into the soup and heat carefully but do not let the soup boil, or the egg yolks will curdle. Taste, add more pepper and salt if needed, stir in the dill, and serve.

HALIBUT SOUP

Lúðusúpa
Serves 4 as a main course

This rather special sweet-sour fish soup, much loved by many Icelanders, is an old one; there are several versions in the earliest Icelandic cookbook, published in 1800, one of them being a "fine fish soup for gentlefolk." That one has currants instead of prunes and raisins, and is thickened with sour cream and decorated with parsley.

There are many variations of this soup. Egg yolks or cream may be used for thickening, and sometimes pearl sago is added. The prunes may be substituted with 1-inch lengths of rhubarb stalks, precooked until softened. Other types of fish may be used, especially salmon and trout, but the halibut version is by far the most common.

2 pounds halibut
1 tablespoon white vinegar
2 bay leaves
Salt
12 pitted prunes
2 to 3 tablespoons raisins
1 tablespoon butter
1 tablespoon flour
Juice of 1/2 lemon
1 tablespoon sugar, or to taste

Clean the halibut and cut it into 1-inch-thick steaks. Combine vinegar, bay leaves, a teaspoon or so of salt and 5 cups water in a large pan and heat to a boil. Add the halibut steaks and simmer slowly until the fish is cooked and can just be separated from the bones.

Skim the broth and strain most of it into another pan. Add prunes and raisins and heat to a boil, but leave a cupful of broth in the pan with the fish to keep it warm. Mix butter and flour and stir into the broth. Let the soup simmer for 5 to 6 minutes.

Stir in the remaining broth, add lemon juice and sugar to taste and serve with the fish.

The fish, rarely served in the soup, is usually put on a separate plate, and is frequently paired with boiled potatoes, which may be sprinkled with some chopped parsley.

FISH SOUP WITH TOMATOES AND PEPPERS

Fiskisúpa með tómötum og papriku
Serves 4 as a main course

This soup combines some very popular ingredients in Icelandic cooking today. Despite the harsh climate, tomatoes and bell peppers are grown almost around the year in hothouses heated by steaming groundwater and illuminated by electricity produced by Iceland's mighty rivers. The cold, unpolluted ocean surrounding Iceland produces slow-growing, tasty fish and shellfish. And garlic—well, what can I say? Icelanders have a love affair with it and use it liberally.

The success of this soup depends very much on the stock. A homemade fish stock, cooked with heads, bones, and maybe a piece or two of fish, and flavored with a carrot, celery stick, bay leaf, and some peppercorns takes less than half an hour to make and keeps for days in the refrigerator, or for months in the freezer. But good store-bought stock can also be used. Other types of fish or shellfish may be used, for instance halibut, haddock, mussels, or langoustines.

2 tablespoons olive oil
1 cup chopped onion
1 tablespoon finely chopped garlic
1 red and 1 green bell pepper, seeded and cut into strips
4 cups chopped tomatoes
6 cups fish stock
Freshly ground pepper
Salt
1/2 pound monkfish tail
1/2 pound trout or salmon
12 to 16 scallops
12 to 16 prawns, shelled
Juice of 1/2 lemon (optional)
2 to 3 tablespoons chopped parsley

Heat the olive oil in a large saucepan. Add onion and cook at moderate heat until softened. Add garlic and peppers and cook for 2 to 3 minutes more. Add tomatoes, cook for a couple of minutes, then stir in the fish stock, bring to a boil, season with pepper and salt, and simmer for 15 to 20 minutes.

Meanwhile, cut the monkfish tail into thin slices and the trout or salmon into small cubes. Halve the scallops if large. Add fish and shellfish to the soup, bring to a boil and simmer for about 5 minutes.

Taste, add pepper and salt if needed, and perhaps some lemon juice, sprinkle parsley over the soup, and serve.

CURRIED LANGOUSTINE SOUP

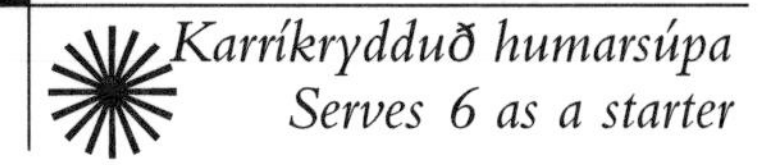

Karríkrydduð humarsúpa
Serves 6 as a starter

There are many versions of the following soup, seasoned with curry powder. Fairly similar curried soups, made with white fish instead of shellfish, can be found in old cookbooks, and many modern fish and shellfish soups are curry-flavored. Prawns may be substituted for the langoustines.

1/2 pound langoustines, in the shell
1 tablespoon oil
1 onion, finely chopped
1 carrot, chopped
1 tablespoon tomato paste
Freshly ground pepper
Salt
2 tablespoons butter
1 garlic clove, chopped
2 teaspoons mild curry powder (or to taste)
1/2 cup dry white wine
1 cup cream, or half-and-half

Shell the langoustines and set them aside. Crush the shells and put them in a pan with oil, half the onion, and the carrot. Cook slowly until the onion is softened. Stir in tomato paste and 6 cups water, add pepper and salt and bring to a boil. Simmer, uncovered, for 30 minutes, then strain through a fine sieve and set aside.

Wash out the pan and melt the butter in it. Add the rest of the onion and cook at moderate heat until softened. Add garlic and curry powder and cook for 1 minute. Stir in the wine and cook briskly until reduced by half, then stir in the langoustine stock, bring to a boil, and simmer for 10 minutes.

Cut the langoustines into thick slices and add them to the soup. Stir in cream, bring to a boil, and simmer for 2 minutes more. Season to taste with pepper and salt and serve at once.

A dash of brandy is sometimes added to the soup.

ICELANDIC LAMB SOUP

Kjötsúpa
Serves 4 as a main course

The Icelandic name of this very traditional soup means simply "meat soup" and for most Icelanders, this is THE Icelandic soup, even though similar soups can be found in other countries. Formerly this soup was often served on Christmas Eve but later it became more of an everyday soup.

Rutabagas, potatoes, and carrots are the traditional vegetables but every housewife used to have her very own recipe for it. Most include a small amount of rice or oatmeal as a thickener—sometimes just a tablespoon or two—but my mother's version did not and I like the soup much better this way. On the other hand, I usually add a tablespoon of "soup herbs" (actually mostly dried finely chopped vegetables and a few herbs), which can be bought in small packets in Iceland. A few tablespoons of chopped lovage leaves would be a good substitute, or even chopped celery leaves. But the soup can be made without this addition, and it is still very popular.

2 pounds lamb on the bone, cut in big chunks
2 teaspoons salt
1/2 teaspoon freshly ground pepper
1 pound rutabagas
1/2 pound potatoes
1/2 pound carrots
1 small onion
1 cup shredded cabbage (optional)

Trim some of the excess fat off the meat. Place it in a large pan, add 6 cups cold water and heat slowly to a boil. Skim the broth, then add salt and pepper and simmer, partly covered, for about 45 minutes.

Meanwhile, peel the rutabagas and cut them into chunks. Peel the potatoes and halve or quarter them unless they are small. Peel or scrape the carrots and cut them into pieces. Peel the onion and slice it thinly. Add the vegetables (except the cabbage, if using) to the soup and simmer for 15 minutes more.

Add cabbage and simmer for 5 to 10 minutes, or until all the vegetables are tender. Taste, add salt and pepper if needed, and serve.

The soup is always eaten with the meat but it is often taken out and served on a separate plate. Soup plates are placed on the right side of the dinner plates. Some people prefer to cut up their meat on the dinner plate, transfer it to the soup plate, and pour soup and vegetables over it. Others prefer taking a forkful of meat and a spoonful of soup alternately.

LAMB SOUP

Lambakjötssúpa
Serves 6 as a starter

A leaner, modern version of the traditional Icelandic lamb soup. This is not a full meal but can easily be made into one with the addition of more meat and vegetables. Other vegetables may also be added, for instance celery, peppers, or mushrooms. Even more modern versions sometimes include things like garlic, ginger, and chili peppers.

1/2 pound lamb, boned and trimmed
2 tablespoons butter
1/2 cup sliced leeks
1 cup sliced carrots
1 cup peeled and roughly chopped potatoes
1/4 cup chopped lovage or celery leaves
1/4 teaspoon dried thyme
1 bay leaf
2 teaspoons salt
1/2 teaspoon freshly ground pepper
2 cups roughly chopped broccoli
2 to 3 tablespoons chopped parsley

Cut the meat into bite-size pieces. Melt the butter in a large saucepan. Add leeks, carrots, and potatoes and fry gently for a few minutes, stirring often. Add meat and fry until colored but not browned. Add 5 cups hot water and bring to a boil. Skim, then add lovage or celery leaves, thyme, bay leaf, salt, and pepper. Simmer, partly covered, for 35 minutes.

Add broccoli and simmer for 5 to 6 minutes more. Add parsley. Taste and adjust seasonings if needed.

SPLIT PEA AND SALTED LAMB SOUP

Saltkjöt og baunir
Serves 4 to 6 as a main meal

This is a very traditional Icelandic dish. It is quite similar to Scandinavian pea soups, except it is always made with salted lamb, not pork. Salted lamb may be very hard to find outside Iceland and as it is so common there, I have provided a recipe for salting lamb (page 219). Salted pork can be substituted but the dish will taste quite different. For many people, this is now a once-a-year treat, always served on Shrove Tuesday, called *Sprengidagur* (Bursting day) in Iceland.

The following is my mother's recipe. The reason for cooking most of the meat separately is simply that if it is properly salted, it may make the soup too salty. If it is very mildly salted, all the meat can be cooked in the soup. Many people now add a piece or a few slices of bacon at the beginning of cooking, and vegetables like leeks and cabbage are sometimes added.

Most people soak the peas for up to 24 hours but this is totally unnecessary and the soup will definitely not gain anything from it. It will, on the other hand, benefit from being made the day before and reheated.

1 cup yellow split peas
1 cup chopped onion
2 teaspoons dried thyme
3 pounds salted lamb on the bone
1 pound rutabagas
1 pound potatoes
1/2 pound carrots
Freshly ground pepper
Salt (optional)

Place the peas in a large pan and add 8 cups cold water. Heat to a boil, skim, and add onion and thyme. Simmer, partly covered, for 1 hour, stirring occasionally.

Add one chunk of meat to the soup but place the rest in a separate pan, cover with water and cook until tender. Let the soup simmer for 30 minutes.

Meanwhile, peel the vegetables and cut them into 1 1/2- to 2-inch cubes. Add them to the soup and simmer for 25 minutes more, or until tender. Stir the soup occasionally and add water if it is becoming rather thick.

When the meat and vegetables are tender, taste the soup and add some pepper and more salt if needed. Remove the meat from the soup and serve on a separate platter.

This soup is eaten with the meat as a main course but the meat is not served in the soup. The table is laid with dinner plates and soup plates side by side and each person will be served a piece of meat on his dinner plate. Many cut it up and add it to the soup but others prefer to eat a piece of meat and a spoon of soup alternately.

PTARMIGAN SOUP

Rjúpnasúpa
Serves 6 as a starter

Ptarmigan is a very popular game bird in Iceland, especially at Christmas. Frequently only the breasts are served and the rest of the bird is used to make some very tasty stock, ideal for a sauce to serve with the bird, or for a soup such as this one—a modern take on a traditional soup.

4 to 6 ptarmigans, minus the breasts
1 tablespoon butter
1 tablespoon oil
2 to 3 chopped shallots
1/2 cup chopped carrot
1/2 cup chopped celeriac or celery stalks
Freshly ground pepper
Salt
1/4 cup dried wild mushrooms
2 tablespoons cream cheese
1 cup cream
1 tablespoon red currant or blueberry jam
1/4 cup red currants or blueberries
Few chives stalks

Roughly chop the skinned ptarmigan cadavers. Heat the butter and oil in a large, heavy saucepan and brown the ptarmigan pieces nicely on all sides at medium-high heat. Add shallots, carrots, and celeriac, lower the heat to medium and cook for a few minutes more, stirring often. Add 4 cups water, bring to a boil, season with some pepper and salt, cover, and simmer at low heat for 1 hour.

Strain the stock through a fine sieve and pour it back into the pan. Check the ptarmigan pieces; if the leg meat is tender enough, it can be reserved and added back to the soup later if desired. Add mushrooms, cream cheese, and cream, bring the soup to a boil and simmer at very low heat for 30 minutes.

If you are using the leg meat, slice or chop it and add it to the soup. Stir in the jam, taste the soup, and add more pepper and salt if needed. Serve on individual plates and decorate each with a few berries and a chives stalk or two.

GOOSE SOUP WITH RAISINS

Gæsasúpa með rúsínum
Serves 6 as a starter

A very tasty game soup, usually made with either pink-footed or greylag goose, the species that breed in Iceland. This is a good method to deal with legs, when the breasts have been cooked separately.

4 wild goose legs
3 tablespoons raisins
2 tablespoons port wine or brandy
2 tablespoons butter
1/2 cup chopped onion
1/2 cup chopped carrot
1 celery stalk, chopped
2 bay leaves
2 to 3 whole cloves
1/2 teaspoon dried thyme, preferably wild
6 cups goose stock or chicken stock
Freshly ground pepper
Salt
1 cup light cream
1 teaspoon sugar, or to taste

Cut each goose leg in two at the joint. Put the raisins in a small bowl, pour the port or brandy over them and let them soak for an hour or two, stirring occasionally. Melt the butter in a wide, heavy-bottomed pan and brown the legs nicely on all sides at medium-high heat. Remove them to a plate, lower the heat and add onions, carrots, and celery. Cook, stirring often, for 5 to 8 minutes, or until the vegetables are beginning to soften.

Add the goose legs back to the pan with the bay leaves, cloves and thyme and pour the stock over them. Bring to a boil. Skim carefully, then add some pepper and salt, lower the heat, and simmer gently, partly covered, for 2 1/2 hours.

Remove the legs from the soup, bone them and cut the meat into small pieces. Strain the soup through a fine sieve, or remove the bay leaves and cloves and purée it in a food processor. Pour it back into the pot, add raisins, port or brandy and the light cream, and bring the soup back to a boil. Season to taste with pepper, salt, and a little sugar. Simmer the soup for a few minutes, then add the meat and heat through. Serve at once.

STARTERS, SPREADS, AND DIPS

Starters were more or less unknown in Iceland until fairly recently. An Icelandic meal had two courses: the main course and a dessert. If anything was served at all before the main course, it was usually soup, and then only on festive occasions. The only recipe in this section that can be called traditional is the herring recipe; the others are more recent and are meant to show newer trends in Iceland. Some are served as starters, others would most likely be found on a cold buffet table.

Gravlax, while very common as a starter in Iceland, is not particularly Icelandic in any way, and recipes for it abound in so many books and magazines, so I decided against including a recipe for it. Most people buy it ready-made anyway. But I give a recipe for a honey-mustard sauce that is usually served with it. Smoked salmon is also very common as a starter.

HERRING WITH SOUR CREAM

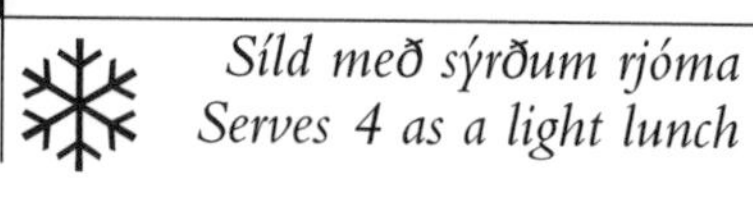

Síld með sýrðum rjóma
Serves 4 as a light lunch

Icelanders have never been very fond of herring and most of them will only eat it marinated or in salads. During the early part of the twentieth century, efforts were made to teach people to appreciate the fish, which was by then being caught in huge quantities by Icelandic boats and had become a very important part of the economy. Cookbooks of the time have many recipes for fresh and salted herring and Helga Sigurðardóttir says in *Matur og drykkur*: "Icelandic housewives, it is our duty to ensure that people eat more herring than they do now," but to no avail; herring never gained much favor, and in the 1960s it largely disappeared from Icelandic waters due to over-exploitation.

The herring has been returning slowly, and the current exploitation is being carefully monitored to protect the stock, but Icelanders still haven't learned to appreciate herring, unless it is marinated. The following recipe is an adaptation of a classic recipe in *Matur og drykkur*. That recipe calls for naturally soured cream and I've found a mixture of commercial sour cream and skyr to be a good alternative. This is a dish for a cold buffet table, or to be served at lunch, perhaps with boiled potatoes.

4 fillets salted herring
1 cup sour cream
3 tablespoons finely chopped chives
1 to 2 teaspoons vinegar
1 teaspoon sugar
Pinch of pepper
Lettuce leaves, for serving

Soak the herring in cold water for 12 to 24 hours to desalt it. Change the water at least once or twice. Drain the herring fillets, pat them dry on a kitchen towel, and cut them across in 1/2-inch slices.

Mix sour cream, 2 tablespoons of the chives, the vinegar, and sugar in a bowl. Season with pepper to taste, and more vinegar or sugar, if desired. Stir in the herring, cover and refrigerate for 3 hours, stirring once or twice.

Arrange a few lettuce leaves on a platter, heap the herring salad on them, and decorate with the remaining 1 tablespoon chopped chives. Serve with thin slices of rye bread.

SALMON TARTAR TIMBALES

Laxatartartoppar
Serves 4 to 6 as a starter

Ten to fifteen years ago, most Icelanders would not have considered eating raw fish, with the exception of smoked and gravad salmon and other similar dishes. Then sushi became trendy and raw fish is now popular, especially as a starter in restaurants, but adventurous cooks also make dishes like this at home. The salmon must be wild and very fresh; frozen farm-raised salmon will not do. Arctic char can be used instead of salmon.

1/2 pound skinned and boned salmon fillet
1/4 cup extra-virgin olive oil
Juice of 1/2 lemon
2 teaspoons Dijon mustard
1 teaspoon grated fresh ginger
1 teaspoon grated horseradish
Freshly ground pepper
Salt
3 tablespoons chopped chives
Lettuce leaves

Finely dice the salmon. Whisk together olive oil, lemon juice, mustard, ginger, horseradish, pepper, and salt. Mix 3 tablespoons of the vinaigrette with the diced salmon. Stir in 1 tablespoon of the chives. Divide the salmon mixture between small timbale molds or cups, press it lightly down, and refrigerate until just before serving.

Arrange lettuce leaves on plates. Turn out the salmon timbales on top of the lettuce leaves. Drizzle with the remaining vinaigrette and sprinkle the remaining 2 tablespoons chives on top.

LANGOUSTINES WITH GARLIC BUTTER

Humar með hvítlaukssmjöri
Serves 4 to 6 as a starter

Although the langoustine is quite common around Iceland, its popularity is fairly recent—it wasn't even eaten until a few decades ago, so there are no old recipes. It is very popular now, though expensive, and recipes for it abound—there was a time a few years ago when every other cooking column in the Icelandic newspapers seemed to have a langoustine recipe. The following recipe is fairly typical, since Icelanders have also become great garlic lovers.

3 garlic cloves
1/2 cup unsalted butter, softened
Juice of 1/2 lemon
16 to 20 langoustines in their shells
Freshly ground pepper
Salt
3 tablespoons chopped parsley

Finely chop the garlic and mix it with the butter and lemon juice. Melt a quarter of the lemon-garlic butter in a large frying pan. Fry the langoustines for 2 to 3 minutes at medium heat, turning them once and sprinkling them with pepper and salt. Add the rest of the butter and the chopped parsley.

When the butter begins to froth, remove the pan from the heat and pour the contents into a serving platter, or divide the langoustines and butter between 4 to 6 heated plates. Serve at once with crusty bread.

SHELLFISH IN WHITE WINE CREAM SAUCE

Skelfiskur í hvítvínsrjómasósu
Serves 6 as a starter

Icelanders love shellfish, especially langoustines, shrimp, and scallops, and often cook it in rich, creamy sauces. The following recipe can also be used for a gratin. In that case, the mixture is spooned into 6 individual ovenproof dishes or one large dish, and placed under a hot broiler until the topping is golden brown.

1 1/2 tablespoons butter
1 1/2 tablespoons flour
1/2 cup fish or shellfish stock
1/2 cup dry white wine
1/2 pound scallops
1/2 pound shrimp, cooked and shelled
3 tablespoons chopped dill
2 teaspoons freshly squeezed lemon juice
Freshly ground pepper
Salt
1/2 cup cream
Lettuce leaves
6 slices toasted bread

Melt the butter in a saucepan and stir in the flour. Cook for 1 minute, then gradually stir in the stock and the wine. Simmer gently for 5 to 8 minutes, stirring often.

Add scallops, shrimp, 2 tablespoons of the dill, and the lemon juice. Bring to a boil, season with pepper and salt, and simmer for 2 minutes. Remove from heat, stir in the cream, taste, and adjust seasonings.

Divide onto 6 plates decorated with lettuce, sprinkle with the remaining 1 tablespoon dill, and serve with the toast.

MARINATED SCALLOP AND PEPPER SALAD

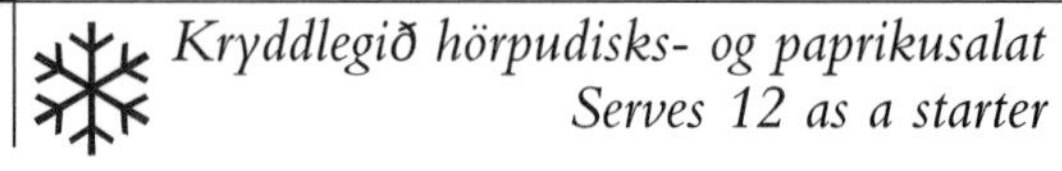
Kryddlegið hörpudisks- og paprikusalat
Serves 12 as a starter

This dish is always extremely popular at parties, even with people who do not normally like scallops. It is also very colorful and festive. I like to serve it straight from the bowl, or from a large earthenware jar, with some nice freshly baked bread to soak up the delicious marinade from the plate. The marinade can also be poured off and the scallops and peppers heaped on a plate.

This salad is very good for a buffet table but can also be served as a kind of antipasto or as a starter, maybe arranged on a lettuce leaf and served with some warm garlic bread.

1 orange, 1 yellow, and 1 red bell pepper
3 to 4 shallots
1 pound scallops
1/2 pound shrimp, shelled and cooked
1 cup roughly chopped pickled gherkins
1 cup dry white wine
1/4 cup white wine vinegar
1/4 cup olive oil
1/4 teaspoon green peppercorns
3 to 4 whole cloves
1 bay leaf, roughly crushed
Freshly ground pepper
Salt

Quarter and seed the peppers and cut them crosswise into narrow strips. Peel the shallots and cut them into wedges. Mix everything except the salt in a bowl or large jar and refrigerate for 12 to 24 hours, stirring occasionally. Salt to taste and serve with freshly baked crusty bread.

COD ROE SALAD

Þorskhrognasalat
Serves 6 as a starter

Cod roe has always been popular during the spawning season in late winter and early spring. Usually the roe was poached and served with the fish and its liver. Sometimes the roe sacks were inverted and stuffed with the liver before being poached. One might suppose the roe would break up when it isn't enclosed by the sack but it doesn't.

Úlfar Eysteinsson, who runs the fish restaurant Thrír Frakkar hjá Úlfari in Reykjavík, has created a modern version of this old dish. He stuffs one of the inverted roe sacks with fish forcemeat instead of liver, poaches the roe for at least 15 minutes, and serves it with potatoes and rye bread, or in thin slices as a starter.

The following recipe is for a roe salad that is commonly used as a starter or served on a buffet table.

1/2 pound cod roe
3/4 cup sour cream
1/4 cup mayonnaise
1 tablespoon grated onion
Pinch of curry powder
Freshly ground pepper
Salt
1 lemon
2 hard-boiled eggs
2 tomatoes
Few sprigs of parsley

Poach the roe in salted water and let them cool (or use canned roe). Remove the roe sacks and break the roe up with a spoon in a bowl. Stir in sour cream, mayonnaise, onion, curry powder, pepper, salt, and a few drops of lemon juice. Taste and adjust seasonings.

Spoon into a serving bowl or arrange on individual plates and decorate with egg and tomato wedges and parsley sprigs. Serve with lemon wedges and toasted bread.

GRAVAD FILLET OF LAMB

Grafinn lambahryggvöðvi
Serves 8 to 12 as a starter

A tender fillet of Icelandic lamb needs very little cooking, or no cooking at all, as it can be treated in a similar manner to gravlax, with salt and herbs. Wild thyme, *blóðberg*, grows abundantly in many places in Iceland and fills meadows and woodlands with its wonderful scent. Its flavor is not very strong, however, and rather a lot of it is needed. It is a popular herb for grilled lamb, and is also used for some sauces and salads.

1 pound lamb fillet
2 pounds coarse salt
2 tablespoons sugar
2 fistfuls wild thyme (or 1 fistful regular thyme)
3 teaspoons chopped chives
1 teaspoon finely chopped fresh rosemary
1 tablespoon coarsely crushed black pepper

Remove all fat and membranes from the fillet. Mix salt and sugar in a bowl. Spread some of it on a nonreactive dish, place the meat on top and cover with the rest of the salt/sugar mixture. Refrigerate for 3 to 4 hours.

Remove the fillet from the salt and wipe it off; if the salt sticks to the meat, you can run some cold water briefly over it and pat it dry. Chop the thyme and mix it with the rest of the herbs and the crushed pepper. Roll the meat in the herb mixture and press it firmly into it. Refrigerate, lightly pressed, for 24 hours.

Cut the meat diagonally into very thin slices and serve as a starter, perhaps with toasted bread, some lettuce, and a mustard or honey-mustard sauce (page 59).

GRAVAD BREAST OF PTARMIGAN

Grafnar rjúpnabringur
Serves 6 to 8 as a starter

The ptarmigan is a fairly strong-tasting game bird, not least because it is usually left to hang for several weeks in a cool place. It will not spoil but the flavor will get increasingly gamy and intense. Most aficionados agree it should hang breast down, to allow flavors from the herb-stuffed gizzard to slowly seep into the breast meat, although there are those who strongly disagree and say the bird should be hung by the head. For this dish, however, the bird should not hang for too long—1 week is ideal, but a couple of days might be enough.

Serve with a good vinaigrette, perhaps a mixture of cider vinegar and a fruity oil, mixed with chopped apples and/or grapes and a little honey or sugar.

6 ptarmigan breast halves, from birds that have hung in a cool airy place for 2 to 7 days
4 tablespoons coarse salt
2 tablespoons sugar
2-3 tablespoons chopped parsley
2 tablespoons fresh thyme, or 1 teaspoon dried
1 tablespoon peppercorns, preferably a 4-color mixture
5-8 juniper berries, crushed
1 garlic clove, crushed
1 tablespoon runny honey

Pat the ptarmigan breasts dry with a kitchen towel. Mix the rest of the ingredients (except the honey) in a bowl and roll the ptarmigan breasts in the mixture, pressing it into the meat. Place the breasts in a nonreactive dish and sprinkle with the remnants of the spice mixture. Drizzle with the honey. Cover and refrigerate for 24 to 36 hours, turning occasionally.

Remove the breasts from the marinade and scrape most of it off. Place the breasts on a cutting board and cut them into thin, diagonal slices. Arrange on a serving dish or individual plates, drizzle with vinaigrette and serve with a salad of wild herbs and red currants, or a nice green salad.

RAW SMOKED LAMB

Hrátt hangikjöt
Serves 8 as a starter

There are those who will tell you that eating uncooked smoked lamb was unheard of in Iceland until a few years ago. They say the custom was invented by a chef who wanted to serve raw Parma ham with melon but couldn't get permission to import it so he thought of using smoked lamb instead. Although this may have happened, many Icelanders happily treated themselves to uncooked smoked lamb long before that. I remember when my mother was cooking the smoked lamb for Christmas, she usually had to guard the meat closely from the moment it was brought into the kitchen until it went into the huge cooking pot, since everyone was trying to cut himself a thin slice of the delicious smoked meat, usually very dark red and almost black on the outside, after having hung for weeks or even months in a smoke-filled hut.

You will need smoked lamb for this, of course. There is no substitute. And even if a friend or relative in Iceland has sent you some smoked lamb, it will probably be a boned and rolled leg, too lightly smoked to be really good. You ideally need a heavily smoked shoulder or leg that must not be too salty. The meat can be cut into thin slices and served plain, with melon wedges or other fruit, or it can be flavored further with a dry herb marinade, as in the following recipe.

1/2 pound smoked lamb
1/2 teaspoon freshly ground pepper
1/4 teaspoon freshly ground allspice
5-6 juniper berries, crushed
a bunch of fresh thyme sprigs

Trim excess fat off the lamb and rub it with a mixture of pepper, allspice, and juniper berries. Wrap it in thyme sprigs, pack it tightly in foil or plastic wrap, and refrigerate for a day or two.

When it is to be served, remove the wrappings and the thyme sprigs and place the meat in the freezer for an hour. With a sharp knife, cut it into very thin slices and arrange them on a plate. Serve with rye bread or toasted white bread, and perhaps some honey-mustard sauce (page 59).

REINDEER CANAPÉS

Snittur með hreindýrasteik
Makes 40 to 50 canapés

The Icelandic reindeer stock is carefully monitored and hunting quotas are very strict. Consequently, reindeer meat has become very expensive and the best cuts are only served at very special occasions, like Christmas. The recipe for these delicious canapés was developed when reindeer was easier to get and less expensive. They can be served as a finger food or hors d'oeuvre.

A reindeer fillet may be hard to come by in many countries but venison or other similar game can be used in most recipes that call for reindeer.

1/2 pound reindeer fillet
1/2 teaspoon freshly ground pepper
1 tablespoon oil
1/2 teaspoon salt, or to taste
4 tablespoons butter, softened
2 teaspoons chopped fresh thyme
1/2 teaspoon Dijon mustard
8 to 10 thin slices rye bread or toasted white bread
Red currant jelly
Few sprigs of fresh thyme (wild or regular)

Season the meat with pepper. Heat the oil in a sauté pan and fry the meat for 3 to 5 minutes on each side, according to taste. Remove from the pan, salt and let cool. Cut the fillet into thin slices. Mix butter, thyme, and mustard in a bowl and season to taste.

Cut the bread slices into small squares or rounds and butter them with the herb butter. Place a slice of meat on each and decorate with a dollop of jelly and a thyme spring.

PUFFIN SPREAD

Lundakæfa
Makes 2 cups

This spread is ideal as a finger food, spread, or piped on small crackers or pieces of toast and perhaps decorated with a slice of pickled gherkin and a small dollop of red currant or black currant jelly.

Puffin may not be widely available but this recipe also works for wild goose legs; simmer or braise them until tender, then chop them up and process them with the rest of the ingredients.

6 puffin breast halves
Salt
1/2 cup butter
4 to 5 pickled gherkins
1/2 teaspoon dried thyme
Pinch of nutmeg
1/2 bay leaf, crushed
3 to 4 juniper berries, crushed
Freshly ground pepper

Simmer the puffin breasts in salted water for around 1 hour. Remove them from the pan and let them cool somewhat.

Take the meat off the bone, cut into pieces, and place in a food processor along with the butter, gherkins, herbs, and spices, and process until smooth. Season to taste. Put the paste into a piping bag with a star-shaped nozzle and pipe it onto small crackers, or spoon it into a mold and refrigerate until stiff.

SMOKED SALMON SPREAD

Laxasmurostur
Makes 2 cups

Smoking was a preservation method much used in Iceland from the earliest times, not least for salmon, trout, and char. The following recipe will work equally well for any of these species.

A wide variety of flavored cream cheeses and cheese spreads can be bought in Iceland but these spreads are also frequently made at home. This fairly typical spread can be served with toast or crackers, or piped on small crackers which are decorated with a sprig of dill or parsley.

8 ounces smoked salmon
8 ounces cream cheese, softened
1 1/2 tablespoons freshly squeezed lemon juice
1 small red onion, finely chopped
2 tablespoons chopped dill
Dash of Tabasco sauce
Freshly ground black pepper
Salt (optional)

Chop the salmon, place it in a food processor with the cream cheese and lemon juice, and process until smooth. Alternatively, run the salmon through a mincer, then mix it with the cheese and lemon juice. Stir in chopped red onion, dill, and Tabasco sauce, and season to taste. Serve the spread with crackers or lightly toasted baguette slices.

LAMB SPREAD FROM LEFTOVERS

Lambasmurkæfa
Makes 3 to 3 1/2 cups

This is a good but slightly untraditional method to deal with a big chunk of leftover roasted lamb. The spread can be kept refrigerated for 2 or 3 days but it can also be frozen. It is very good on some crusty bread, dark rye bread, or rye flatbread.

1 pound cooked lamb, off the bone
6 tablespoons butter, softened
1/2 onion, chopped
2 to 3 garlic cloves, finely chopped
1/4 cup leftover gravy or good stock
2 tablespoons port or brandy (optional)
Freshly ground pepper
Salt

Cut the meat into cubes and remove all fat. Melt the butter in a saucepan and sauté the onion and garlic at medium-low heat until softened, but do not let it brown. Place meat, onion mixture, and the gravy or stock in the bowl of a food processor and process until fairly smooth. Add port or brandy, if desired, and season with pepper and salt to taste. Spoon into a jar or bowl and refrigerate.

SHRIMP DIP

Rækjusalat
Makes 4 cups

Dips like this were served at almost every party in the 1970s—cocktail parties, youth parties, confirmations, birthdays, funerals, sewing clubs—always with Ritz crackers and other similar crackers. It is still popular, but not quite as common as it used to be.

A tablespoon or two of grated onion is sometimes added to the dip, and maybe a pinch or two of curry powder. Many newer versions include finely cubed bell peppers, often in two or three colors.

3 eggs
1/2 pound shrimp, peeled and cooked
1 small (5 ounces) can crushed pineapple
1/2 cup mayonnaise
1/2 cup sour cream
1/2 teaspoon paprika
1 teaspoon lemon juice
Dash of Tabasco sauce
Freshly ground pepper
Salt

Hard-boil the eggs, cool, peel, and chop. Chop the shrimp, unless it is small. Drain the crushed pineapple well.

Mix mayonnaise and sour cream in a bowl and stir in paprika, lemon juice, Tabasco sauce, pepper, and salt. Add shrimp, chopped eggs, and crushed pineapple and blend well. Refrigerate until serving.

COCKTAIL SAUCE

Kokkteilsósa
Makes 1 cup

If you buy fast food in Iceland—especially if it is accompanied with French fries—chances are you will get or be offered this immensely popular dipping sauce. It is also often served at home with fried fish or chicken, and several other dishes. It became popular in the 1960s.

The original version, developed by a restaurant owner in Keflavík around 1960, was a mixture of cold béchamel sauce and mayonnaise, mixed with tomato ketchup, pineapple juice, and spices. Modern fast-food versions are often made of a mixture of mayonnaise, ketchup, mustard, and seasonings. The following recipe is a slightly refined version I was taught in a cookery course in Akureyri in 1976.

1 cup mayonnaise
1/2 cup sour cream (optional)
4 tablespoons tomato ketchup
1 tablespoon pineapple juice
1 tablespoon sherry (optional)
1 teaspoon paprika, preferably Hungarian
Dash of Tabasco sauce
Freshly ground pepper
Salt

Mix the mayonnaise, sour cream, ketchup, pineapple juice, and sherry, if using, until well combined and smooth. Stir in the paprika and add Tabasco sauce, pepper, and salt to taste. This sauce can be kept in a covered bowl in the refrigerator for a couple of days.

HONEY-MUSTARD SAUCE

Graflaxsósa
Makes 1 cup

This sauce is commonly served with gravlax and also with other dry-marinated fish and meat, and sometimes with smoked salmon and raw smoked lamb. The recipe calls for making the mayonnaise base from scratch but you can also omit the egg yolk, vinegar, and oil and use a ready-made mayonnaise instead, especially if salmonella in raw eggs is a concern.

4 tablespoons Dijon mustard
1 egg yolk
1 to 2 tablespoons honey
1 tablespoon white wine vinegar
Freshly ground pepper
Salt
1/2 cup vegetable oil
2 tablespoon finely chopped dill

All ingredients should be at room temperature. Whisk mustard, egg yolk, honey, vinegar, pepper, and salt in a bowl until well combined, or use a blender. Gradually whisk in the oil. Stir in the chopped dill and adjust seasonings.

Should the sauce curdle or fail to thicken, just pour it into a bowl, add another egg yolk to the blender, whisk it and gradually whisk in the sauce again.

DILL-MUSTARD SAUCE

Dill-sinnepssósa
Makes 1 1/2 cups

Here is another popular sauce to serve with gravlax. This is a creamy, fairly mild mustard sauce, flavored with dill.

1 cup sour cream or full-fat yogurt
1/4 cup mayonnaise
3 tablespoons chopped dill
2 tablespoons mild mustard
1 teaspoon sugar or honey
1/2 teaspoon freshly ground pepper
Salt

Mix sour cream and mayonnaise. Add dill, mustard, sugar, pepper, and salt to taste. Refrigerate for at least 2 hours. Serve with smoked or gravad salmon or trout, or marinated raw fish.

CUCUMBER SAUCE

Gúrkusósa
Makes 2 cups

Several versions of cucumber sauces and dips are made to go with salmon, trout, and other fish. Most of them are dairy-based and flavored with herbs.

5-inch piece of cucumber
Salt
1 cup sour cream, skyr, or yogurt
1/4 cup finely chopped pickled gherkins
1 tablespoon finely chopped capers
1 tablespoon chopped dill or parsley
1/4 teaspoon freshly ground pepper

Grate the cucumber on a coarse grater, sprinkle a little salt on it and set aside for 15 to 30 minutes. Squeeze out as much juice as possible. Mix sour cream, gherkins, and capers, or process in a food processor for a smooth sauce. Add the grated cucumber and stir in dill, pepper, and salt to taste. Refrigerate for at least an hour. Serve with fried or grilled salmon or other fish.

FISH AND SHELLFISH DISHES

Iceland is surrounded by some of the best fishing grounds in the world and the catches of the trawlers and fishing boats have made it one of the richest nations in the world, but this has really only fairly recently begun to show to any extent in the cuisine. Icelanders used to boil their fish, or fry it—usually breaded—using the same simple recipes over and over again, and they tended to overcook the fish.

This has more or less changed. There is now a wealth of fish recipes to chose from and people have been getting more adventurous, although most still don't like cod. Many new trends have emerged and fish and shellfish species that few would have dared to eat a few decades ago are now very popular and fetch high prices.

The recipes here are a mixture of old and new, traditional simple recipes like poached haddock and fried fishballs and spicy dishes that are meant to show what the ordinary Icelander is cooking at home these days.

POACHED HADDOCK

Soðin ýsa
Serves 4

A survey published a few years ago revealed that poached haddock with boiled potatoes was still the most popular meal in Iceland, closely followed by pan-fried haddock. This may now have changed somewhat, not least because prices have been rising, but haddock is still what most Icelanders think of when they say "fish."

Icelander's attitude towards cod is somewhat of an enigma. It is caught in large quantities and is vitally important for the economy. Yet many Icelanders have never tasted fresh cod, and it can even sometimes be hard to find. Most people prefer its smaller relative, the haddock.

If the haddock is truly fresh, this simple dish can be quite delicious. Cross-cut whole steaks are vastly preferred over fillets, but even in Iceland, many shops now only sell haddock fillets.

One 2-pound haddock, cleaned and beheaded but whole
1 tablespoon coarse salt
1 tablespoons lemon juice or vinegar (optional)
3 to 4 peppercorns (optional)
1 bay leaf (optional)

Rinse the fish in cold water and scrape it. The fins are sometimes cut off but that isn't necessary. Cut the fish into 1 1/2-inch thick steaks and place them in a wide pan with the salt. Add lemon juice or vinegar, peppercorns, and bay leaf, if using. Add cold water to cover. Bring to a boil, skim, cover, and simmer at very low heat for 8 to 10 minutes, or until just cooked through.

Remove with a slotted spoon and arrange on a serving platter. Serve with boiled potatoes and melted tallow with cracklings, or with butter.

During the spawning season, in late winter and spring, the haddock is often served with poached cod liver and roe. This is usually cooked in a separate pan and a little vinegar or lemon is often added to the cooking water, along with salt and peppercorns.

BREADED PAN-FRIED HADDOCK

Steikt ýsa í raspi
Serves 4

This has for decades been the second most popular method (after poaching) to prepare haddock and other white fish. The fish pieces are sometimes just dusted in a little seasoned flour but it used to be much more common to cover them with dried bread crumbs. Garishly colored Paxo bread crumbs were almost a requirement in the 1960s and 70s but people now tend to use plain bread crumbs, sometimes homemade. The bread crumbs were sometimes seasoned with a little curry powder or paprika but a modern cook might add some fresh or dried herbs and maybe a pinch of cayenne pepper.

1 1/2 pounds haddock fillets (or other white fish)
1 egg
1 tablespoon milk
1/2 cup dried bread crumbs
Freshly ground pepper
Salt
4 to 6 tablespoons margarine or butter
1 lemon
Few sprigs of parsley (optional)

Skin and bone the fish fillets and cut them into pieces. Lightly whisk egg and milk in a shallow bowl. Mix the bread crumbs and seasonings in another bowl.

Melt the margarine in a frying pan. When it is no longer frothy, dip the fish pieces into the egg mixture, roll them in bread crumbs and arrange them in the pan. Lower the heat somewhat and fry the fish at medium heat for 3 to 4 minutes on each side.

Arrange the fish pieces on a serving platter and decorate with lemon wedges and parsley sprigs. Serve with boiled potatoes.

FRIED FISH WITH ONIONS

Steiktur fiskur með lauk
Serves 4

Another traditional method for frying fish is to roll it in seasoned flour instead of bread crumbs and serve it with a thick onion sauce or stew. The recipe can be used for almost any white fish but some only use it for ocean catfish, others only for halibut, and so on.

Onions, while not grown in Iceland, were being imported in the nineteenth century and became a very popular accompaniment to pan-fried fish dishes, either browned and cooked in liquid, as in the following recipe, or simply fried in fat until lightly browned and heaped on the fish.

1 1/2 pounds white fish fillets
3 tablespoons flour
Freshly ground pepper
Salt
3 medium onions
4 tablespoons butter
1 cup meat stock (or water and a stock cube)

Skin and bone the fish fillets and cut them into pieces. Dust them with flour seasoned with pepper and salt and let stand for a few minutes. Peel the onions and thinly slice them.

Melt 2 tablespoons of the butter in a frying pan and fry the fish at medium heat for 3 to 4 minutes on each side, or until just cooked through. Remove with a slotted spoon and keep warm.

Add the remaining 2 tablespoons butter to the pan, raise the heat, and add the onion slices. Cook at fairly high heat, stirring often, until the onions begin to brown.

Meanwhile, bring the stock or water to a boil in a saucepan. Pour it over the onions, stir and cook briskly until not much liquid is left. Lower the heat again, arrange the fish pieces on top of the onions, cover and simmer for a minute or two.

Serve immediately, perhaps with some mashed potatoes.

BAKED FISH WITH VEGETABLES I

Bakaður fiskur með grænmeti
Serves 4

This is a fairly typical recipe for a warm and filling fish dish that is just right on cold winter days. The small amount of curry called for in the recipe is about as spicy and daring as a traditional Icelandic fish recipe gets. On leafing through my old Home Economics cookbook, I note that pepper and curry are the only spices used for fish, unless one counts a couple of tablespoons of tomato ketchup here and there as a spice. That doesn't mean the dish is bland, though. This depends entirely on the type and quality of the fish used. Haddock is fine but cod, halibut, ocean catfish, ling, and other white fish should be good, too.

1 pound fish fillets, skinned and boned
Freshly ground pepper
Salt
4 medium potatoes
4 medium carrots
1 medium rutabaga
1 small leek
2 tablespoons butter
2 tablespoons flour
1/4 teaspoon curry powder

Preheat the oven to 375°F. Cut the fish into pieces, season with pepper and salt, and arrange them in a buttered ovenproof dish. Peel the potatoes, carrots, and rutabaga and cut them into chunks. Split and clean the leek and cut it into 3-inch pieces. Parboil the vegetables in 2 cups lightly salted water for 8 to 10 minutes.

Drain but do not discard the water. Melt the butter in a saucepan. Stir in the flour and curry powder and cook for 1 minute, stirring continuously. Gradually whisk in around 1 cup of the hot vegetable stock—the sauce should neither be too thick nor too thin. Season to taste and cook for 3 to 4 minutes.

Arrange the vegetables on top of the fish, pour the sauce over them, and bake for 15 minutes or so, or until the fish is cooked through and the vegetables are tender.

BAKED FISH WITH VEGETABLES II

Bakaður fiskur með grænmeti
Serves 4

Another fish and root vegetable dish that uses more or less the same ingredients as the previous recipe, although the finished dish is very different. Many modern versions would leave out the rutabagas, perhaps substituting them with another vegetable, such as bell peppers or broccoli.

1 1/2 pounds white fish fillets, such as haddock or ling
Freshly ground pepper
Salt
4 tablespoons butter
1 cup peeled and thinly sliced carrots
2 cups peeled and cubed rutabagas
2 cups peeled and cubed potatoes
1 cup thinly sliced onions
1/2 cup chopped celery
1 to 2 garlic cloves
1 cup fish stock
1/2 cup white wine or whey

Preheat the oven to 350°F. Skin and bone the fish, cut it into pieces and season it with pepper and salt. Butter an ovenproof dish with some of the butter.

Mix all the vegetables and the garlic in a bowl and cover the bottom of the ovenproof dish with half the mixture. Season with pepper and salt. Arrange half the fish on top, add the rest of the vegetables, more seasonings, and top with the rest of the fish.

Mix the fish stock and wine or whey and pour over the fish. Dot with the remaining butter, place a tight lid on the dish or cover with foil, and bake for 40 minutes.

CURRIED HADDOCK WITH SHRIMP AND PINEAPPLE

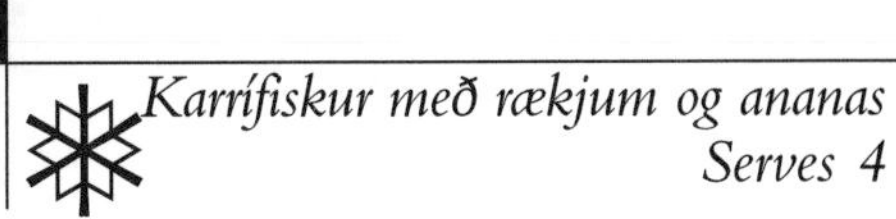
Karrífiskur með rækjum og ananas
Serves 4

The following recipe is a fairly representative example of how many Icelanders might cook their haddock when they want to make something special out of it. I've seen variations on this recipe featured several times in newspapers and magazines in recent years, especially when featuring favorite recipes. It is a festive way of serving the rather bland haddock.

This particular version includes no cheese or butter but I have a feeling that the original recipe probably contained a sizeable amount of cream cheese or cheese spread.

2 to 3 tablespoons vegetable oil
1 1/2 pounds haddock fillets, boned and skinned
1 medium leek
1 garlic clove
1 cup chopped red bell pepper
1 cup shrimp, cooked and peeled
1 cup sour cream
1 small can pineapple chunks
2 teaspoons Worcestershire sauce
1 teaspoon curry powder, or to taste
1 teaspoon paprika (preferably Hungarian)
Freshly ground pepper
Salt

Preheat the oven to 400°F and brush an ovenproof dish with some of the oil. Cut the haddock into fairly small pieces. Wash and clean the leek and thinly slice it. Crush the garlic or finely chop it. Heat the remaining oil in a skillet and sauté the leek and garlic for a few minutes, until softened. Add the bell pepper and cook for another 3 minutes.

Add the shrimp, sour cream, pineapple chunks, the juice from the pineapple can, Worcestershire sauce, curry powder, paprika, pepper, and some salt and stir until well combined. Add the fish and bring to a boil. Remove the skillet from the heat, pour the contents into the prepared ovenproof dish and bake for 15 to 20 minutes, or until the fish is cooked through. Serve with rice.

FISH GRATIN WITH SHRIMP SAUCE

Fiskgratín með rækjusósu
Serves 4

I'm usually not fond of combining fish and cheese in a dish but most of my countrymen seem to disagree with me there. Many add some form of cheese to almost any fish dish they cook—grated cheese, cream cheese, flavored cheese spreads, Parmesan cheese, and so on. Several of these recipes probably originated in the test kitchen of the Icelandic Dairy Produce Marketing Association, which has for decades been publishing recipe booklets and cookbooks to promote its products. The following is a fairly basic example of a dish of this kind.

1 1/2 pounds white fish fillets (i.e. haddock or cod)
3 tablespoons butter
1 1/2 cups milk
1/2 cup chopped onion
1 1/2 tablespoons flour
1/2 cup grated cheese
1/4 pound shrimp, peeled and cooked
Pinch of cayenne pepper
Freshly ground pepper
Salt

Skin and bone the fish fillets and cut them into pieces. Preheat the oven to 400°F. Butter an ovenproof dish with 1 tablespoon of the butter and arrange the fish pieces in it.

Heat the milk in a saucepan. Melt the remaining 2 tablespoons butter in a skillet and sauté the onion for around 5 minutes, or until softened. Add the flour and stir constantly until it begins to color. Gradually stir in the hot milk and bring to a boil, stirring until the sauce is smooth. Simmer for 2 to 3 minutes, then stir in the cheese and remove from the heat.

Chop the shrimp roughly and stir them into the sauce along with cayenne pepper and ground pepper and add salt to taste. Pour the sauce over the fish and bake for around 20 minutes, or until the topping has colored nicely.

OVERNIGHT-SALTED HADDOCK

Nætursöltuð ýsa
Serves 6

Overnight-salted fish is just that; the fish is usually cured for only a day or two, although it can be left in the salt for up to a week (then it will need some soaking in cold water before cooking). Haddock is the preferred fish for this, although cod and other white fish may be used, and this is also a good method for trout.

Icelanders usually do not prepare this at home, as most stores sell the lightly salted haddock, but it is easy to do.

2 pounds haddock fillets
4 tablespoons salt

Arrange the fillets, skin side down, on a shallow tray, and sprinkle the salt evenly over them. Cover with plastic wrap and refrigerate for 24 to 48 hours.

When the fillets are to be cooked, they are washed in cold running water and drained well. Cut them into pieces and place them in a large pan. Cover with cold water, bring slowly to a boil and simmer for a minute, then remove from heat and let the fish remain in the hot liquid for 5 minutes or so, or until cooked through.

Serve with boiled potatoes and vegetables, and some butter.

SALTED HADDOCK IN A CREAM SAUCE

Nætursöltuð ýsa í rjómasósu
Serves 4

Although the overnight-salted haddock is usually just poached and served with boiled potatoes and other vegetables, it can be used for other recipes, too, and here is one way of dealing with it. The lightly salted fish is much firmer and tastier than ordinary fresh haddock, which can be a bit bland and boring, especially if it has been frozen.

1 1/2 pounds overnight-salted haddock, see the previous recipe
2 tablespoons flour
1/2 teaspoon ground pepper
1/2 teaspoon paprika
1/4 teaspoon garlic powder
Pinch of cayenne pepper
2 tablespoons butter
1 cup thinly sliced onion
1 large red or yellow bell pepper, seeded and chopped
1 cup light cream
1/2 teaspoon soy sauce

Wash the fillets in cold running water, drain well, and pat dry with a kitchen towel. Skin and bone them and cut them into pieces. Mix flour and spices in a plastic bag, throw in the fish pieces, and toss to coat them completely.

Melt the butter in a large heavy pan and sauté the onion for a few minutes at medium heat, until it is soft and transparent. Push towards the sides of the pan and raise the heat somewhat. Place the fish pieces on the pan and fry them for 2 to 3 minutes, or until golden brown. Turn them, add peppers and fry for 1 to 2 minutes more.

Add cream and soy sauce, bring to a boil, cover and simmer at low heat for a few minutes, or until the fish is cooked through and the peppers are tender.

Serve with rice or mashed potatoes.

SALT COD WITH VEGETABLES

Saltfiskur með grænmeti
Serves 6

The important role that salt fish has played for over two centuries in the Icelandic economy is not reflected in the traditional cuisine. It has often been said that the Portuguese—and probably some other southern European nations as well—have 365 recipes for salt fish. It is also often said that the Icelanders, who are major producers of salt fish and eat a lot of it themselves, have only one recipe, which can be described in two words: Boil it.

While not quite correct, this is not far from the truth either. The first Icelandic fish cookbook, *160 Fish Dishes*, published in 1939, does have five salt fish recipes—but one of them is for poached salt fish, and three are for dealing with leftover poached salt fish.

The fish is traditionally served with boiled potatoes and rutabagas, and some melted fat—sheep tallow, margarine, or butter. These days carrots are often served with salt fish, and sometimes broccoli or other vegetables as well. Most people buy their fish already soaked.

4 medium carrots
2 medium rutabagas
Salt
8 medium potatoes
2 pounds soaked salt cod

Peel or scrape the carrots and cut them into pieces. Peel the rutabagas and cut them into chunks. Place carrots and rutabagas in a saucepan, add water to cover, bring to a boil, salt lightly and simmer for around 20 minutes, or until tender. Drain.

Meanwhile, boil the potatoes until tender, let them cool slightly, and peel them. Cut the salt cod into fairly large pieces and place them in a saucepan. Add cold water to cover, bring slowly to a boil and simmer for 6 to 8 minutes, or until just cooked through.

Arrange fish on a serving platter with the vegetables and serve with melted butter, or maybe a mustard sauce (page 60) or lemon butter sauce (page 78).

PAN-FRIED SALT COD WITH TOMATO SAUCE

Pönnusteiktur saltfiskur með tómatsósu
Serves 4

It wasn't really until the late 1980s that Icelanders discovered there were other methods to cook their beloved salt cod, and its popularity underwent a renewal when Mediterranean recipes swept the nation. Tomatoes, garlic, olives, and herbs are now very common ingredients in salt fish recipes, along with chili peppers and exotic spices.

The following modern recipe has a definite Mediterranean flavor but it is still Icelandic in character—no exotic spices and vegetables here, just ingredients that have earned themselves a solid place in local cooking. The whey is a very Icelandic addition.

1 1/2 pounds soaked salt cod
2 tablespoons oil
1/2 medium onion, chopped
1 garlic clove, finely chopped
1 cup chopped canned tomatoes
1 bay leaf
1/2 teaspoon dried thyme
Freshly ground pepper
1/2 cup whey or white wine
6 tablespoons flour
3 tablespoons butter

The salt cod, which needs to be well soaked, should be boneless and skinned. Cut it into 4 to 6 fairly equal pieces.

Heat the oil in a saucepan and sauté the chopped onion and garlic for a few minutes, or until softened. Add tomatoes, bay leaf, thyme, pepper, and whey or wine, bring to a boil, and simmer for 10 to 15 minutes. Season to taste.

Meanwhile, roll the fish in flour liberally seasoned with pepper. Melt the butter in a frying pan and fry the fish at medium heat for 3 to 4 minutes on each side, or until just cooked through.

Serve with the tomato sauce and boiled or mashed potatoes.

BREADED COD CHEEKS

Þorskkinnar í raspi
Serves 4

Cod cheeks are scallop-size, with a dense, fibrous texture, like monkfish or scallops (and they can, in fact, be substituted for scallops in most recipes, and vice versa). Since the cod is not known for chewing its food much, the cheek muscles are little used and are tender and cook rather quickly, despite their density. They were usually poached or pan-fried and here is one traditional recipe.

12 skinned cod cheeks
2 eggs
1 cup fresh bread crumbs
Freshly ground pepper
Salt
4 tablespoons butter or margarine

Wash the cheeks and pat them dry. Break the eggs into a bowl and whisk them lightly. Mix bread crumbs, pepper, and salt on a plate. Melt the butter in a large frying pan. Dip the cheeks in the egg, roll them in the bread crumbs, and fry them at fairly high heat for 2 to 3 minutes on each side.

Serve with boiled potatoes and other vegetables, and some melted butter.

The bread crumbs can be flavored in various ways, for instance with paprika, basil, tarragon, and parsley.

CHEEKS IN PEPPER CREAM SAUCE

Kinnar í paprikurjómasósu
Serves 4

Modern cooks have used cheeks in many innovative ways: cooked in various types of sauces, baked au gratin, grilled or broiled, quick-fried with vegetables, and so on. Or they may be quickly fried in hot oil, then marinated for several hours in olive oil and lemon juice with herbs and spices, and served at room temperature as a starter or a part of a cold buffet. One of the most popular methods is to simmer the cheeks in a creamy sauce.

2 large red bell peppers
1 large green bell pepper
2 shallots, chopped
1 cup cream
Pinch of cayenne pepper
Freshly ground pepper
Salt
1 1/2 pounds cod or halibut cheeks, skinned
1 tablespoon olive oil

Core the peppers and thinly slice them. Put the green pepper and one of the red peppers aside. Place the remaining red pepper in a saucepan, pour over the cream, bring to a boil, and simmer, covered, for around 20 minutes.

Let cool slightly, then transfer to a food processor or blender and process until smooth. Season with cayenne pepper, ground pepper, and salt. Pour back into the saucepan, add the fish cheeks, bring to a boil, and simmer for 4 to 5 minutes, or until the cheeks are cooked.

Meanwhile, heat the oil in another pan and sauté the reserved peppers for a few minutes. Transfer the cheeks to a serving platter, pour the sauce over them, and arrange the pepper slices around the edges.

GARLICKY COD TONGUE GRATIN

Gratíneraðar hvítlauksgellur
Serves 4

Cod tongues—or rather, throat muscles (*gellur* in Icelandic)—have long been regarded as a delicacy in Iceland, as well as in other cod fishing communities all around the North Atlantic. Boys (and sometimes girls) used to earn a little pocket money by cutting out the tongues from fish heads they were given by fishermen on the dock and selling them, either to neighbors or to shops.

The cod tongues are usually fried or baked au gratin, or they may be salted and poached. Take care to remove membranes before cooking.

1 pound cod tongues
Freshly ground pepper
Salt
3 tablespoons butter
3 tablespoons olive oil
3 slices white bread
5 to 6 garlic cloves
4 to 5 tablespoons chopped parsley
1 teaspoon chopped fresh rosemary, or 1/4 teaspoon dried

Preheat the oven to 400°F and season the cod tongues with pepper and salt. Put the butter and oil into a fairly large ovenproof dish and place it in the oven until the dish is hot and the butter has melted.

Meanwhile, place the bread in a food processor or blender along with garlic, parsley, and rosemary and run the machine until you have fine crumbs. Season them with a little pepper and salt and transfer them to a plate.

Remove the hot dish from the oven and roll the cod tongues in the melted butter. Press one side firmly into the bread crumb mixture and arrange them in the dish, breaded side up. Return to the oven and bake for 10 to 12 minutes, or until the bread crumbs begin to brown.

Serve with boiled potatoes or rice.

POACHED HALIBUT WITH LEMON BUTTER SAUCE

Soðin lúða með sítrónusmjörsósu
Serves 4

Halibut is another fish that has always been popular in Iceland, from the earliest times onward. It is quite common, especially by the western and southern coast. The halibut can grow extremely large; the largest ever caught in Icelandic waters was over 10 feet long and weighed around 550 pounds. Although large specimens are occasionally caught these days, small halibuts of a few pounds make up most of the catch. Halibut is no longer actively pursued but will often be mixed in with a catch of other species, so it is always available in shops. An Icelandic fish farm has been having very good results with halibut farming recently.

One of the Icelandic names of the halibut is *heilagfiski*, "holy fish." Many legends surround it and a large halibut was usually (but not universally) considered a lucky catch. One legend says that any fisherman who catches increasingly large halibuts in the same spot, especially if they seem be just under the surface, should beware and row away as fast as he can, because the Halibut Mother, supposedly a fearsome creature, is drawing near.

Salt
10 black peppercorns
1 bay leaf
Finely grated zest and juice of 1 lemon
4 cross-cut slices of small halibut (around 1/2 pound each)
1/2 cup butter
1/2 teaspoon Dijon mustard
1/4 teaspoon curry powder
1 to 2 tablespoons chopped chives
Freshly ground pepper

Bring water to a boil in a pan large enough to accommodate the halibut slices in a single layer and add 1 teaspoon salt, the peppercorns, bay leaf, and a little juice from the lemon. Simmer for a few minutes. Add the halibut and simmer for 8 to 10 minutes, or until the halibut is just cooked through.

Meanwhile, melt the butter in a small saucepan at very low heat; it should be only just melted, not hot. Remove from heat and stir in lemon zest, 1 tablespoon lemon juice, mustard, curry powder, and chives. Season with salt and pepper and add more lemon juice, if desired. Remove the cooked halibut slices from the pan with a slotted spoon and arrange them on a serving platter.

Serve with boiled potatoes and the butter sauce.

HALIBUT WITH LEEK AND MUSHROOMS

Lúða með blaðlauk og sveppum
Serves 4

Halibut is a versatile fish that will stand up to most cooking methods. It is often just poached, as in the preceding recipe, but it may also be used for soups and stews, pan-fried, grilled, or baked, often au gratin, as in this recipe.

1 1/2 pounds halibut fillets
1 lemon
Freshly ground pepper
Salt
2 tablespoons oil
3 cups chopped leeks
1 tablespoon butter
2 cups thinly sliced mushrooms
1 cup cream
4 tablespoons cream cheese
1/4 teaspoon paprika
2 to 3 tablespoons chopped parsley

Preheat the oven to 350°F. Skin and bone the halibut fillets and cut them into pieces. Cut the lemon in two, press the juice from one half and sprinkle it over the fish. Season with pepper and salt and let sit for 10 minutes or so.

Meanwhile, heat the oil in a heavy skillet and sauté the leek for around 5 minutes, but do not let it brown. Remove the leek with a slotted spoon and set aside. Melt the butter in the skillet and fry the sliced mushrooms for a few minutes at medium heat. Add the leek back to the pan, pour in the cream and when it bubbles, stir in the cream cheese, paprika, parsley, and a little pepper.

Arrange the halibut in an ovenproof dish, pour the leek and mushroom sauce over it, and bake for around 20 minutes, or until the halibut is just cooked through.

CURRIED OCEAN CATFISH

Steinbítur í karrísósu
Serves 6

The Icelandic name of this large fish, *steinbítur*, means "stone biter" and it needs its ferocious-looking teeth to crush the clams and sea urchins that make up part of its diet. Ocean catfish is fairly common in Icelandic waters, especially by the Western Fjords. It was usually dried—and many people still prefer it to any other dried fish—but it was also eaten fresh, either poached or pan-fried.

The fish has to be very fresh, as ocean catfish spoils quickly. This could be one reason why curry is often used in older ocean catfish recipes—it might be an attempt to disguise that the fish is just beginning to go off. It doesn't work, of course, but as a matter of fact curry fits the fish quite well.

2 pounds ocean catfish fillets
1/2 lemon
Freshly ground pepper
Salt
2 medium onions
5 tablespoons butter or margarine
2 tablespoons flour
1/2 teaspoon curry powder, or to taste
1 cup fish stock or water

Skin and bone the fish fillets and cut them crosswise into 1-inch strips. Sprinkle them with juice from the lemon, season with pepper and salt, and let stand for 10 to 15 minutes.

Peel the onions and slice them thin. Melt 3 tablespoons butter in a frying pan and fry the onion slices at medium heat until they begin to color. Remove them with a slotted spoon and set aside.

Melt the remaining 2 tablespoons butter in the pan. Mix flour, curry powder, and some pepper and salt and dust the fish pieces with some of it. Fry them quickly at high heat until browned on both sides. Pour in the fish stock or water and bring to a boil.

Place the remaining flour in a jar with 1/4 cup cold water, put on a lid, and shake until well combined and smooth. Stir the mixture into the pan to thicken the sauce. Add the onions when the sauce is smooth.

Simmer for 5 minutes, adjust seasonings, and serve with boiled potatoes and perhaps some vegetables.

OCEAN PERCH IN MUSTARD CREAM SAUCE

Karfi í sinnepsrjómasósu
Serves 4

Icelandic trawlers catch a lot of ocean perch (redfish) but until fairly recently, it was not often seen in stores and there are no traditional recipes. Modern Icelandic chefs cook it quite often, sometimes with lots of spices and other exotic ingredients, sometimes with a creamy sauce which can be hot or mild, according to taste, such as this one.

1 1/2 pounds ocean perch fillets
3 tablespoons flour
Freshly ground pepper
Salt
2 tablespoons butter
1 cup matchstick-cut carrots
1 cup matchstick-cut zucchini
1 cup cream
1 tablespoon Dijon mustard, or to taste

Skin and bone the fillets and cut them into pieces, unless they are very small. Dust them liberally with flour seasoned with pepper and salt.

Melt the butter in a sauté pan and fry the fish at high heat until browned on one side. Turn them over and add the vegetables. Fry for 1 minute, then add cream and mustard and simmer for a few minutes, or until the fish is just cooked through and the vegetables are tender.

Adjust seasonings and serve the fish in the pan, or transfer to a heated serving platter.

GRILLED MONKFISH

Grillaður skötuselur
Serves 4

If the first sunny spring day in Reykjavík happens to be a Saturday or Sunday, it is a safe bet that barbecue smells will waft through the streets. Iceland is not the ideal barbecue country, weatherwise, but almost everyone owns a gas or charcoal grill and has been waiting throughout the long, cold winter for an opportunity to use it again. Meat is the first choice of most but grilled fish and shellfish are becoming increasingly popular and this grilled monkfish recipe is a fairly typical example. Monkfish is a firm-fleshed fish that lends itself beautifully to grilling.

1 1/2 pounds monkfish tail (1 large tail or 2 smaller)
2 garlic cloves
Grated zest and juice of 1 lemon
2 tablespoons chopped fresh parsley
1 tablespoon chopped fresh thyme
1 tablespoon chopped fresh basil
1 teaspoon freshly ground pepper
Pinch of cayenne pepper
2 tablespoons olive oil
Salt

Clean the fish and remove all membranes. Chop the garlic very fine and put it in a bowl with the lemon juice and zest, the herbs, ground pepper, and cayenne pepper. Mix thoroughly and stir in the oil.

Place the fish in a nonreactive dish and spread half the marinade on top. Turn the fish and spread the rest of the marinade over it. Let stand at room temperature for half an hour.

Preheat the grill. Remove the fish from the marinade, salt it and grill it for 5 to 8 minutes on each side, depending on size.

Serve with grilled potato wedges or boiled potatoes and a green salad or a tomato salad.

POACHED LUMPFISH

Soðinn rauðmagi
Serves 4

The female lumpfish is rarely eaten fresh but when it is caught before the spawning season, it is gutted and beheaded, scored deeply with a knife and hung in a cool place until the flesh turns yellow. Then it is poached. This is called *sigin grásleppa* and is considered a delicacy by many. My grandfather told me that when he was a newly engaged farm boy with little taste for fish, he visited his fiancée and her family in the fishing village of Húsavík. *Sigin grásleppa* was on the menu every day and he stayed for a whole week. He simply couldn't eat it, no matter how he tried, and was terribly embarrassed because his mother-in-law-to-be had to cook a piece of male lumpfish just for him, every single day. Nothing else was on offer; they were poor and during early spring, lumpfish was abundant and very inexpensive.

Male lumpfish can be quite good. It can be pan-fried or poached and served cold in a gelatin mold, but usually it is just poached in the following manner.

2 medium-size male lumpfish
1 bay leaf
6 to 8 peppercorns
1 tablespoon white vinegar
Salt
1 lemon, or more vinegar

Pour boiling water on the fish and scrape off the bony lumps which sit in rows on the sides and across the belly. Cut the fish crosswise into fairly thin slices. Often it is simply scored down to the bone, not cut quite through.

Pour 2 quarts water into a large saucepan, add bay leaf, peppercorns, vinegar, and salt, and bring to a boil. Simmer for a few minutes. Add the lumpfish and simmer for 5 to 8 minutes, depending on thickness.

Remove with a slotted spoon and serve with boiled potatoes and vinegar (traditional) or lemon juice.

The stock can be used for a fish soup, similar to the halibut soup (page 35). Just add prunes and sugar and thicken with a little flour.

GRILLED SALMON

Grillaður lax
Serves 4

Salmon is a very popular fish for grilling. Often it is just drizzled with lemon juice, seasoned with pepper and salt and left to marinate for half an hour or so, then grilled directly on the rack for 4 to 5 minutes on each side, but variations on the following method, where the fish is really baked or steamed on the grill, rather than grilled, are also common.

The original recipe uses a mixture of colored peppercorns but ordinary black peppercorns can be used instead.

1 1/2 pounds salmon fillet
4 tablespoons oil
1/2 garlic clove, finely chopped
2 teaspoons roughly crushed peppercorns (see above)
3 to 4 tablespoons chopped parsley
1 tablespoon chopped wild thyme (or regular thyme)
Salt

Cut out a piece of double-thickness foil, somewhat larger than the salmon fillet, and brush it with oil. Place the fillet on the foil, skin side down, and turn up the edges of the foil to make a tray of sorts. Mix oil, garlic, crushed peppercorns, parsley, thyme, and a little salt and drizzle on the salmon.

Preheat the grill. When it is hot, place the foil with the salmon fillet on the rack, cover loosely with more foil, and grill at moderate heat until the thickest part of the salmon is just cooked through. Baste a couple of times with hot oil from the foil tray.

Serve with a green salad or a tomato salad and maybe some baked or grilled potatoes.

SALMON WITH WILD SORREL AND MUSHROOMS

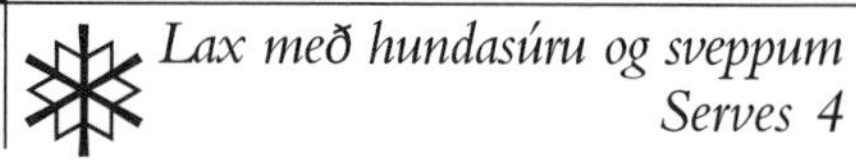

In *The Iceland Journal* of Henry Holland, later physician to Queen Victoria, who traveled the country as a young man in 1810, he often describes the food he was served during his visits to some of Iceland's leading men. One of the dishes he describes is salmon with wild sorrel, cooked like spinach.

Several types of edible mushrooms grow in Iceland but they were not commonly eaten in earlier times, although eighteenth- and nineteenth-century sources often say that they "used to be eaten more widely than now." Those who knew how to use them either cooked them in butter and some whey, or preserved them in a whey marinade.

The following is not an actual old recipe, rather a reconstruction of a dish that may well have been cooked in the early nineteenth century and is equally good today. Two or three cups of chopped spinach can be substituted for the sorrel.

1 1/2 pounds salmon fillets
Freshly ground pepper
Salt
2 tablespoons butter
2 cups sliced mushrooms
2 tablespoons oil
2 tablespoons flour
1 cup roughly chopped sorrel leaves
1/2 cup whey (or dry white wine)

Bone the salmon fillets and cut them into pieces. Sprinkle them with pepper and salt and refrigerate for 15 minutes or so.

Melt the butter in a sauté pan and cook the mushrooms at medium heat for 8 to 10 minutes. Season with pepper and salt.

Meanwhile, heat the oil in a frying pan. Dust the salmon with a little flour and fry it at medium-high heat for 3 to 4 minutes on each side, or until just cooked through.

Add the chopped sorrel to the mushrooms, mix well, and cook for 1 minute, stirring often. Add whey or wine and cook briskly for a minute or two. Pour the mushrooms and sorrel mixture onto a heated serving platter and arrange the salmon on top. Serve with boiled potatoes.

POACHED TROUT

Soðinn urriði
Serves 4

Both trout and char have been caught and eaten ever since the Settlement, and are often mentioned in old documents. They are traditionally cooked in various ways but poaching was always the most common method.

Although most people would cut the fish into rather thick steaks and just poach it in simmering water, flavored with salt, peppercorns, and probably a bay leaf, this very gentle method will provide even better results. The thin steaks will cook perfectly in the less-than-simmering aromatic stock.

1 whole trout, around 2 pounds
1 carrot, chopped
1 celery stalk, chopped
1/4 onion, whole
1 bay leaf
Juice of 1/2 lemon
1/4 teaspoon black peppercorns
2 teaspoons salt

Wash and scale the trout and cut it crosswise into fairly thin slices—3/4 inch is ideal. Pour 6 cups water into a saucepan and add carrot, celery, onion, bay leaf, lemon juice, peppercorns, and salt. Bring to a boil and simmer for 15 minutes.

Strain the stock, or remove the vegetables with a slotted spoon. Add the trout pieces to a boiling stock, immediately remove from the heat, cover, and let stand for 6 to 8 minutes.

Remove to a heated serving platter and serve with boiled potatoes and melted butter.

PAN-FRIED TROUT

Pönnusteiktur urriði
Serves 4

In Iceland, trout fillets are traditionally coated in seasoned bread crumbs or flour and fried until browned on both sides and cooked through. This is another, more gentle method that allows the fresh, delicious flavor of the trout from the Icelandic rivers to come through very cleanly, without any masking or overcooking.

The temperature of the butter when the fish goes in is important because if it is not hot enough, the skin will not crisp up properly; if too hot, it will add an unwanted flavor to the trout. It should sizzle when the fish is placed in it but not splatter much. A thin, white film may have formed on the surface of the salmon when it is cooked. That is a good thing and means the trout is fat and succulent, certainly not dry.

2 trout fillets, around 1 pound each
Freshly ground pepper
Salt
6 tablespoons butter
1/2 lemon
1 tablespoon chopped fresh thyme

Pat the trout fillets with a kitchen towel and sprinkle both sides generously with pepper and salt. Melt the butter in a large frying pan and heat it until it is no longer frothy but has not begun to brown. Place the trout in the pan, skin side down, and fry at high heat for 2 to 3 minutes.

Squeeze the juice from the lemon over the trout, lower the heat, cover, and cook at very low heat until just about cooked through (about 5 minutes, depending on thickness of fillets). Do not turn.

Sprinkle with chopped thyme and a little more pepper, and serve with the pan juices, boiled potatoes, and a good salad or some lightly sautéed vegetables.

GRILLED ROSEMARY-FLAVORED CHAR

Grilluð rósmarínkrydduð bleikja
Serves 4

Grilling is a very popular method to cook Arctic char, a fish found in innumerable Icelandic lakes and rivers. The best char for this recipe would undoubtedly be the sea char *(sjóbleikja)*, recently returned from its feeding grounds in the ocean, considered by many to be the best tasting fish caught in Icelandic rivers and lakes, superior even to the salmon.

2 pounds small char fillets
juice of 1 lemon
1 tablespoon olive oil
2 teaspoons finely chopped fresh rosemary
Freshly ground pepper
Salt

Mix lemon juice, olive oil, rosemary, and pepper in a bowl. Add the char fillets and turn them in the marinade to coat them. Refrigerate for half an hour, turning once or twice.

Meanwhile, heat the grill. Remove the char fillets from the marinade, salt them and place them on the hot grill rack, skin side down. Grill for 3 minutes, then turn them carefully and grill them for 2 to 4 minutes on the other side, or until just cooked through. Brush the fillets with the marinade once or twice while they cook.

Serve with a grilled vegetable salad and lemon wedges.

MASHED FISH

Plokkfiskur
Serves 4

Old accounts from the school at the bishop's seat of Skálholt in southern Iceland show that in 1771, the schoolboys were served *plokkfiskur* every other day, but that dish must have been rather different from the modern version. Probably it was just cooked fish, mashed with lots of butter—and since the fish must have been salted or dried most of the time, this dish can be called an Icelandic version of the famous Provençal *brandade de morue*—now often made from Icelandic salt cod.

This used to be—and still is—a very popular way of dealing with leftover boiled fish but since most people buy smaller portions these days—and fillets instead of whole fish—there usually aren't enough leftovers, so fish is often bought especially for this dish. It should then be poached in salted water, drained, and left until cool enough to handle.

In the following version the fish is completely broken up and mashed into the sauce but some prefer a flaky version, in which case the sauce should be stirred as little as possible after the fish and potatoes have been added. Others want their *plokkfiskur* to be as smooth and creamy as possible so they mash their potatoes with a fork or put them through a ricer before adding them to the pan. There are even recipes where both fish and potatoes are put through a mincer.

3 to 4 cups cooked haddock or cod
1 1/2 cups milk
2 tablespoons butter
1 medium onion, finely chopped
2 tablespoons flour
3 to 4 cups cubed cooked potatoes
Freshly ground pepper
Salt
Chives for decoration (optional)

Pick over the fish to ensure that all bones and skin have been removed. Break it up into flakes. Heat the milk in a saucepan, almost to boiling point. Melt the butter in a pan and sauté the onion at medium heat until soft and opaque. Do not let it brown.

Sprinkle the flour over the onion, stir and cook for a minute or two, stirring continuously. Gradually stir in the warm milk, bring to a boil, and simmer for 5 minutes, stirring often. Add the fish and stir briskly to break up the flakes. Add the potatoes and simmer until they are heated through. Season to taste with pepper and salt.

Spoon into a bowl and sprinkle with chives, if desired. Serve hot with dark rye bread and butter.

Many people make a pile of piping hot *plokkfiskur* on their plate, make an indentation in the top with their fork, and add a large knob of butter.

FISHBALLS

Fiskbollur
Serves 4

Almost every Icelandic housewife has her own recipe for fishballs, and this is mine. I usually make the balls from haddock, but almost any fish can be used, if it isn't too oily. These fishballs can also be used as an appetizer or finger food—just use a teaspoon to shape the balls, fry them fairly quickly, turning continuously, and serve them hot or cold with a dip.

If half the potato starch and half the flour is omitted, or a little more cream used, the recipe can also be used for a fish pudding. Just spoon the mixture into a well-buttered ovenproof dish, smooth the surface, dot with a little more butter, and bake at 400°F until cooked through and browned on top. The fish mixture can also be layered with some parboiled vegetables, such as broccoli, carrots, and bell peppers.

1 pound fish fillets, skinned and boned
1 medium onion
3 tablespoons cream or milk
2 tablespoons butter, softened
2 tablespoons chopped parsley or chives
a small pinch of cayenne pepper
1/2 teaspoon freshly ground pepper
1 teaspoon salt
4 tablespoons potato starch or cornstarch
3 tablespoons flour
Oil or margarine for frying

Cut the fish into pieces, peel and chop the onion, and mince them finely in a mincer, or use a food processor. Add cream, butter, herbs, and seasonings and mix well. Stir in potato starch or cornstarch and flour. The mixture should be fairly thick and hold its shape well.

Heat the oil or melt the margarine in a large frying pan. Scoop up the fish mixture with a tablespoon, shape it into slightly oblong balls (you can use 2 tablespoons to shape the balls if that is more convenient) and fry them at medium heat for a few minutes on each side, or until nicely browned and cooked through.

Serve with melted butter and boiled potatoes.

FISHBALLS WITH BROWN SAUCE

Fiskbollur í brúnni sósu
Serves 4

Here is another popular method for making fishballs; these are served in a sauce, flavored with a little tomato ketchup, which was often the only tomato product available around the year in earlier times. Other types of sauces were used instead, for instance a currant sauce, where 3 to 4 tablespoons of dried currants were cooked in the sauce, which was flavored with a little vinegar and sugar, but no ketchup. Instead of a sauce, the fishballs may be served with melted butter, perhaps with a couple of tablespoons of chopped chives mixed in.

The traditional shape of the fishball is three-sided and somewhat oblong but two-sided, flat patties are also common.

1 pound fish fillets, skinned and boned
1 medium onion
1 teaspoon salt
1/4 teaspoon freshly ground pepper
2 tablespoons potato starch or cornstarch
4 tablespoons flour
1 egg
1 cup milk
4 tablespoons margarine or butter
1 stock cube
2 to 3 tablespoons tomato ketchup
Gravy browning or soy sauce (optional)

Cut the fish into pieces, peel and chop the onion, and mince them finely in a mincer, or use a food processor. Add salt, pepper, potato starch or cornstarch and 2 tablespoons of the flour and mix well. Stir in the egg, then stir in the milk gradually—you may not need all of it. The mixture should be fairly thick and hold its shape well.

Melt the margarine in a large frying pan. Scoop up the fish mixture with a tablespoon, shape it into slightly oblong balls (you can use 2 tablespoons to shape the balls if that is more convenient) and fry them at medium heat for a few minutes on each side, or until nicely browned and cooked through. Remove them with a slotted spoon and keep them warm.

Dissolve the stock cube in 1 1/2 cups hot water. Sprinkle the remaining 2 tablespoons flour on the pan and stir until lightly browned. Stir in the hot water and the tomato ketchup, bring to a boil, and continue stirring until smooth. Simmer for 5 minutes.

If the sauce looks too pale, a few drops of gravy browning or soy sauce may be added to darken it. Adjust seasonings. Pour the hot sauce over the fishballs, or add them back to the pan and serve them in the sauce.

GRILLED LANGOUSTINES

Grillaður humar
Serves 4

The popular but expensive langoustines are favorites for summertime grill parties, when company is coming. They are often grilled on foil trays, or they are threaded on a spit, as is done in the following recipe. Garlic is a very common flavoring.

1 1/2 pounds langoustines, shelled
3 tablespoons olive oil
2 to 3 garlic cloves, chopped
3 to 4 tablespoons chopped parsley
1 cup dry bread crumbs
Freshly ground pepper
Salt

Place the shelled langoustines in a bowl with oil and garlic and stir to coat the langoustines in oil. Add parsley, bread crumbs, pepper, and salt and mix well. Thread the langoustines onto presoaked wooden sticks or metal spits and refrigerate while the grill is heating up.

Place the spits on an oiled rack and grill the langoustines for 2 minutes on each side, or until the bread crumb coating has colored nicely.

Serve with lemon wedges, a green salad, and garlic bread.

SHRIMP GRATIN WITH MUSHROOMS

Rækjugratín með sveppum
Serves 6

Seafood gratins like this are always popular but ingredients vary widely. They may include haddock, cod, halibut, ocean catfish, plaice, and many other species, shrimp, langoustines, or scallops, and many kinds of vegetables, such as carrots, potatoes, cauliflower, or tomatoes. With so many different ingredients, the cooking time can be a bit hit-or-miss—the seafood may be overcooked before the firmer vegetables are ready—so a bit of planning is essential for success. Some vegetables may need to be parboiled, for instance. But the result is usually a crowd pleaser.

1 pound cooked and shelled frozen shrimp
1 pound haddock or other white fish
1/2 pound mushrooms
4 tablespoons butter
2 garlic cloves, finely chopped
Freshly ground pepper
Salt
2 tablespoons flour
2 teaspoons paprika
2 1/2 cups hot fish stock
4 ounces cream cheese
1/2 cup freshly grated Parmesan cheese
1 cup chopped red bell pepper
2 cups chopped broccoli florets (not stalks)

Defrost the shrimp. Skin and bone the fish and cut it into small pieces. Slice the mushrooms thin. Melt 1 tablespoon butter in a pan and sauté the mushrooms and garlic at medium-low heat for 10 minutes. Season with pepper and salt and remove from heat.

Preheat the oven to 425°F. Melt 2 tablespoons butter in a saucepan and stir in flour and paprika. Cook for 1 minute, then gradually stir in the hot fish stock and bring to a boil. Stir the sauce until absolutely smooth, season it with pepper and salt, and let it simmer for 10 minutes.

Stir in the cream cheese and 1/4 cup of the Parmesan cheese. Remove the pan from heat, taste, and adjust seasonings.

Butter a fairly large ovenproof dish with the remaining 1 tablespoon butter and cover the bottom with bell pepper and broccoli florets. Arrange the fish pieces on top, then the shrimp, and finally distribute the mushrooms evenly over all. Pour the cheese sauce over the mushrooms, sprinkle with the remaining 1/4 cup Parmesan cheese, and bake for around 25 minutes, or until the topping is golden brown.

Serve with a green salad and freshly baked bread.

MEAT DISHES

Lamb and mutton used to be by far the most common meat in Iceland, probably from the earliest times. Beef has always been eaten to some extent but cows were reared for milk, not meat, and most of the beef that was available came from old and tough cows. The meat was sometimes marinated in sour whey to tenderize it. Veal was eaten fresh but there are no traditional veal dishes; the meat was just cooked in a similar manner to lamb. There was no pork, because pigs became extinct in Iceland, probably in the sixteenth century, and were not imported again for over 300 years.

This has rapidly changed in recent years. The consumption of lamb has diminished considerably and beef and pork are now just as popular. The trend has been towards shorter cooking times—roasts and steaks were traditionally well done or very well done. A leg of lamb that was rosy at the bone would have been considered partly raw by most.

It is impossible to write about Icelandic cooking without giving a recipe for the classic Sunday roast leg of lamb, but I've also included two rather different recipes for this very popular cut. There are other festive dishes as well, such as pork roast and leg of reindeer, not to mention smoked lamb, but also traditional everyday dishes like curried meat and meat patties.

SUNDAY ROAST

Sunnudagslærið
Serves 8 to 10

What most Icelanders over thirty still think of when somebody mentions Sunday roast is definitely leg or saddle of lamb, well done, probably served with sugar-glazed potatoes and canned green peas—maybe also carrots and other cooked vegetables, sweet-sour red cabbage, pickled cucumber, canned corn, sautéed mushroom, or a coleslaw—but invariably with a thick and rich gravy.

This recipe for leg of lamb is very traditional, except the pepper would not have been freshly ground. Older cookbooks often give roasting times as long as half an hour per pound, which is rather excessive for most modern tastes, but most people used to prefer their meat well done. These days, the roasting time is usually much shorter and the roast is often spiked with garlic slivers and more herbs are used.

1 leg of lamb on the bone, 5 to 6 pounds
Freshly ground pepper
Salt
1/2 teaspoon dried thyme or rosemary (optional)
2 tablespoons butter or margarine
2 to 3 cups lamb stock or water (more as needed)
3 tablespoons flour
Gravy browning or soy sauce (optional)

Preheat the oven to 450°F. Rub the leg of lamb liberally with seasoning and herbs, if using. Butter a roasting pan, place the roast in it, top with dots of butter and place in the hot oven. Roast for 15 to 20 minutes, then lower the heat to 325°F.

Meanwhile, heat the stock or water in a saucepan. Pour it over the roast and into the roasting pan. Roast for an additional hour or so, depending on the size of the leg and desired doneness. Baste occasionally and add more stock or water if needed.

Remove the roast from the oven when ready, place it on a heated serving plate, cover with foil and keep warm. Skim some of the fat from the stock in the roasting pan, then pour it through a sieve into a saucepan and bring to a boil. Mix the flour and some cold water into a smooth paste and stir it into the stock to thicken it.

Simmer for 5 to 10 minutes, season to taste, and add a little gravy browning or soy sauce if the sauce is very pale. A splash of cream is sometimes added to round out the flavor.

The roast is usually carved at the table.

Saddle of lamb is traditionally cooked in exactly the same way but needs shorter cooking time: 45 to 60 minutes, according to size.

SALTED AND SLOW-ROASTED LEG OF LAMB

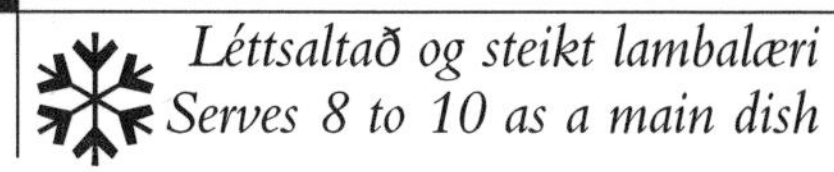

Léttsaltað og steikt lambalæri
Serves 8 to 10 as a main dish

This is a very popular regular at my annual St. Thorlak´s party on Dec 23. It is served cold and can be left on the table all day and people just cut slices from it and eat it with rye flatbread or freshly baked crusty bread, and often a potato salad as well. It can also be served hot as a main course, for example with boiled or roasted vegetables, or peas and boiled potatoes in a white sauce.

A leg of lamb that has been cured in brine would traditionally be smoked, then boiled, but there are also old recipes for brine-cured lamb that is simply roasted. Here I use a rather spicy brine and slow-roast the meat for a couple of hours, since I prefer it pink and juicy.

1 leg of lamb on the bone, 5 to 6 pounds
1 cup coarse salt
1/2 cup sugar
1 teaspoon chili pepper
1 teaspoon black peppercorns
1 teaspoon coriander seeds
6 bay leaves
2 cinnamon sticks
Oil

Trim the meat and remove some fat. Pour 4 quarts of water into a large saucepan and stir in salt, sugar, and spices. Bring to a boil and simmer for a few minutes, then remove from heat and let cool completely.

When the brine is cold, place the leg of lamb in a deep roasting pan or other container and pour the brine over it. Add ice-cold water as needed to cover the meat completely. Refrigerate or keep cold for 2 to 3 days.

Remove the meat from the brine and discard it. Rinse the meat in cold water, pat it dry, and let stand at room temperature for half an hour. Preheat the oven to 260°F.

Brush the meat with some oil, place it in a roasting pan and roast slowly for around 2 hours, or until a meat thermometer inserted in the thickest part shows 130°F.

Let stand, covered, for 10 to 15 minutes and serve hot, or let cool completely and serve cold, cut into thin slices.

For a more attractive color, turn the broiler on towards the end of the roasting time.

PIT-ROASTED LEG OF LAMB

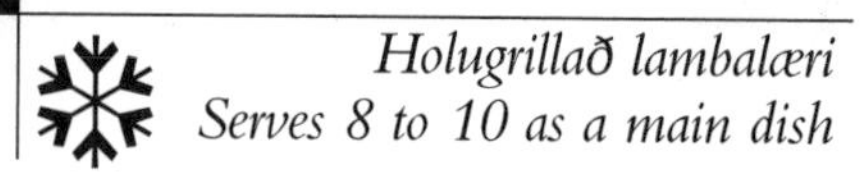

Holugrillað lambalæri
Serves 8 to 10 as a main dish

I'm not sure what to call this—it is called hole-grilling or pit-grilling in Iceland but it isn't really grilling or barbecuing, since the meat is completely enclosed in foil and is really steaming in its own juices. But it is delicious all the same.

Not everyone can just dig a pit in the ground anywhere he pleases to cook a leg of lamb in it, not even in Iceland, but many do have a pit in their backyard or close to their summer cottage, because this is really very much a summer cottage dish. If you can dig a pit, take care to cover the bottom with gravel or bricks, and place a double layer of foil on top of that. The pit should be around 1 1/2 feet deep and big enough to accommodate a large leg of lamb.

1 leg of lamb, 5 to 6 pounds
Fistful of fresh wild thyme, or 1 teaspoon dried thyme
1 tablespoon chopped fresh rosemary, or 1 teaspoon dried
4 garlic cloves, finely chopped
Freshly ground pepper
Salt
1/4 cup olive oil

Trim excess fat off the meat. Chop the fresh thyme roughly, if using. Mix herbs, garlic, seasonings, and oil and rub all over the meat. Wrap tightly in a double thickness of foil and refrigerate for 12 to 24 hours.

Prepare the grilling pit. Spread charcoal briquettes on top and light them. Let them burn until they are gray all over. Place the foil-wrapped leg of lamb on top, partly cover the pit, and leave undisturbed for 40 minutes.

Turn it and leave for 30 minutes more. Remove from the pit and let stand for 10 minutes before unwrapping. Scrape off most of the herbs and serve.

Foil-wrapped baking potatoes can be cooked alongside the lamb and served with it. A potato salad is also a good side dish, along with fresh, ripe tomatoes and cucumbers, or some grilled corn on the cob.

SMOKED LEG OF LAMB

Hangilæri
Serves 8 to 10

Smoked leg of lamb is a very popular feast dish in Iceland and it is one of the least bothersome meals possible, since the meat is usually served cold. It is cooked a day or two in advance and only has to be sliced. The traditional side dishes are also easy: boiled potatoes in white sauce, canned marrowfat peas (probably very hard to find outside Iceland, so other green peas can be substituted), boiled carrots, and sometimes boiled red cabbage.

Since few people own a pan large enough to boil a whole leg of lamb on the bone, the leg is often cut into two or three large chunks before cooking. This should be avoided, however, as the meat tends to dry out too much. Even a large leg of lamb can easily be poached in a large covered roasting pan on top of the stove, or in the oven. The following instructions are for stovetop cooking.

1 smoked leg of lamb on the bone (5 to 6 pounds)
1 tablespoon sugar (optional)

Place the leg of lamb in a large roasting pan (unless you have a stockpot large enough to accommodate the whole leg) and add cold water; it doesn't have to cover the meat completely. Add the sugar, if using, place the roasting pan on two burners on the stove, and heat slowly; it may take 30 to 45 minutes to bring the water to boiling point. Simmer for 10 to 15 minutes, then turn off the heat and let cool in the cooking water for several hours. Remove to a tray, cover, and refrigerate until serving time.

If you want to serve the meat hot, you should let it simmer for 20 to 30 minutes before the heat is turned off. Let it cool for 15 to 20 minutes in the cooking water, then remove, cut into thick slices, and serve.

STUFFED SHOULDER OF LAMB

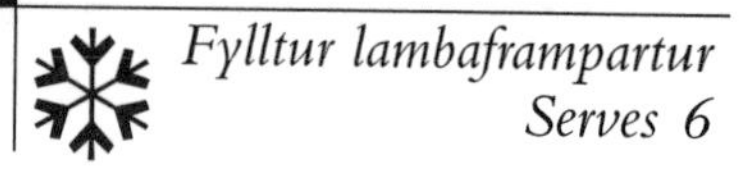

Fylltur lambaframpartur
Serves 6

This used to be a popular method for turning the shoulder, less expensive than leg or rack of lamb, into a fancy Sunday roast for the family. The sauce is, however, a deluxe version of the traditional brown sauce that used to accompany almost any meat dish.

2 1/2 pounds boned and trimmed shoulder of lamb
1 large apple
1/2 cup pitted prunes
2 tablespoons chopped wild thyme, or 1 teaspoon dried
Freshly ground pepper
Salt
2 cups lamb or beef stock
1 tablespoon butter, softened
1 1/2 tablespoons flour
1/2 cup cream
1 tablespoon brandy
Gravy browning or soy sauce (optional)

Preheat the oven to 350°F. Spread the boned shoulder out on a work surface, skin side down. Peel, core, and chop the apple and chop the prunes. Mix half the thyme with the fruit along with some pepper and salt.

Arrange the fruit on the meat, roll it and tie it with a string, and season the roll with the remaining thyme, along with more pepper and salt. Place on a rack over roasting pan, pour the stock into the pan, and roast for 1 hour.

Remove the meat from the oven to a cutting board, cover, and let stand for a few minutes. Strain the stock into a saucepan and bring to a boil. Mix butter and flour in a bowl and stir into the stock to thicken. Simmer for 5 minutes.

Add cream and brandy, bring to a boil again, and simmer for a few minutes more. Season to taste with pepper and salt and add a little gravy browning or soy sauce, if desired, to darken the color of the sauce. Remove the string from the meat, cut it into thick slices, and arrange them on a serving platter.

Serve with the sauce, along with glazed or roasted potatoes.

BREADED LAMB CUTLETS

Lambakótelettur í raspi
Serves 4

Icelandic lamb cutlets are small and thinly cut but a part of the flank is often included, so they tend to be more fatty than other cutlets. In these health-conscious times, some or all of the fat is trimmed before cooking.

When I was growing up, this was the accepted method to cook the cutlets and they were a popular Sunday dinner, as were breaded lamb chops. They were often cooked in exactly the same way, although a few tablespoons of water were often added to the pan after they had been browned on both sides and the chops were then covered and cooked on low heat until ready. These cuts were always cooked through, never just until pink in the middle.

12 small lamb cutlets (about 2 pounds)
1 egg
3 tablespoons milk
1 cup dry bread crumbs
Freshly ground pepper
Salt
6 tablespoons margarine or vegetable oil

Pat the cutlets dry with paper towels and trim some of the fat. Beat them with a mallet to make them even thinner. Lightly whisk egg and milk in a shallow bowl. Season the bread crumbs with pepper and salt.

Melt the margarine in a large skillet. Dip the cutlets into the egg mixture, roll them in the bread crumbs, and arrange them on the pan. Brown them on both sides at fairly high heat, then lower the heat and cook the cutlets for 8 to 10 minutes, turning once. Remove them from the pan and arrange them on a heated serving plate.

Serve with more melted margarine, boiled potatoes, and vegetables.

FILLET OF LAMB WITH BILBERRY SAUCE

Lambahryggvöðvi með sveppa- og bláberjasósu
Serves 4

The tender fillet of a young Icelandic lamb is absolutely delicious, with a sweet, herbaceous and delicate taste. The Icelandic sheep are sturdy, free-range animals; they are transferred to the mountainous wilderness in early summer, when the lambs are a month or two old, and there they graze on hardy mountain grasses and herbs until they are rounded up in autumn, so the animals can almost be said to season themselves. And that is all most of the lambs ever eat—no hay or other feed crops, and no grain.

When dealing with a tender, quick-cooking cut like the fillet, care should be taken not to drown the delicate taste of the meat itself by too much spicing, but a small amount of herbs and garlic enhances the flavor of the meat.

2 pounds lamb fillet, with a thin layer of fat
Freshly ground pepper
1/2 teaspoon chopped fresh rosemary
Handful of thyme sprigs
3 tablespoons olive oil
1/4 cup dried wild mushrooms
1 tablespoon butter
3 to 4 shallots, chopped
1 garlic clove, finely chopped
Salt
1/2 cup lamb or chicken stock
1/4 cup ruby port
1/2 cup bilberries (or blueberries)
Cornstarch (optional)

Cut the fillet into 3- to 4-inch pieces and score the fat side with shallow crisscross cuts, around 1/2 inch apart, using the tip of a sharp knife. Season with freshly ground pepper and rosemary. Wrap a few thyme sprigs around each piece and arrange the pieces on a plate, fat side down. Sprinkle 2 tablespoons olive oil on them. Let stand at room temperature for 30 minutes, turning once.

Meanwhile, soak the dried mushrooms in 1 cup hot water. Preheat the oven to 450°F. Melt the butter in a saucepan and sauté the shallots and garlic for a couple of minutes at medium heat, taking care not to brown. Add the mushrooms and their soaking water, bring to a boil, and cook rapidly until reduced to 1/2 cup.

Heat the remaining 1 tablespoon of oil in a heavy ovenproof pan until almost smoking. Salt the meat pieces sparingly, place them in the pan, fat side down, and fry at high heat for 2 minutes. Turn and immediately place the pan in the oven for 6 to 8 minutes.

Add stock and port to the mushroom sauce and continue cooking rapidly for 5 minutes. Add the berries, lower the heat, and season to taste. The sauce can be thickened with a little cornstarch, mixed with cold water, if desired.

Arrange the lamb fillet pieces on a heated serving platter and pour some of the sauce over them. Serve the rest of the sauce separately.

LAMB CURRY

Kjöt í karríi
Serves 4

Mild curry spice mixtures were used in Iceland from the late nineteenth century and were one of the very few spices to be found in most kitchens up until the 1960s. It was used to flavor some fish soups and sauces and a few other things, but its main use was for this dish. The following recipe may not sound terribly exciting but this was probably the spiciest dish I tasted during my childhood. And the simple curry sauce actually makes a good foil for the slightly bland boiled lamb.

1 1/2 pounds shoulder of lamb, on the bone
Salt
1 bay leaf (optional)
6 medium potatoes
3 medium carrots
2 tablespoons flour
1 teaspoon curry powder
1 1/2 tablespoons butter, softened
Freshly ground pepper (optional)

The meat should be cut into fairly large chunks. Cut away excess fat, wash the meat, and put it into a pan. Add enough hot water to cover and bring to a boil. Skim and add 1 teaspoon salt and the bay leaf if using. Simmer for 30 to 35 minutes.

Meanwhile, peel and cube the potatoes. Scrape the carrots and cut them into pieces. Add to the meat and cook for another 15 minutes, or until the vegetables are tender and the meat is cooked through. Remove the meat and vegetables to a plate and keep hot.

Strain and measure the cooking liquid, add 1 1/2 cups of it back to the pan, and bring back to a boil. Mix the flour with the curry powder and butter and add to the stock, stirring until smooth. Simmer for 5 minutes and season to taste with pepper and salt. Serve with the meat and vegetables, along with boiled long-grained rice.

SPICED LAMB STEW

Krydduð smásteik
Serves 6

This is probably the Icelandic version of Hungarian goulash, since one popular name for it is *gúllas*, and it does have some paprika—at least this version does, but sometimes pepper was the only spice used. My mother made a stew like that, and we called it *glás*, which can also mean "a lot," but was probably a distortion of goulash.

Virtually any meat could be used but lamb was most common. The stew could be very good but sometimes the meat was tough and gristly. Since it was covered with a thick, dark brown sauce, you didn't always know what you were being served, so stews of this kind were sometimes jokingly called *kjöt í myrkri* ("meat in the dark") or other similar names.

2 pounds boneless lamb or other meat
2 medium onions
4 medium carrots
5 tablespoons margarine or butter
4 tablespoons flour
3 cups meat stock
2 bay leaves
1 teaspoon paprika
1/2 teaspoon freshly ground pepper
1/4 teaspoon allspice
Salt
Gravy browning or soy sauce

Cut the meat into 1-inch cubes and trim excess fat. Peel the onions and slice them thin. Scrape the carrots and cut them into pieces.

Melt 2 tablespoons of the margarine in a frying pan and fry the onion slices at fairly high heat until they begin to brown. Remove them to a heavy-bottomed pan and melt the remaining 3 tablespoons margarine in the frying pan. Toss the meat in the flour to coat it, then brown it on all sides in the frying pan at high heat. Reserve the remaining flour. Add the meat to the onion in the pan.

Pour some of the stock into the frying pan, let it boil briskly for a minute or two, and scrape the bottom of the pan. Pour it over the meat and add the remaining stock, the carrots, bay leaves, paprika, pepper, allspice, and salt. Bring to a boil and simmer, partly covered, for 40 minutes or more, depending on type and age of meat.

Put the remaining flour into a jar with a little cold water, shake until thoroughly combined, and stir into the pan to thicken the sauce. Simmer for 5 to 10 minutes. Season to taste and stir in enough gravy browning or soy sauce to make the sauce fairly dark.

Serve with mashed potatoes.

BONELESS BIRDS

Beinlausir fuglar
Serves 4

This is one of those old-fashioned dishes rarely encountered these days, not because it isn't good, probably rather because it is seen as bothersome and time-consuming, although there are recipes that simply skip the rolling part and just cook the bacon in a stew with the meat slices. The rolls are supposed to resemble boned small birds. Similar dishes are found all over Europe—for example French *oiseau sans tête* (headless birds) or Mallorcan *perdices de capellán* (the chaplain's doves).

This recipe is slightly adapted from Jóninna Sigurdarðóttir's cookbook, originally published in 1915, and is closely modeled on a Danish recipe. Most older Icelandic cookbooks include a recipe for boneless birds and there are several variations—some add chopped onion and parsley with the bacon, or a carrot stick. Other, more modern recipes may include dried fruit, ham, and fresh herbs in the filling, and the sauce is sometimes a reduced red wine sauce instead of a cream sauce. The type of meat varies; usually beef or veal but horsemeat and lamb are also used.

1 pound veal or beef
8 bacon slices
1/2 teaspoon freshly ground pepper
1/4 teaspoon ground cloves
3 tablespoons flour
Salt
3 tablespoons butter
1/2 cup cream

Cut the meat into 8 elongated slices and beat them with a mallet until they are quite thin. Sprinkle each bacon slice with a little pepper and cloves. Fold it, place it on one end of a meat slice, and roll the meat slice around the bacon. Tie it with a string and try to keep a nice shape to it. Dust the rolls with flour mixed with the remaining spices and a little salt, unless the bacon is very salty. Reserve the remaining flour.

Melt the butter in a heavy sauté pan and fry the "birds" until well browned on all sides. Pour in the cream and add water to barely cover. Simmer gently for 1 hour, adding water as needed.

Lift the birds from the sauce with a slotted spoon, remove the strings, and keep them warm on a heated serving platter. Put the reserved flour in a jar with a little cold water, shake until well combined and smooth, and stir into the sauce. Simmer for 5 minutes and season to taste with pepper and salt.

Pour the sauce over the birds and serve with glazed or boiled potatoes and vegetables.

PORK ROAST WITH CRACKLINGS

Svínasteik með stökkri pöru
Serves 10 to 16

Pigs were reared in Iceland from the Settlement up until the late Middle Ages and seem to have more or less run wild. Deforestation and a worsening climate, along with a shortage of grain, led to their gradual disappearance and they were not imported again until the early twentieth century.

The two best-known Icelandic pork dishes are both large roasts, served at Christmas and other feasts. One is *hamborgarhryggur*, a salted and lightly smoked pork rack, usually simmered in water, then spread with a glaze (a mixture of mustard and brown sugar is popular), and cooked in the oven until nicely glazed. The other is pork roast with cracklings, often called Danish pork roast.

Various methods are employed to ensure really crisp cracklings, like rubbing the skin liberally with salt, or pouring boiling water on it, but the one I use and have found to be infallible is to prick the skin all over—hundreds of times, maybe—with the point of a really sharp knife, before scoring it in the usual manner.

1 leg or shoulder of pork, 6 to 10 pounds
2 teaspoons freshly crushed allspice berries
1 tablespoon coarse salt
1 teaspoon peppercorns
1 teaspoon whole mustard grains
3 tablespoons butter
3 tablespoons flour

Preheat the oven to 450°F. Score the skin deeply with the tip of a sharp knife, cutting into the fat layer but not into the meat itself. Use the pricking method described above, if desired.

Rub the skin with a mixture of allspice and salt and stud the cuts with peppercorns and mustard grains. Place the roast on a rack above a roasting pan and roast for 20 to 30 minutes, or until the skin is crisp and brown.

Lower the heat to 300°F, pour 3 cups boiling water into the roasting pan, and roast for 3 to 4 hours, or until a steak thermometer inserted into the thickest part of the leg shows 150°F. Do not baste the steak while it roasts. Remove the roast from the oven, cover it loosely with foil and keep warm for 20 to 30 minutes.

Meanwhile, strain the pan juices and skim off most of the fat. Melt the butter in a saucepan, add the flour and stir until the flour begins to brown. Gradually stir in hot stock. Simmer for 10 minutes and season to taste. Stir in any juices that may have seeped out of the roast. If the sauce is a bit dull, it can be perked up with some mustard.

Serve the roast with the sauce and serve boiled or glazed potatoes, red cabbage, and green peas on the side.

LEG OF REINDEER WITH ROSEMARY

Rósmarínkryddað hreindýralæri
Serves 10 to 12

A whole leg or rack of reindeer is a rare treat these days, since prices have risen so high. Other cuts can be had more cheaply but are still pretty expensive. The quality of the meat can vary widely, depending on the age of the animal. The leg of an older animal is probably best fit for braising or stewing but the leg of a young reindeer can be amazingly tender, sweet, and tasty.

There are no traditional recipes to speak of but the following recipe is fairly typical of the way a leg of reindeer may be treated these days.

1 leg of young reindeer (8 to 10 pounds)
3 to 4 rosemary sprigs
3 tablespoons olive oil
1 tablespoon red wine vinegar
2 to 3 tablespoons chopped fresh basil
2 teaspoons roughly crushed black pepper
Salt
2 tablespoons red currant jelly
12 bacon slices
8 to 10 shallots
8 to 10 small carrots

Make several deep incisions into the meat with the point of a sharp knife and insert pieces of rosemary into each cut. Chop the remaining rosemary fine and mix with oil, vinegar, and basil. Rub the reindeer leg with pepper and salt and place it in a large ovenproof dish. Drizzle the marinade over it and let stand at room temperature for 1 hour or refrigerated for up to 12 hours, turning occasionally.

Preheat the oven to 400°F. Remove the meat from the marinade, pat it loosely with a paper towel, and spread the red currant jelly on it. Arrange the bacon slices in a crisscross pattern on top. Insert a meat thermometer in the thickest muscle.

Peel the shallots and arrange them around the meat along with the carrots, turning them to cover with marinade. Place in the oven.

Lower the heat to 275°F after 10 to 15 minutes and continue roasting until the thermometer shows 132 to 140°F, according to taste. Remove the meat from the oven, cover loosely with foil, and let it rest in a warm place for 20 minutes before serving.

Meanwhile, you can deglaze the roasting pan with some stock or red wine, reduce the sauce heavily, and perhaps enhance it with some port wine, a little red currant jelly, and/or some berries.

MEAT MASH

Kjötkássa
Serves 4

This is a traditional way of using leftover meat, especially tough or dull meat, since it is finely minced and spiced with pepper and onions. Salted lamb is the best meat for this recipe but fresh meat will work fine, too. Many versions omit the potatoes but then the mash is usually served with mashed potatoes. They are often piped or arranged in a circle around the meat mash on a serving platter.

3 to 4 cups cooked lamb or other meat, preferably salted
2 medium onions
2 tablespoons butter
2 tablespoons flour
1 cup meat stock or milk, or as needed
4 cups cooked, cubed potatoes
Freshly ground pepper
Salt (if using unsalted meat)
Gravy browning or soy sauce

Mince the meat and 1 onion in a mincer. Melt the butter in a skillet. Chop the other onion and sauté it for a few minutes, until it begins to soften.

Add the flour, stir until smooth, and cook for 2 to 3 minutes at fairly low heat, stirring continuously. Raise the heat and gradually stir in the stock or milk. The sauce should be fairly thick. Cook for a couple of minutes, stir in meat and potatoes, and simmer for 5 minutes.

Season to taste, add enough gravy browning or soy sauce to color the mixture medium brown, and serve hot.

MEATBALLS IN BROWN SAUCE

Kjötbollur í brúnni sósu
Serves 4

These traditional Icelandic meatballs were usually made from lamb or mutton, but ground beef or pork is at least as likely to be used now. The usual recipe requires the cook to mix ground meat and onion in a bowl, smooth the surface, and cut the mixture into quarters. Then one quarter is taken out and the cavity is filled with flour. For this quantity of meat, that translates into around 1/2 cup. Helga Sigurðardóttir says in the original 1947 edition of *Matur og drykkur* that the mixture should then be stirred for half an hour. It does need a good stirring or kneading but if an electric mixer is used, a few minutes should be quite enough.

The same recipe can be used for poached meatballs but the meat is often ground more finely and half the flour is often replaced with potato starch.

1 pound ground meat
1 onion, finely chopped
Salt
Freshly ground pepper
1/2 cup flour
1 egg (optional)
1/2 cup milk, or as needed
4 tablespoons margarine, or 2 tablespoons butter and 2 tablespoons oil
1 cup stock or water
1 1/2 tablespoons flour
Gravy browning or soy sauce (optional)

Mix ground meat and onion in a bowl and season with 1 teaspoon salt and 1/2 teaspoon pepper. Stir in the flour and the egg. Gradually add milk, until the mixture has the desired consistency. Stir or knead the mixture thoroughly.

Melt the margarine in a large frying pan. Shape fairly large balls from the forcemeat, using 2 tablespoons, and fry the balls on 3 sides at medium-high heat until well browned. Pour off most of the fat, then add the stock and simmer, covered, for 5 minutes.

Put the flour and a few tablespoons cold water in a small jar, shake until smooth, and stir into the stock. Simmer for 5 minutes, stirring occasionally. Season to taste with pepper and salt, and add a few drops of gravy browning or soy sauce if the sauce is very pale.

Serve with boiled potatoes, green peas, and jam.

MEAT PATTIES WITH ONION SAUCE

Buff með lauk og brúnni sósu
Serves 4

This used to be a very popular dish. It can be enhanced in various ways with spices and herbs. The wild thyme, although not strictly traditional, is a very nice addition and adds a dimension of flavor to the dish.

1 1/4 pounds ground beef
1/2 teaspoon dried thyme (preferably wild)
Freshly ground pepper
Salt
3 tablespoons flour
2 to 3 medium onions
4 tablespoons butter
Gravy browning or soy sauce (optional)

Mix the ground beef with thyme, 1/2 teaspoon pepper, and 1 teaspoon salt. Divide it into 8 even parts and shape each one into a patty, around 1/4 inch thick. Roll the patties in flour, reserving the remaining flour to thicken the sauce.

Peel the onions and slice them fairly thin. Melt 2 tablespoons butter in a large, heavy pan and fry the onions at medium heat, stirring often, until they are browned. Remove to a plate.

Melt the remaining 2 tablespoons butter in the pan and fry the patties at medium-high heat until browned on both sides. Pour 1 cup water into the pan, add the onions, and bring to a boil.

Put the reserved flour into a jar with a little cold water, shake until smooth, and stir the mixture into the boiling water in the pan. Stir well to ensure there are no lumps. Simmer at low heat for 5 minutes. Season the sauce with pepper and salt and add a little gravy browning or soy sauce, if desired.

Serve the patties in the onion sauce with boiled potatoes and green peas on the side, and if you want to be authentic, add some jam and a few pickled gherkins or cucumbers.

SALTED MEAT PATTIES WITH FISH

Saltkjötsbuff með fiski
Serves 4

Many Icelanders will tell you they have never heard of this dish, others have fond childhood memories of it. It was probably much more common by the seaside, where fresh fish was usually readily available; salt fish will not do, as the patties will be way too salty. It is a leftover dish and can also be made using cooked fish instead of raw.

As the consumption of salted meat has dropped drastically in the last fifty years, there are rarely any leftovers to deal with, so this dish is not often made. Not that it isn't well worth making, though. The unusual meat-fish combination works well and the patties are surprisingly light and tasty.

In Iceland, salted lamb or mutton would be used, or perhaps salted horsemeat, but pork works, too. I've made this recipe using haddock or cod, but I'm told saithe is the best choice for this dish. The meat-fish proportions vary widely, as is to be expected of a leftover dish; you go with what you have. A couple of tablespoons of chopped parsley may be added to the forcemeat if desired.

2 cups chopped cooked salted meat
1 cup chopped raw fish
2 to 3 medium onions
1/2 teaspoon freshly ground pepper
1 cup fresh bread crumbs
1 cup milk
6 tablespoons margarine or oil for frying

Run the meat, the fish, and 1 onion through a mincer and mix thoroughly. Add pepper, bread crumbs, and milk and stir to combine. Divide into 8 to 10 portions and shape into 1/2 inch thick patties.

Heat the margarine or oil in a large frying pan and fry the patties at medium heat for around 5 minutes on each side. Peel and halve the remaining 1 to 2 onions, slice the halves thin and add them to the pan when the patties have been turned. Remove the patties to a serving platter when ready and keep warm.

Continue cooking the onion slices for a couple of minutes, then spoon them over the patties and serve with boiled potatoes.

STUFFED LAMB HEARTS

Fyllt lambahjörtu
Serves 4

Organ meats, especially hearts, livers and kidneys, have always had their place in Icelandic cooking. In earlier times, they were often used in various kinds of sausages, or they were boiled and preserved in whey, but in the twentieth century, various kinds of dishes involving organ meats were developed. The following recipe is a slightly adapted version of a recipe from the 1947 edition of *Matur og drykkur.*

The usual method for cooking lamb hearts, however, was to cut them into 4 to 6 sections and brown them in margarine, often along with sliced onions and maybe some carrots. Water was then added and the stew was cooked until the hearts were tender. The sauce was thickened with flour and the stew was often served with mashed potatoes.

4 to 6 lamb hearts, depending on size
1/2 cup chopped dried apples
1/4 cup chopped dried apricots
1/4 cup chopped prunes
Pinch of thyme
Freshly ground pepper
Salt
3 tablespoons butter or margarine
2 cups lamb or beef stock
2 tablespoons flour

Wash the hearts to remove all blood and soak them in cold water for a few hours. Drain them and pat them dry, inside and out.

Mix the dried fruit with a little thyme, pepper, and salt and stuff the hearts with the mixture. Sew or pin them shut.

Melt 1 1/2 tablespoons of butter in a heavy casserole and fry the hearts until well browned on all sides. Pour in the stock, bring to a boil, and simmer, covered, for 1 hour, or until the hearts are tender.

Remove them with a slotted spoon and keep them warm. Mix the remaining 1 1/2 tablespoons butter and the flour in a small bowl and stir into a boiling stock. Simmer for 5 minutes and season to taste.

Slice the stuffed hearts into thick slices and arrange them on a heated serving platter. Pour a little sauce over them and serve the rest on the side, along with boiled or mashed potatoes and poached vegetables.

LIVER PATTIES

Lifrarbuff
Serves 4

The most common way to cook lamb's liver in Iceland is simply to cut it diagonally into thin slices, dust them in seasoned flour, brown them quickly on both sides, and make a brown sauce, often with bacon bits and chopped onion, to serve with them.

Another method, and one that often finds favor with children and people who do not normally like liver, is to mince the liver with potatoes and onions and make thin patties or pancakes, which are then fried and served with melted butter or with a sauce. These patties are often more highly spiced than most other traditional foods.

1 lamb's liver, around 1 pound
1 pound raw potatoes, peeled and chopped
2 medium onions
1/4 cup flour
1 1/2 teaspoons salt
1/2 teaspoon freshly ground pepper
1/2 teaspoon dried thyme
1/4 teaspoon allspice
1/4 cup butter or oil for frying

Clean the liver and cut it into pieces. Run it through a mincer with the potatoes and 1 onion, or process it in a food processor. Stir in flour, salt, pepper, thyme, and allspice.

Melt the butter in a heavy frying pan and spoon the mixture onto the pan—the patties should be pancake-sized. Fry the patties at medium heat until browned on both sides. Remove them from the pan with a slotted spoon and keep warm on a heated serving platter.

Slice the remaining onion thinly and fry it in the remaining fat until lightly browned. Arrange on top of the patties and serve them with boiled potatoes, pickled beets, or red cabbage and gherkins.

GAME BIRDS

There are no chicken or turkey recipes in this book, because although both are very popular now, there are no specific Icelandic recipes for them, but game birds are another story.

The settlers of Iceland probably brought some hens and they are mentioned several times in the sagas and in other medieval sources, but they gradually became less common, probably because of lack of grain to feed them. Cold weather and lack of housing may also have played a part. Hens never disappeared completely, though, and at the beginning of the twentieth century, many housewives kept a few hens to provide eggs for their baking. Up until the 1960s, hens were mostly bred for egg production, not for chicken meat. Almost the only hens that were cooked were old birds that had finished their egg-laying, so it is no wonder most people had a rather low opinion of chicken.

On the other hand, many game birds have been hunted and eaten from the earliest times. Among these are the ptarmigan, the greylag goose and the pink-footed goose, and several species of wild duck, such as mallard and teal. Whooper swans were hunted well into the twentieth century, mostly during the molting season, when the large birds could not fly. They were then rounded up like sheep. And many seabirds were and still are hunted and used to be a large part of the diet in some regions. Among those are puffins, guillemots, gannets, cormorants, shags, and fulmars.

CHRISTMAS PTARMIGAN

Jólarjúpa
Serves 4 to 6

After smoked lamb, ptarmigan can be considered as the most typical Icelandic Christmas dish. But it didn't begin to gain popularity until the 1920s. Before that, the only people who served it at Christmas were those who were so poor they couldn't afford lamb but managed to snare or shoot a couple of birds.

These days ptarmigan is served on Christmas Eve in 15 to 20 percent of all Icelandic homes, and those who serve it usually say they simply couldn't imagine Christmas without it. This means that in a "bad ptarmigan year," when the hunting has not been good, prices—never moderate—can go sky-high, but that doesn't stop people from buying the birds.

This is more or less the classic method to serve ptarmigan, although the birds are often cooked whole. The sauce is the traditional Icelandic ptarmigan sauce, although some versions use less red currant jelly and blue cheese, and older versions would be more likely to include brown cheese rather than blue cheese, or no cheese at all. The classic side dishes are sugar-glazed potatoes, boiled red cabbage, green peas, and a Waldorf salad or other apple salad. Sautéed vegetables like carrots and string beans are also suitable, as are baked apples or pears.

8 ptarmigans, skinned and cleaned
2 tablespoons oil
Freshly ground pepper
Salt
2 bay leaves
1 medium carrot, chopped
4 tablespoons butter
Pinch of thyme
2 tablespoons flour
1 cup heavy cream
2 tablespoons red currant jelly, or to taste
1 tablespoon blue cheese

Cut the breasts and breastbone from the birds (each breast should be left whole, not cut into halves). Chop the rest of the birds up roughly along with the giblets.

Heat the oil in a large skillet and sauté the cut-up birds at high heat until well browned on all sides. Season with pepper and salt and add water to cover. Bring to a boil, skim well, add the bay leaves and chopped carrot, and simmer for 1 hour, adding more water if needed.

Strain the stock through a sieve. Melt 2 tablespoons of the butter in the skillet, season the ptarmigan breasts with salt, pepper, and a little thyme, and brown them in the butter. Pour the hot stock over them, cover, and simmer for 45 minutes.

Remove the breasts from the pan and keep them hot. Mix the remaining 2 tablespoons butter with the flour and stir half of it into the stock, adding the rest if the sauce is very thin, but it shouldn't be thick.

Cook for 5 minutes, add cream, red currant jelly, and blue cheese, and stir until combined. Cook for 5 minutes more, adjust seasonings, and serve with the ptarmigan breasts.

BRAISED WILD GOOSE WITH FRUIT STUFFING

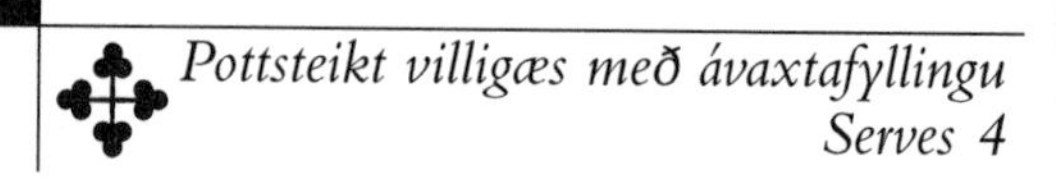

Pottsteikt villigæs með ávaxtafyllingu
Serves 4

Greylag goose, pink-footed goose, or any other similar wild goose may be used for this recipe. A fruit stuffing is traditional for roast goose, usually prunes and dried or fresh apples, but other fruit may be used as well. This fairly quick method works best for a young bird but another popular method, especially if you are not too sure about the age of the goose, is to slow-roast it at 300°F for around 3 hours.

1 wild goose, around 5 pounds, cleaned
1 lemon
Freshly ground pepper
Salt
1 cup mixed dried fruit
2 apples (Jonagold is good)
1/2 teaspoon dried thyme
4 tablespoons butter
2 1/2 cups goose or chicken stock
2 tablespoons flour
1/2 cup cream

Pat the goose dry with a paper towel. Cut the lemon in two and rub the goose inside and out with the cut surfaces. Press the remaining juice from the lemon halves and set aside. Season it well with pepper and salt and refrigerate for an hour or two.

Meanwhile, soak the mixed dried fruit in warm water. Preheat the oven to 450°F. Peel the apples, core, and cut into wedges. Roll them in the lemon juice and stuff the goose with them, along with the drained dried fruit, the thyme, and dots of butter.

Place the bird, breast side down, in a Dutch oven or covered roasting pan. Roast for 15 minutes, then turn the bird over, add 1 cup of the goose or chicken stock, and lower the heat to 350°F. Cover and roast for 1 hour, or until juices run clear.

Remove from the oven and let stand for 10 to 15 minutes. Meanwhile, place the roasting pan on the cooker and turn up the heat. Stir in the remaining 1 1/2 cups stock, bring to a boil, and scrape the bottom of the pan. Pour into a saucepan and boil briskly for a few minutes.

Put the flour in a jar with a little cold water and shake well to combine. Stir the mixture into the stock to thicken the sauce and simmer for 5 minutes. Stir in the cream and simmer for a few minutes more.

Season to taste and serve the sauce with the goose, along with sugar-glazed or roasted potatoes, some sautéed vegetables, and perhaps some poached or pan-fried pears or peaches.

QUICK-FRIED WILD GOOSE BREAST

Léttsteiktar villigæsabringur
Serves 4

Recipes like this have been gaining popularity in recent years, as people have been discovering that there are other methods of cooking game birds than just roasting them until cooked through.

1 young wild goose
2 onions
1 cup stout
1 tablespoon white wine vinegar
5 juniper berries, crushed
5 peppercorns
2 bay leaves
2 medium carrots
Freshly ground pepper
Salt
1 teaspoon fresh wild thyme, or 1/4 teaspoon dried thyme
1/4 teaspoon dried rosemary
1 tablespoon butter
1 tablespoon oil
1 1/2 tablespoons flour
Red currants for decoration (optional)

Carve the breast halves off the goose and pat them dry with a paper towel. Chop 1 of the onions fine and mix it with stout, vinegar, juniper berries, peppercorns, and 1 crushed bay leaf. Place the goose breasts in a nonreactive dish, pour the marinade over them, and turn to coat. Refrigerate for 4 to 8 hours, turning occasionally.

Cut the legs off the goose and chop the rest into pieces. Place the legs and the chopped up carcass in a saucepan. Chop the remaining onion and the carrots and add to the saucepan with the remaining 1 bay leaf, pepper, salt, and water to cover. Bring to a boil and simmer for 2 to 3 hours. (The goose legs can be removed when cooked through and reserved for another dish.) Strain the broth and let it cool.

Preheat the oven to 350°F. Remove the goose breasts from the marinade, strain it, and combine it with the stock in a saucepan. Bring to a boil and reduce down to 1 1/2 cups. Pat the breasts dry, sprinkle them with thyme, rosemary, and pepper, and fry them in butter and oil at medium heat for 3 to 5 minutes on each side, until nicely browned. Remove them to an ovenproof dish and place them in the oven while finishing the sauce, or for 10 minutes or so.

CONTINUED

Sprinkle flour into the remaining fat on the pan and stir until it begins to brown. Gradually stir in the hot stock, bring to a boil, and simmer for a few minutes. Taste and adjust seasonings, perhaps adding a teaspoon or two of red currant jelly.

Remove the breasts from the oven, cut them into thin slices, arrange them on a serving dish or individual plates and pour some of the sauce over them or around them. Decorate with red currants, if desired.

GUILLEMOT IN BROWN SAUCE

Svartfugl í brúnni sósu
Serves 4

The following recipe comes from a stenciled cookery textbook my mother used when she attended a homemaker's academy in the late 1940s, although that recipe is actually for the very similar razorbill. This is a very traditional method to cook *svartfugl*, "blackbird," which is the collective name for the auk family, including razorbill and guillemot, and any bird from that family can be used. The birds can have a somewhat fishy taste and to reduce this, they are often soaked overnight in a mixture of milk and water, or in water to which some vinegar and/or salt has been added.

Lardoons are thin strips of pork fat that are inserted into lean meat to prevent it from drying out during cooking. Fat bacon slices can be used for larding instead.

2 guillemots (or razorbills), skinned and cleaned
4 lardoons or fat bacon slices
6 tablespoons butter
2 onions
1 celery stalk, chopped
1 bay leaf
10 peppercorns
Pinch of thyme
1 pound carrots
1 pound leeks (white and pale green parts only)
2 tablespoons flour
Freshly ground pepper
Salt
1/2 cup cream
1 teaspoon jam (optional)

Soak the birds overnight, as described above, then pat them dry. Lard the breasts with lardoons or bacon.

Melt 4 tablespoons of the butter in a frying pan and brown the birds on all sides. Transfer them to a heavy pan or Dutch oven, breast side down, and add cold water to barely cover. Bring to a boil and skim well.

Peel the onions but do not chop them. Add them to the pan along with celery, bay leaf, peppercorns, and thyme. Cover and simmer for an hour. Clean and trim the carrots and leeks and simmer for an additional half hour. Remove the birds and the whole vegetables and keep hot. Strain the stock.

Melt the remaining 2 tablespoons butter in a saucepan, stir in the flour, and cook for a minute or two. Gradually stir in hot stock, until the sauce has the desired thickness. Season with pepper and salt and simmer for 5 to 10 minutes.

Stir in cream and jam, if using, adjust seasonings, and serve with the birds and some

FLAMED PUFFIN BREASTS

Eldsteiktar lundabringur
Serves 4

The puffin is considered a delicacy by many, not least in the Westmann Islands off the south coast of Iceland. It has been estimated that at least 4 million puffins reside in these rocky volcanic islands. This small bird was usually boiled for at least 3 hours and often eaten with a soup made from the stock, flavored with a little vinegar, and thickened with rice or oatmeal.

My mother-in-law, a native of the Westmann Islands, was quite shocked when I told her I only cooked the puffin for 1 hour. "Three hours is the minimum," she said, shaking her head. I never dared to offer her the quick-fried puffin breasts from the following recipe, popular with younger cooks.

8 puffins
2 cups milk
2 tablespoons flour
1/2 teaspoon dried thyme
Freshly ground pepper
Salt
1 tablespoon butter
1 tablespoon oil
1/2 pound mushrooms
2 tablespoons brandy
1 cup cream

Carve the breasts off the birds and place them in a large bowl. Pour the milk over them and add cold water to cover. Cover and refrigerate for several hours or overnight.

Remove the breasts from the milk marinade, pat dry with a towel, and dust with flour seasoned with thyme, pepper, and salt. Melt butter and oil in a large frying pan and fry the breast at high heat for 1 minute on each side. Stir in the mushrooms.

Pour the brandy into the pan and ignite. When the flames die down, pour in the cream, bring to a boil, and cook for 2 to 3 minutes. Season with pepper and salt and serve.

VEGETABLES AND SALADS

The produce section of a large Reykjavík supermarket is not much different from supermarkets in other European or American cities, although prices tend to be much higher. But this was not always so. Twenty years ago, there were only relatively few types of vegetables to be had. One hundred years ago, one might have been able to buy potatoes, rutabagas, turnips, onions, and a handful of other vegetables. Two hundred and fifty years ago, nothing at all.

There is no concrete evidence that any vegetables at all were grown in Iceland before the eighteenth century, except in a few herb and vegetable gardens at the monasteries. Very little is known about these gardens and what was grown there but whatever it was, it seems not to have spread. Enthusiastic gardeners began experimenting again in the mid-eighteenth century and the first potatoes were planted in 1758. It took them until the early twentieth century to spread all over Iceland. Other vegetables were even slower to gain acceptance.

Given this, it is no wonder that there are not many traditional vegetable dishes to choose from. Most of them include boiled potatoes. I know people who eat potatoes twice a day and would not consider a meal complete without them but regard any other vegetable with suspicion.

GLAZED POTATOES

Brúnaðar kartöflur
Serves 6

Caramelized or sugar-glazed potatoes are certainly not an Icelandic innovation. We learned from the Danes to make them, but they became immensely popular and used to be served with most roasted lamb and pork dishes, and often with pan-fried meat as well.

They are still popular but not as common as they used to be. I once heard a story about an Italian who was working here on an assignment and had to make a two-week tour around the island and eat at village hotels and restaurants. He was half-starving when he came back and said: "The potatoes were horrible everywhere—I just can't imagine what they had done to them—it was as if they had been rolled in melted sugar." No one had the heart to tell him that this was just what had been done to the potatoes.

It has to be said that while glazed potatoes can be really good, they can also be pretty dreary, especially if they have been sitting around for some time and have gotten soggy and fluffy. But I've known children who sat down to a sumptuous Christmas dinner and decided that the only thing they wanted was a heaped plate of glazed potatoes.

I prefer to replace half the sugar with honey—I feel it gives a better taste and is easier to manage. Another version replaces the butter with 1/4 cup of cream and some people simply add a little hot water to the sugar when it has caramelized.

2 pounds potatoes
6 tablespoons sugar
3 tablespoons butter

Boil the potatoes until tender, drain them, and peel them when they have cooled enough to handle (or peel them before boiling them). Cut them into even-size pieces, unless they are very small.

Sprinkle the sugar evenly on a heavy frying pan and heat it. Watch the sugar carefully; it should melt and begin to brown but it must not burn. Stir in the butter when it is melted and cook for a minute or two.

Add the potatoes and stir until they are covered in the caramel and heated through.

MASHED POTATOES

Kartöflustappa
Serves 6

One of my earliest kitchen memories is being allowed to pop freshly peeled potatoes into my mother's potato ricer. Mashed potatoes are popular in Iceland, served with stews, meat sauces, and many traditional dishes. Most recipes—at least in older cookbooks—call for adding at least a pinch of sugar to the mashed potatoes along with milk and butter or margarine, and some versions are decidedly sweet. The nutmeg is traditional in some families, others have never used it.

Icelandic mashed potatoes are rarely made with the aid of a mixer or food processor and they are not beaten until fluffy. Usually the potatoes are riced or mashed, butter and milk are stirred in with a wooden spoon, the mash is seasoned to taste, and that's it.

One of the many language-related things Icelanders will get heated up about is the proper name of this dish in Icelandic. *Kartöflustappa* literally means "mashed potatoes" but many people prefer *kartöflumús*, which may sound a bit strange, considering that *mús* usually means "mouse." *Kartöflumús* is, however, a distortion of the Danish name of the dish, *kartoffelmos*, which also means "mashed potatoes."

2 pounds potatoes
6 tablespoons butter
1/2 cup milk, heated (or more)
1 teaspoon sugar, or to taste (optional)
1/4 teaspoon freshly ground nutmeg (optional)
Freshly ground pepper
Salt

Boil the potatoes until tender. Drain them and let them cool until they can be handled, then peel them. (Or peel and cube them before cooking.) Melt the butter in a saucepan over a low flame. Remove the pan from the heat.

Press the potatoes through a ricer into the saucepan, or add them to the saucepan and mash them thoroughly with a potato masher. Gradually stir in warm milk, until the mash has the desired consistency. Season to taste.

POTATOES IN A WHITE SAUCE

Kartöfluuppstúf
Serves 6

There is a well-known scene in an Icelandic movie where an old woman, in a conversation with her daughter, talks about boiling potatoes twice a day for fifty years. She is not exaggerating. For the greater part of the twentieth century, most Icelanders ate potatoes once or twice a day, 365 days of the year, and they knew four ways to serve them, all involving potatoes boiled in their skins: Plain boiled potatoes, sugar-glazed potatoes, mashed potatoes, and potatoes in a white sauce. There were other recipes, of course, but these are the variations familiar to everyone.

Each variety was served with certain types of dishes. Potatoes in a white sauce were—and still are—served with salted and smoked lamb and horsemeat, smoked sausages and a few other similar dishes, and they are commonly eaten with the smoked leg of lamb on Christmas Day. The sauce is a simple béchamel sauce but a pinch of sugar is often added to it.

2 pounds medium potatoes
1 1/2 cups milk
2 tablespoons butter
2 tablespoons flour
Pinch of freshly grated nutmeg (optional)
Pinch of sugar (optional)
Freshly ground white pepper
Salt

Cook the potatoes until tender. Drain them and let them cool until they can be handled, then peel them and cut them up if they are large. Warm the milk in a small saucepan.

Melt the butter in another saucepan, stir in the flour and cook for 1 to 2 minutes, stirring constantly. Gradually stir in the milk and bring the sauce to a boil. Season with nutmeg, sugar, pepper, and salt, add the potatoes and simmer for 5 minutes, stirring occasionally. Serve hot.

MASHED RUTABAGAS

Rófustappa
Serves 6

Mashed rutabagas are always served with certain traditional dishes, like blood pudding, boiled lamb's heads, and various whey-pickled foods. They are also sometimes served with salted lamb, some stews, or poached salt cod. The mash is sometimes seasoned with a pinch of nutmeg or ginger.

1 1/2 pounds rutabagas
Salt
2 tablespoons butter or margarine
1 teaspoon sugar, or to taste
Freshly ground pepper

Peel the rutabagas, cut them into pieces, and cook them in lightly salted water until tender. Drain them, put them back into the hot pan and let them sit for a couple of minutes. Add butter and mash the rutabagas with a potato masher. Season with sugar, pepper, and salt.

BOILED RED CABBAGE

Soðið rauðkál
Serves 8

Red cabbage is a very common accompaniment to roasted and fried meat and poultry in Iceland. An old-fashioned Sunday roast is almost always served with red cabbage, as is a pork roast, roasted goose or duck, and other such dishes. Pan-fried lamb or pork chops are often served with red cabbage, and it often accompanies sausages and meatballs.

For everyday occasions, people will probably just buy canned red cabbage, but many prefer to cook their own for Christmas and other festive occasions. There are many versions; some include apples, currants, and spices, others are very plain.

1 red cabbage, around 2 pounds
1 apple
1 cup red currant or black currant juice
2 to 3 tablespoons red wine vinegar
3 to 4 whole cloves
1 to 2 teaspoons sugar
Salt

Cut the cabbage into thin strips and place it in a medium saucepan. Peel, core, and cube the apple and add it to the cabbage with the rest of the ingredients. Bring to a boil, cover, and simmer for about 1 hour, stirring occasionally. Remove the cover for the last 10 to 15 minutes of the cooking time, if there is still a lot of liquid in the pan. Season to taste with sugar and salt. Serve hot or cold.

GLAZED CABBAGE

Brúnkál
Serves 8

This is an old-fashioned dish that is not much seen these days but is treasured in some families as a side dish to certain roasts, sausages, or meatballs. It originates in Denmark, where it is usually served with bacon or pork ribs.

Another method is to caramelize some sugar and butter in a pan, then add the shredded cabbage and stir until it is well browned. Then a little stock or water is added and the cabbage left to simmer, covered, for an hour or more. Sometimes the cabbage was divided into two layers after the initial browning. One half was left in the pan, covered with a layer of sausage meat, which was then covered with the rest of the cabbage, and this was then simmered for 30 to 40 minutes.

1 medium cabbage head, around 2 pounds
6 tablespoons butter or margarine
1 tablespoon sugar
Freshly ground pepper
Salt

Cut the cabbage into quarters, remove the core, discard it, and slice the cabbage thin.

Melt the butter in a large heavy pan or Dutch oven and stir-fry the cabbage at fairly high heat until it begins to brown nicely, but take care that it doesn't burn. Sprinkle with sugar, pepper, and salt, add 1/2 cup water, cover, and simmer for an hour, stirring occasionally. Add a little water if the cabbage is about to boil dry. Serve hot with meat dishes.

CABBAGE AND APPLE SLAW

Hvítkálssalat með eplum
Serves 6

Vegetable salads and slaws (called *hrásalat*, "raw salad") were relatively uncommon in Iceland until the 1960s or even later and the early versions were often mostly shredded cabbage and/or grated carrots, mixed with lots of mayonnaise. Butterhead lettuce was usually the only lettuce variety available and this was mostly used as a decoration rather than in salads.

If "raw salad" was mentioned to an Icelander in the 1970s, he would probably have thought of something like the following recipe. This slaw was extremely popular and could be served with all kinds of food—fast food, home-cooked dishes, even the Christmas dinner. Even though a wide selection of salad greens and vegetables is now available, it is still popular. It may not be made at home as much as it used to be but several versions are available in shops and supermarkets.

1/2 cup sour cream
1/2 cup mayonnaise
1/2 teaspoon paprika (preferably Hungarian)
Dash of Tabasco sauce
Freshly ground pepper
Salt
1 red apple
2 slices canned pineapple
4 cups shredded cabbage
1 tablespoon chopped parsley (optional)

Mix the sour cream and mayonnaise with the paprika and Tabasco sauce and season to taste. Wash, core, and chop the apple and chop the pineapple. Mix apple and pineapple with the shredded cabbage in a salad bowl.

Pour the sour cream dressing on the salad and toss to blend. Garnish with parsley if desired.

The dressing is sometimes thinned a little with some juice from the pineapple can.

CARROT AND RAISIN SALAD

Gulróta- og rúsínusalat
Serves 6

This simple salad was often served with fish in the 1960s and 70s, and also with some meat dishes. It is especially good with fried fishballs and meatballs. Helga Sigurdardóttir adds half a cup of whipped cream to it in her *Matur og drykkur* and recommends serving it with crackers and wheat buns. If cream is added, she says, it must first be mixed with the carrots, then the sugar, and finally raisins and lemon juice. If the mixing is not done in this order, the cream may curdle.

3 to 4 large carrots
1/4 cup raisins
1 lemon
1 tablespoon sugar
1 head lettuce (Butterhead)

Scrape or peel the carrots and finely grate them. Place the raisins in a bowl and squeeze the juice from the lemon on them. Mix well. Blend in the sugar and the carrots.

Wash and drain the lettuce, break off the leaves and arrange them in a shallow salad bowl or on a platter. Pile the carrot salad in the center.

APPLE SALAD

Eplasalat
Serves 6

Waldorf salad is a popular accompaniment to roasted game, turkey, and several other festive dishes in Iceland but this version is popular also, not least with those who do not care for the taste of celery, although there are versions that use celery instead of cabbage.

The selection of apple varieties available in stores is generally pretty poor (often just divided into red, green, and yellow) but the apples used in this salad are usually Granny Smith and Red Delicious.

2 green, tart apples
1 red, sweet apple
2 canned pineapple slices
2 cups finely shredded cabbage
1 cup sour cream
2 tablespoons mayonnaise (optional)
Sugar

Peel and core the green apples and wash and core the red apple but do not peel it. Chop all the apples fairly coarsely. Chop the pineapple slices and combine with the apples and cabbage in a bowl.

Mix sour cream and mayonnaise in another bowl, add sugar to taste (many use honey or maple syrup instead) and perhaps a little juice from the pineapple can. Pour over the apple mixture and stir to combine thoroughly.

POTATO SALAD

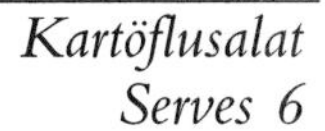

Kartöflusalat
Serves 6

This is a fairly standard potato salad, although some may prefer to use less onion, especially if the salad is made some time in advance.You might also add chopped apples, a little shredded cabbage, or chopped hard-boiled eggs.

Waxy, not too large potatoes are ideal and many prefer a variety called Red Icelandic. In Iceland, potatoes are usually boiled in their skins and peeled while still warm.

2 pounds potatoes, cooked and peeled
1 onion
1 cup mayonnaise
1/2 cup sour cream
1 tablespoon lemon juice
1 teaspoon Dijon mustard
1/4 cup chopped parsley
2 tablespoons chopped chives
Freshly ground pepper
Salt

Cut the potatoes into cubes or chunks and place them in a bowl. Peel the onion and finely chop it. Mix it with mayonnaise, sour cream, lemon juice, mustard, herbs and seasonings, pour over the potatoes and blend well. Refrigerate for 15 minutes before serving.

The salad will be improved if everything but the potatoes is mixed well and refrigerated for a few hours.The potatoes are then mixed with the dressing just before serving.

DESSERTS

Desserts used to be a very important part of the Icelandic diet. A few decades ago, a dessert of some sort was served at least once and often twice a day in every Icelandic household.

"It is a good idea to use a different sort of grains for each day of the week," says home economist Jóninna Sigurðardóttir in her cookbook, and this wasn't difficult to follow; the first 11 dessert soup recipes that come under the heading *Everyday dishes* in the book contain 11 different grains or types of grain: Rice, corn flakes, buckwheat, rice flour, cornflour, oatmeal, pearl barley, German millet, flour (in the form of macaroni), pearl sago, and semolina. Sundays, on the other hand, called for sweet soups and fruit compotes, or maybe a cocoa soup.

I've included here some everyday soups and porridges, some fruit soups and compotes, and a few traditional festive desserts as well. Most of these dishes are still served occasionally but since desserts are now rarely a part of an everyday meal, some of the simpler desserts have turned into real treats, just because people who remember them from their childhood seldom get them any more, so they appreciate them all the more when they are served.

SKYR WITH BERRIES

Berjaskyr
Serves 4

In Iceland, the berries used for this very traditional delicacy are crowberries, bog bilberries, and bilberries, where available—sometimes just one type, sometimes a mixture. American blueberries can be used instead, and I've also used strawberries and raspberries, and substituted honey for some of the sugar—but none of that is traditional.

4 cups skyr
Milk (optional)
Sugar
2 to 4 cups berries
Light cream or half-and-half

Stir the skyr until smooth, with a little milk if it is very thick, and add sugar to taste. Wash the berries and pick them over. Mix them with the skyr. Serve with cream and more sugar.

COCOA SOUP

Kakósúpa
Serves 4

This unusual soup often surprises visitors to Iceland, who will not encounter it at restaurants but may be served it in private homes or canteens. Cocoa soup is rarely seen elsewhere but it came from Denmark and I've seen recipes in old Danish cookbooks.

It is very popular with children and can be a very nice occasional treat. But it shouldn't be served too often. My father worked with a bridge-constructing crew in his youth and soon noticed that none of his workmates seemed overly fond of cocoa soup, to say the least. When he asked why, he was told that a year or two earlier, they had been building a bridge close to a remote farm and the farmer's wife had undertaken to feed them. They were served cocoa soup for dessert at lunch and at supper, and got the leftovers for breakfast, every single day for three weeks.

3 tablespoons cocoa powder
3 tablespoons sugar
1/2 teaspoon cinnamon (optional)
3 cups milk
1 tablespoon potato starch or cornstarch
Salt

Mix cocoa powder, sugar, cinnamon, and 2 cups water in a saucepan and stir until smooth. Bring to a boil and simmer for 5 minutes. Add the milk, heat again to boiling point, and simmer for 2 to 3 minutes.

Mix the potato starch or cornstarch with a little cold water, stir it into the soup, and remove from the heat. Salt to taste. Serve with crushed zwiebacks.

For a more fancy version, use 3 ounces semisweet chocolate instead of the cocoa powder and serve the soup with whipped cream instead of zwiebacks.

RYE BREAD SOUP

Brauðsúpa
Serves 4

I know lots of people, myself included, who get a nostalgic craving for this soup about once or twice a year, but most of them admit they would not want it served every week. It used to be a Sunday treat but it is really nothing more than an ingenious way to use up stale bread. Other types of bread can be mixed in, providing the main part is dark rye.

There is no jam in my mother's recipe but I came across this addition in an old cookbook some time ago, tried it out, and decided I liked it. The thickness of the soup varies; some are quite thin but I prefer a thick, porridge-like version. This one is fairly coarse but some like a smoother soup and press the soaked bread through a sieve before cooking.

1 pound dark rye bread
1/4 cup raisins
1 tablespoon jam (optional)
1/2 lemon
Sugar
Whipped cream

Cut the bread into small cubes. If the bread is old and stale or hard, it should be soaked in cold water for a few hours or overnight.

Place the bread cubes in a medium-size saucepan. Add water to cover (use the soaking water if the bread was soaked) and bring to a boil. Simmer for a few minutes, then break the bread cubes up with the back of a spoon, or mash them with a potato masher; the soup should be fairly smooth.

Add raisins, jam, and a couple of slices of lemon, and simmer for 8 to 10 minutes. Stir in sugar and lemon juice to taste. Serve hot with lots of whipped cream.

VELVET PUDDING

Flauelsgrautur
Serves 4

"I wonder why it tasted so good," people who remember this pudding from their childhood sometimes say—and that is understandable, because, after all, this old-fashioned dessert is really nothing more than a very thick béchamel sauce, eaten with cinnamon sugar and sweetened fruit juice. But it is quick and easy to make, it is velvet smooth, and children usually like it. The recipe originally came from Denmark in the nineteenth century.

Smjörgrautur (butter pudding) is similar but uses water instead of milk. Chocolate velvet pudding is a fancy version where 3 to 4 ounces chopped chocolate is stirred into the hot pudding along with 1/2 cup sugar and a little vanilla extract. The pudding is then either eaten hot or left to cool.

3 1/2 cups milk
1/2 cup butter
1 cup flour
1/2 teaspoon salt, or to taste
Cinnamon sugar

Bring the milk to a boil in a saucepan. Melt the butter in another pan, stir in the flour and gradually whisk in the hot milk. Stir until absolutely smooth and velvety. Add a little more milk if needed; the mixture should be like a very thick sauce.

Simmer for 5 minutes at very low heat, stirring often and taking great care that the pudding doesn't burn. Salt to taste and serve hot with cinnamon sugar.

ELBOW MACARONI SOUP

Makkarónusúpa
Serves 6

A simple milk soup, usually very popular with children. This was virtually the only form of pasta I encountered before my tenth birthday—using macaroni for anything other than a sweet dish would have been considered a revolutionary idea.

Soups of this type are traditional in Iceland and there is even a version in the earliest Icelandic cookbook, published in 1800. That one uses homemade pasta strips and the soup is called "worm milk," as the strips are said to resemble worms. However, few Icelandic housewives ventured upon pasta making for another 190 years or so.

1 cup elbow macaroni
3 cups milk
4 to 6 tablespoons sugar or brown sugar
1/2 teaspoon vanilla extract
Salt

Bring 2 cups water to a boil in a saucepan and stir in the macaroni. Simmer until tender, stirring occasionally. Add milk and sugar, bring to a boil, and simmer for 1 to 2 minutes. Stir in vanilla extract and a pinch of salt and serve.

A little cinnamon is sometimes added to the soup, or sprinkled over it before serving.

EGG MILK SOUP

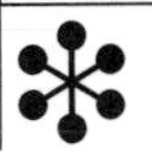

Eggjamjólk
Serves 6

This is the Icelandic version of the classic French dessert *oeufs à la neige*, by way of Denmark. A few prunes or raisins were sometimes added to the soup.

4 cups milk
1/2 vanilla bean
2 tablespoons flour
2 eggs, separated
3 tablespoons sugar, or to taste

Bring the milk to a boil with the vanilla bean. Remove from heat and let stand for 10 minutes or so.

Remove the vanilla bean and bring the milk back to a boil. Put the flour and 1/2 cup cold water in a jar, shake until smooth, and stir into a boiling milk to thicken slightly. Simmer for 5 minutes.

Meanwhile, whisk the egg yolks with the sugar in a bowl. Slowly whisk in the hot milk. Whip the egg whites until they form stiff peaks. Pour the soup into a serving bowl and spoon the egg whites on top with a tablespoon; they should form small floating balls. Serve immediately.

RICE PUDDING

Hrísgrjónagrautur
Serves 6

Rice desserts have long been popular in Iceland. Creamy *ris a l'amande* for Christmas, thick raisin-studded rice pudding for Sundays, thinner rice porridge for everyday desserts—the latter two versions always served with cinnamon sugar. The following recipe is for the thick raisin-y version—the thinner, gruel-like version is not often seen these days.

There are several variations but most start the rice off in water, then continue cooking in milk, sometimes for an hour or more, and in some versions the cooking is even begun the day before. Most recipes use ordinary long-grain rice, not short-grain pudding rice.

1 1/2 cups rice
2 cups milk, or as needed
1/2 cup raisins (optional)
Salt
Sugar
Cinnamon

Bring 3 cups of water to a boil in a saucepan. Stir in the rice and cook, partly covered, for 10 to 15 minutes over medium-low heat, or until most of the water has been absorbed.

Add the milk, bring back to a boil, and simmer for 30 to 40 minutes, stirring often. Add more milk as needed, but the pudding should be thick. If raisins are used, they should be added 10 minutes before the pudding is ready.

Salt to taste and serve with cold milk and cinnamon sugar (5 to 6 tablespoons sugar to each tablespoon of cinnamon).

SAGO FRUIT SOUP

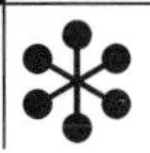

Sagósúpa með ávöxtum
Serves 6

In Icelandic cooking, sago has mostly been used for sweet dessert soups to thicken them and add texture. However, many people dislike the texture and say the transparent sago pellets remind them of fish spawn. But sago soups have their aficionados, too. The following recipe is fairly typical but often the eggs were omitted and some fruit juice was added instead.

1/4 cup pearl sago
1/2 cup raisins
1/4 cup pitted prunes
1/4 cup sugar, or to taste
2 egg yolks
Pinch of salt

Bring 4 cups of water to a boil in a saucepan. Stir in the sago, then add raisins and prunes. Lower the heat and simmer for 20 to 30 minutes.

Whisk sugar, egg yolks, and salt in a large bowl. Gradually whisk in the hot soup, taking care that the egg yolks do not curdle. Taste, add more sugar if needed, and serve hot.

BILBERRY SOUP

Bláberjasúpa
Serves 6

This is an old Icelandic recipe that makes use of bilberries, abundant in some regions, or bog bilberries, which can be found in all regions. Fresh berries were used in season, in August and September, but dried berries were much more common.

2 cups bilberries or blueberries
1/2 cup sugar
2 tablespoons potato starch or cornstarch

Place the berries in a saucepan, add 4 cups water, and bring slowly to a boil. Stir in sugar and simmer at low heat for 5 minutes. Mix the potato starch with a little cold water.

Remove the pan from the heat, and stir in the potato starch mixture. Take care to stir back and forth, not in a circular motion, until the soup thickens somewhat. Do not let the mixture boil after adding the potato starch. (If using cornstarch, do not remove the pan from the heat. Stir in the cornstarch and boil until the soup thickens.) Serve hot.

The soup is usually served with crushed zwiebacks or dried bread but can also be served with cream.

RHUBARB COMPOTE

Rabarbaragrautur
Serves 8

In the virtually fruit-less Iceland, rhubarb was used to make jams, juices, cakes, and soups, but the most popular dish was rhubarb compote, a common Sunday dessert, sometimes eaten hot but usually cold, sprinkled with sugar and with a generous amount of milk, light cream, or sometimes whipped cream poured over it.

The same recipe was also used to make rhubarb soup, using less rhubarb and less thickener. This soup, which was more of an everyday dish, was served hot, usually with crushed zwiebacks, and people would spoon the zwieback crumbs into their soup and stir until the crumbs were soaked and beginning to soften.

Both compote and soup could be made from rhubarb jam, when fresh or preserved rhubarb wasn't available, but those versions were not as popular.

2 pounds red rhubarb stalks
1 cup sugar, or to taste
Red food coloring (optional)
3 tablespoons potato starch or cornstarch
Light cream

Wash and trim the rhubarb and cut it into 1-inch pieces. Place it in a saucepan, add sugar and 2 cups cold water, and bring slowly to a boil. Simmer at low heat until the rhubarb is very soft, stirring often. Add a few drops of red food coloring, if desired.

Mix the potato starch with a little cold water, remove the pan from the heat, and stir in the potato starch mixture. Take care to stir back and forth, not in a circular motion, until the compote thickens. Do not let boil after adding the potato starch. (If using cornstarch, do not remove the pan from the heat. Stir in the cornstarch and boil until thickened.) Serve the pudding hot or cold, with sugar and light cream.

If the compote is to be served cold, it is poured into a serving bowl and a little sugar is sprinkled on top to prevent skin forming.

STEWED MIXED FRUIT COMPOTE

Ávaxtagrautur
Serves 6

Modern dried fruit usually needs no soaking before stewing but older recipes usually call for soaking the fruit for several hours or overnight, then cooking it in the soaking water. The dried fruit mixtures available in Icelandic shops usually include prunes, apricots, apples, and pears, but no raisins. Chopped rhubarb was sometimes added as an extra treat.

If the compote is to be served cold, it is poured into a serving bowl and a tablespoon or so of sugar is sprinkled on top to prevent skin forming.

1 1/2 cups mixed dried fruit
1/4 cup sugar, or to taste
3 tablespoons potato starch or cornstarch
Light cream or whipping cream

Place the fruit in a saucepan with 4 cups water and cook it until very soft and tender, stirring occasionally. Add sugar to taste.

Mix the potato starch with a little cold water, remove the pan from the heat, and stir in the potato starch mixture. Take care to stir back and forth, not in a circular motion, until the pudding thickens. Do not let the mixture boil after adding the potato starch. (If using cornstarch, do not remove the pan from the heat. Stir in the cornstarch and boil until thickened.)

Serve hot or cold and pour some cream over the compote.

The same recipe is used for stewed prune compote, another popular old dessert. These fruit compotes can be served hot or cold but they are usually served cold now, as rather good ready-made boxed versions are available in stores and most people buy them instead of making the compotes at home.

SPICED FRUIT SOUP

Krydduð sætsúpa
Serves 6

Sætsúpa, "sweet soup," usually means a soup containing dried fruit, and often pearl sago as well. Although it is optional in this recipe, I like the texture it provides and wouldn't want to leave it out.

Various versions of *sætsúpa* used to be a very common Sunday dessert in Iceland. Some recipes use spices, others omit them. Other dried fruit, such as apple or pear, may be used. The fruit is usually chopped for soup but in a compote, it is left whole.

1 tablespoon pearl sago (optional)
1/2 cup raisins
1/4 cup pitted prunes
1/4 cup chopped dried apricots
1-inch piece of cinnamon stick
3 whole cloves
1 cup fruit or berry juice (cranberry juice is fine)
Sugar
Freshly squeezed lemon juice

Heat 4 cups water in a saucepan. When it boils, stir in the pearl sago, if using. Add the dried fruit and spices and simmer for 20 to 25 minutes.

Stir in fruit juice. Add sugar and lemon juice to taste and cook for a few minutes more. Serve hot, perhaps with some cream.

GRANDMOTHER'S TRIFLE

Ömmutrifli
Serves 6

This very English dessert came to Iceland via Denmark, probably in the late nineteenth century and was always a slightly upper-class dish, something you would be much more likely to encounter in Reykjavík or the towns than on a farm, and usually only served at Christmas and other grand occasions. For many it is the ultimate nostalgic Granny's dessert, fondly remembered but rarely made. Modern cooks are much more likely to try their hand at other layered desserts, like trifle's fashionable Italian distant cousin, tiramisu.

There are many versions of trifle in old Icelandic cookbooks and among the ingredients mentioned are rhubarb purée or jam; red currant, black currant, or bilberry jam; canned fruit; and, in the most recent versions, fresh fruit. The base is usually almond macaroons but occasionally stale cake cubes are used, often soaked with wine, sherry, or rum, sometimes a shockingly large amount. This old recipe calls for rhubarb jam but other types of jam can be substituted.

1 1/2 cups milk
1 vanilla bean
1 egg
3 egg yolks
5 tablespoons sugar, or to taste
2 cups roughly crushed almond macaroons
4 to 5 tablespoons sherry or port
1/2 cup rhubarb jam, not too sweet
1 cup whipping cream
1 ounce chocolate (1 square), grated or chopped

First make the custard: Pour the milk into a saucepan. Split the vanilla bean, scrape out the seeds and add both bean and seeds to the pan.

Bring the milk to a boil, then remove from heat and let stand for a few minutes. Whisk the whole egg and the yolks with the sugar until golden and frothy. Strain the milk gradually into the egg mixture, whisking thoroughly. Pour the custard back into the saucepan and whisk at very low heat until thickened. Let cool.

Spread the crumbled macaroons on the bottom of a nice looking glass bowl. Drizzle with sherry or port, then spoon the jam over the macaroons. Pour the cooled custard over the jam and refrigerate until set.

Whip the cream, spoon it into a piping bag with a wide star nozzle, and pipe decorations on the surface of the trifle. Sprinkle grated chocolate on top and serve.

LEMON MOUSSE

Sítrónubúðingur
Serves 6

The alternative name for this dessert, *sítrónufrómas* or "lemon fromage," may sound confusing, considering that *fromage* is cheese in French. For some reason, however, fromage has come to mean a mousse in the Scandinavian languages.

Gelatin-stiffened mousses like this used to be popular desserts and many still make them for festive occasions like Christmas and Easter. They are also sometimes used as a filling for layer cakes.

5 teaspoons gelatin powder
3 eggs, separated
1/2 cup sugar
Juice and grated zest of 1 lemon
1 cup whipping cream

Soak the gelatin powder in a little cold water. Whisk the egg yolks and sugar until pale yellow, then gradually whisk in the lemon juice. In another bowl, whip the egg whites until they form stiff peaks. Whip the cream until stiff in a third bowl and reserve some of it if you wish to use it for decoration.

Melt the gelatin over very low heat, or in a bain-marie, and gradually stir it into the egg yolks. Fold in the egg whites with a spatula and finally the whipped cream. Pour the mousse into a pretty glass bowl and refrigerate until set.

Decorate, if desired, with reserved whipped cream and a little grated lemon zest.

The recipe can be used for other similar mousses. For orange mousse, simply substitute an orange for the lemon and use a little more gelatin since there will be more juice. For pineapple mousse, use a can of pineapple slices. Keep some of them for decoration but chop the rest and fold them into the mousse along with 1/4 cup juice from the pineapple can and 1 tablespoon lemon juice.

RICE À L'AMANDE

Ris a l'amande
Serves 6

This delicious rice pudding is a popular Christmas dessert all over Scandinavia. It usually retains its French name (in Sweden it is known as *ris à la Malta*), and it has been served on Christmas Eve in many Icelandic homes for over a century.

1 tablespoon butter
3 cups milk
1 vanilla bean
1/2 cup pudding rice (short-grain)
1/2 teaspoon salt
1/4 cup chopped almonds
2 tablespoons sugar
1 tablespoon sherry (optional)
1 1/2 cups whipping cream

Grease a saucepan with the butter before pouring the milk into it. Bring to a boil. Split the vanilla bean, scrape out the seeds into the milk, and add the split bean. Gradually stir in the rice.

Simmer, covered, for 45 minutes at very low heat. Stir occasionally and add a little more milk if needed. Remove from heat, take out the vanilla bean, salt the rice pudding, and let it cool, covered, preferably overnight.

Stir almonds, sugar, and sherry, if using, into the cold rice pudding. Whip the cream until stiff and fold it in carefully.

Refrigerate and serve with a fruit sauce, such as the apricot sauce in the following recipe, or canned fruit.

Some prefer to stiffen their pudding with some gelatin. To do that, dissolve 4 teaspoons gelatin in a little hot water, stir into the still-warm pudding along with almonds, sugar, and sherry, and fold in the whipped cream before the pudding begins to stiffen. Refrigerate for a few hours or overnight.

APRICOT SAUCE

Apríkósusósa
Makes 1/2 cup

This sauce can be served with *ris a l'amande* (page 154) and other puddings, or with ice cream. The same recipe can be used for other fruit. Fresh berries, for instance, need only be cooked for a few minutes.

1/2 cup chopped dried apricots
1/4 cup sugar, or to taste
1 teaspoon potato starch or cornstarch

Soak the apricots in 2 cups water for a couple of hours. Turn them into a saucepan with the soaking water and cook them gently until tender. Press them through a sieve and pour them back into the saucepan. Stir in sugar to taste and bring to a boil again.

Dissolve the potato starch or cornstarch in a little cold water, remove the saucepan from the heat and immediately stir in the starch mixture. Stir until slightly thickened. Cool and serve.

CHRISTMAS ICE CREAM

Jólaís
Serves 6

I know people who don't like glacé cherries at all but wouldn't dream of serving anything other than this ice cream as a dessert at Christmas because it looks so festive and besides, this is what their mother always served. It is a very good dessert, simple to make—and of course, the cherries can always be omitted.

Egg safety has not really been an issue in Iceland, as there have been no documented cases of salmonella poisoning from eggs, but uncooked eggs are a concern in many countries. The ice cream can also be made with a simple custard that cooks the eggs and makes them safe. Just whisk the eggs, sugar, and half the cream over very low heat or in a bain-marie until the mixture thickens. Cool, fold in the whipped cream, and proceed as described in the recipe.

5 egg yolks
6 tablespoons sugar
1 teaspoon vanilla extract
2 cups whipping cream
1/2 cup chopped dark chocolate
1/4 cup chopped mixed red and green glacé cherries

Whisk the egg yolks thoroughly with the sugar and the vanilla extract. Whip the cream until stiff and fold it gently into the egg mixture.

If you have an ice cream machine, pour the mixture into it and let it run until the ice cream begins to thicken. Add the chocolate and the chopped cherries and let the machine run until the mixture has thickened. Spoon into a decorative ice cream mold and freeze.

If you don't have an ice cream machine, just pour the egg and cream mixture into a metal bowl and freeze until it begins to thicken. Stir in the chocolate and cherries, then spoon the mixture into a mold and freeze again.

Remove the ice cream from the freezer 20 to 30 minutes before serving and let it soften in the refrigerator. Turn it out on a plate it and serve it with fresh or canned fruit, and/or a chocolate sauce.

BILBERRY ICE CREAM

Aðalbláberjaís
Serves 6

A simple but delicious dessert. The tasty Icelandic wild bilberries are just right for this ice cream but it can also be made with American bilberries or blueberries.

If egg safety is a concern, then whisk the eggs, 1/4 cup sugar, and 1/2 cup cream over very low heat or in a bain-marie until the mixture thickens. Let cool. Whip the remaining 1/2 cup cream and fold it into the egg mixture. Add the berries and their syrup and freeze as described in the recipe.

1/2 cup sugar
2 cups bilberries (or blueberries)
3 eggs
1 teaspoon vanilla extract
1 cup whipping cream

Heat 1/2 cup water with 1/4 cup sugar in a saucepan, stirring until the sugar is dissolved. Boil for 2 minutes or so, then add the berries and boil briskly for 2 minutes more. Pour into a bowl and let cool. Refrigerate until cold.

Whisk the eggs with the remaining 1/4 cup sugar and the vanilla extract. Whip the cream until stiff and fold it gently into the egg mixture. If you have an ice cream maker, pour the mixture into it and let it run until the ice cream begins to thicken. Add the berries and their syrup and let the machine run until the mixture has thickened. Spoon into a mold and freeze.

If an ice cream maker is not available, then pour the egg and cream mixture into a metal bowl and freeze for an hour. Stir in the ice cold berries and syrup, spoon into a mold and freeze again, perhaps stirring once or twice.

Remove the ice cream from the freezer 20 to 30 minutes before serving and let it soften in the refrigerator.

CAKES, PASTRIES, AND COOKIES

My father remembers being sent, as a teenager, on an errand to the next farm. This was not long after Christmas and the housewife offered him a cup of coffee. He was the only guest but she proceeded to bring all kinds of baked goods to the table, despite his protests. He says he counted seventeen different sorts of cakes and cookies there. And she probably went on and on excusing herself for her poor hospitality—Icelandic housewives used to do that all the time, while heaping goodies on the table.

This woman was not an exception, and Nobel laureate Halldór Laxness has written a famous description of just such a one-man pastry extravaganza in one of his novels. This was an ordinary Icelandic housewife, caught up in the baking frenzy that gripped Icelandic women in the early twentieth century, when they finally had both ovens for baking and enough flour to play with. Before that, most "coffee bread," as cakes, cookies, and sweet pastries are called collectively in Iceland, had been fried, in the form of crepes, pancakes, crullers, love balls, and so on.

I have included recipes for the traditional fried cakes, and for several cakes and cookies that date from the first half of the twentieth century. Most of these are still frequently baked today, or are at least well known and appreciated when someone bothers to make them. I've also added a couple of more recent cakes, to show what people like best today. And there is, of course, a recipe for rhubarb jam.

CREPES

Pönnukökur
Makes 20 to 25 crepes

Don't expect an American-type pancake if an Icelander offers you pancakes with jam and whipped cream. An Icelandic *pönnukaka* (literally, pancake) is a very thin crepe, almost always cooked in a special heavy crepe pan that is around 7 1/2 inches in diameter, with only 1/4-inch-high sides. This pan is rarely used for anything but crepes, pancakes, and scones. Nothing sticks to it and it is *never* washed. (One of my children did wash my pan in 1991. The incident has not been quite forgiven.)

The crepes are either drizzled liberally with sugar while still warm, rolled fairly tightly into cigar shapes and stacked up like logs, or they are left to cool, then spread with jam (rhubarb is traditional, but strawberry or raspberry jam is more popular now). A liberal amount of stiffly whipped cream is heaped on the center of the crepe, which is then folded in half and again into a triangle. The filled crepes are arranged in overlapping rows on a serving plate and served with coffee. Almost everybody loves them and many will tell you that they consider either this or crepes rolled with sugar the most Icelandic dish there is.

Add a little more milk to the batter if the crepe is too thick; whisk in a little flour if it is too thin and is difficult to turn.

2 eggs
2 cups milk
1 teaspoon vanilla or lemon extract
1 cup flour
2 tablespoons sugar
1/2 teaspoon baking powder
Pinch of salt
4 tablespoons butter

Whisk the eggs with the milk and flavoring. Stir in flour, sugar, baking powder and salt and whisk until smooth.

Heat the crepe pan. Melt the butter in the hot pan and stir it into the batter. Pour around 2 tablespoons of the batter into the hot pan, tilting it and rotating it while pouring to enable the batter to spread all over the surface before it begins to cook. The crepe should be very thin. Cook at medium-high heat for a minute or less, or until the underside is golden brown.

While the crepe cooks, run the tip of the spatula around the outer edge to loosen it and prevent it from burning. Turn it with the spatula and cook for 10 to 15 seconds on the other side. Continue cooking until the batter is used up.

Roll the pancakes with sugar, or spread them out on a work surface to cool if they are to be filled with cream.

RICE PUDDING PANCAKES

Grautarlummur
Makes around 12 pancakes

These thick, irregular rustic pancakes are a really old-fashioned type of treat that is still served at many countryside homes. They are usually made from leftover rice pudding (page 146) but some people are so fond of them that they will cook a plateful of rice just to make the pancakes. Ordinary boiled rice will not do, however; it must be slowly simmered in milk until very tender but not too mushy, and ideally it should absorb virtually all the milk and be stiff enough to cut when cold.

The pancakes are best freshly made. Usually they are just served with sugar but jam is another option. If leftover pudding is used there should be no need for more salt but it might be a good idea to cook one small test pancake to check this and also the thickness of the batter.

2 cups leftover rice pudding
2 eggs
2 tablespoons sugar, and more for serving
1 teaspoon freshly ground cardamom or
  1 teaspoon vanilla extract
1 1/4 cups flour
1 1/2 teaspoons baking powder
1 cup milk
1/4 cup raisins
6 tablespoons butter or margarine

Mix cold rice pudding and eggs until the rice pudding is completely broken up. Stir in sugar and cardamom or vanilla extract. Mix flour and baking powder and stir into the batter along with the milk. Add a little more flour or milk as needed; the batter should be thick but not so thick that it doesn't spread in the pan. Stir in raisins.

Melt the butter in a pancake pan or frying pan and stir it into the batter. Spoon the batter into the pan—1/4 cup or so for each pancake—and cook the pancakes at medium heat until nicely browned on both sides, turning once.

Stack the pancakes on a serving plate and sprinkle sugar on each layer. Serve with more sugar.

WAFFLES

Vöfflur
Makes around 8 waffles

Waffles, along with crepes, pancakes, crullers, and a few other fried cookies, are one of the few sweet treats that were commonly served in Iceland in the nineteenth century, when there was hardly an oven on the whole island and baked cakes and cookies were practically unknown. Waffles, although requiring a special tool and not as simple to make as *lummur* (pancakes), gained a popularity that has never diminished. There is a waffle recipe in the earliest Icelandic cookbook, published in 1800, which goes something like this:

"Waffles are made of wheat flour stirred with good milk or cream, a few eggs, or some beestings (colostrum) until you have a thick batter, into which is stirred some unsalted melted butter ... Thoroughly mix in a little ground cinnamon, sugar, and grated lemon zest, if available, and let the batter stand for a while in a warm place or by the fire, to make it swell. Heat the waffle irons on the fire and butter them well with unmelted butter." The following modern recipe really is not that much different (although no suggestion is made of substituting beestings for eggs). The only addition is the baking powder, not yet invented in 1800. I can't recall any twentieth-century waffle recipes that include cinnamon, though. Cardamom was sometimes used as flavoring but that is not often seen these days. In a few versions, some or all the milk is substituted with cream.

Most Icelandic homes have a waffle iron, usually the Scandinavian type that makes heart-shaped waffles. Waffles are rarely cooked for breakfast or lunch; they are served with afternoon or evening coffee, especially when unexpected guests arrive or when the family deserves a treat. The waffles may be served with sugar, jam, or jam and whipped cream, rarely with a savory topping. Warm, crisp waffles with strawberry or blueberry jam and a big dollop of whipped cream are a very fine treat indeed.

2 eggs
1 cup milk
1 3/4 cups flour
1 teaspoon baking powder
2 tablespoons sugar
Pinch of salt
1/2 teaspoon vanilla or lemon extract
4 to 6 tablespoons butter

Whisk the eggs and milk in a bowl. Stir in the flour, baking powder, sugar, and salt and continue stirring until the batter is smooth. Add the flavoring.

Heat the waffle iron. Melt the butter and brush the grids with some of it but stir the remainder into the batter. Spoon 3 to 4 tablespoons batter onto the hot iron and cook until nicely browned and crisp—it is better to slightly overcook the waffle than to undercook it.

The waffles are usually consumed as soon as they are cooked and there may be a waiting line. If serving the waffles all at once, do not stack them, or they will go limp and soggy. Spread them out on kitchen towels, or keep them warm on racks in the oven.

DEEP-FRIED BOWS (CRULLERS)

Kleinur
Makes around 30 bows

Almost every European nation has a recipe for deep-fried bows of some kind. I've seen them in Russian, Polish, Romanian, German, French, and Italian cookbooks, not to mention the Scandinavian versions, like Norwegian *fattigmenn*. I've even come across recipes in African cookbooks; it seems they are sold as street food in Western Africa. They have been known in Denmark since medieval times. In Iceland, they are first mentioned in the old cookbook published in 1800. They became widespread in the nineteenth century, originally as a festive treat, but later they were regarded as everyday cookies.

Most Icelandic *kleinur* are plump and soft but some prefer them to be thinner and more crisp. For that, just add a little less buttermilk to obtain a stiffer dough and roll it out more thinly. Icelandic *kleinur* are never sprinkled with sugar while hot, as is done with some similar cookies elsewhere. They are always eaten plain with coffee and are at their best when still warm.

Kleinur seem to be very closely knit to a grandmotherly image and youngish Icelandic grannies are sometimes heard to say: "Yes, sure, I'm a grandmother, but I'm not so old that I stay at home and make *kleinur*!"

2 cups flour
1/2 cup sugar
1 teaspoon baking soda
1/2 teaspoon baker's ammonia (optional)
Pinch of salt
6 tablespoons butter or margarine, softened
2 eggs
1 teaspoon freshly ground cardamom or lemon extract
1/4 cup buttermilk, or as needed
Shortening or Crisco for deep-frying

Mix flour, sugar, baking soda, baker's ammonia, if using, and salt in a bowl. Add the butter and stir until combined. Add eggs and flavoring and mix well. Gradually add buttermilk, until the dough is fairly soft but not sticky.

Roll the dough out on a floured work surface to 1/8- to 1/6-inch thickness. Cut it into elongated diamonds (around 3 inches long and 1 1/2 inches wide). Make a diagonal slit in the center of each and pull one end through the slit.

Heat the fat to 375°F. Fry the bows, 4 to 6 at a time, in the hot fat until golden brown, which should take around 2 minutes. Turn them once for even cooking. Remove the crullers with a slotted spoon and drain them on paper towels.

LOVE BALLS

Ástarpungar
Makes around 20 balls

These round, dark golden doughnuts have been made in Iceland for over a century. They are easier and quicker to make than *kleinur* but have lost out in the popularity stakes in later years, probably because not many people make deep-fried cookies at home any more. Love balls really need to be freshly fried and eaten warm to be fully appreciated. *Kleinur*, while at their best when freshly cooked, usually hold up to storage better and are packaged and sold in shops. And they can always be dunked in hot coffee to freshen them up if they get stale. Love balls somehow don't lend themselves as easily to that treatment.

Do not make the balls too large, or they will be too dark on the outside before the center is fully cooked. The raw dough balls should be somewhat larger than walnuts. They will expand considerably in the hot fat and should ideally be perfectly round. They can be flavored with grated lemon zest or some vanilla sugar instead of the cardamom.

2 eggs
6 tablespoons sugar
3 1/2 cups flour
1 tablespoon baking powder
1/2 teaspoon freshly ground cardamom
1 cup milk, or as needed
1/2 cup raisins
Shortening or Crisco for deep-frying

Whisk eggs and sugar in a bowl. Mix flour, baking powder, and cardamom and stir it in gradually, alternating with milk. You may not need all the milk—the batter should be thick and almost able to hold its shape. Stir in raisins.

Heat the fat to around 390°F. Shape balls out of the batter, using 2 tablespoons, and fry 5 to 6 at a time until medium brown and puffy, turning several times to make them cook evenly. They should be ready in 3 to 4 minutes.

Remove with a slotted spoon and drain on paper towels.

VINARTERTA

Vínarterta
Makes a 9-inch, 6-layer cake

Vínarterta is sometimes just about the only Icelandic word that Canadians and Americans of Icelandic descent know. When their ancestors left Iceland in the late nineteenth or early twentieth century, *vínarterta* was at the height of its popularity. It is a grand-looking cake that was, due to the thin layers, much easier to make in the primitive ovens of the time than thicker cakes would have been, and could even be baked without an oven. The prune filling was the closest thing to a jam that most Icelandic housewives could make but when rhubarb patches became widespread, rhubarb jam largely replaced the more expensive prunes.

The name has nothing to do with wine *(vín)* or friends *(vinir)*, as many believe. It means literally "Vienna Cake." The cake came to Iceland from Denmark but it probably does originate in Vienna; I've seen almost identical recipes for *Wiener Torte* in German cookbooks from the late nineteenth century. These cakes are flavored with cardamom and filled with jam.

Here is a slightly adapted early twentieth-century Icelandic recipe that may be somewhat different to what Americans familiar with the cake expect, although not as different as many of the *vínarterta* versions they will encounter in Iceland today. These are often made of soft, spongy layers, filled with strawberry or raspberry jam, and rarely flavored with cardamom or other spices.

The original recipe does not specify how many layers should be made but when my mother made this cake (not round layers but big sheets), she usually baked four layers. I'm told that for Canadian vinarterta, five layers are a minimum, and six layers are even better.

1 cup margarine or butter, softened
1 cup sugar
2 small eggs
4 cups flour, or as needed
1 1/2 teaspoons baker's ammonia or baking powder
1 teaspoon freshly ground cardamom
1/2 cup milk
1 1/2 cups rhubarb jam or prune filling (page 195)

Cream butter and sugar. Add eggs, one at a time, whisking well between additions. Add flour, baker's ammonia and cardamom along with the milk and stir to combine. Knead the dough until smooth; it should be soft and just short of sticky. Shape it into a ball, cover with plastic wrap and refrigerate for at least an hour.

Preheat the oven to 375°F. Divide the dough into 6 equal parts. On a floured work surface, roll each part out into a thin disc, around 9 inches in diameter. Arrange the circles on baking sheets lined with parchment paper and bake in the center of the oven for 12 minutes, or until just beginning to brown at the edges.

Sandwich the layers with the jam while still warm. Let cool completely, wrap in foil, and keep for at least a couple of days. If stored in a cool place, the cake will keep for weeks and improve with age.

Sometimes a four-layer cake is made, with each layer a distinct color—one is white, one is colored brown with cocoa powder, and food coloring is used to make the remaining layers pink and green. This cake is usually called *regnbogaterta*, rainbow cake, and it is especially popular in the Westmann Islands.

BROWN STRIPED CAKE

Brún randalín
Makes a 5x10-inch, 3-layer cake

This popular traditional cake is really a spiced version of the *vínarterta*, filled with a buttercream instead of prunes or jam. It was customary to make large sheet cakes of this type and the following recipe is originally meant for one layer only. Sometimes the cake is four-layered and then the filling between the two center layers is often jam, making the cake tricolored.

Modern versions of this cake are often made using more butter and eggs, so instead of a soft but kneadable dough you have a thick batter, which is then spread on parchment paper and baked. The soft cake is then cut into three or four strips when cold and these are layered. To make this type of cake, add 1/2 cup butter and two eggs to the following recipe.

1 cup sugar
1 cup butter, softened
2 eggs
2 1/2 cups flour, or as needed
2 tablespoons cocoa powder
2 teaspoons baking powder
1/2 teaspoon baking soda
1 teaspoon cinnamon
1/2 teaspoon ground cloves

Cream sugar and butter in a bowl. Add the eggs, one at a time, whisking well between additions. Sift flour, cocoa powder, leavenings, and spices into the bowl and mix until well combined. Knead the dough until smooth. Add flour if it is sticky, but it should be rather soft. Shape it into a ball, wrap it in plastic wrap and refrigerate for an hour.

Preheat the oven to 350°F. On a floured work surface, roll out the dough into a rectangle, around 10 x 15 inches. Trim edges, cut the rectangle into three 5-inch-wide strips, and place them on baking sheets lined with parchment paper. Bake in the center of the oven for 12 to 15 minutes. Let cool on a rack.

Meanwhile, make a buttercream (page 193). Spread one cake layer with half the buttercream, place another layer on top, spread the rest of the buttercream on it, cover with the third layer, and press down firmly but not too hard. The cake layers will be hard and brittle at first but they soften somewhat after a day or two. If no egg yolk is used in the buttercream, the cake will keep for weeks in a cool place, if it is well wrapped.

SPICE CAKE WITH CURRANTS

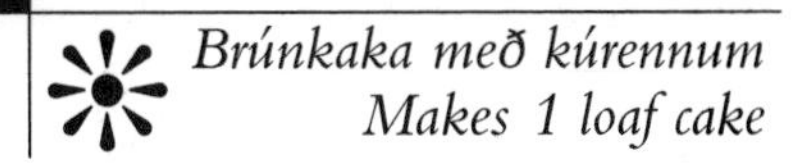

Brúnkaka með kúrennum
Makes 1 loaf cake

Traditionally Icelandic spice cakes are dry rather than moist, and not too sweet. Even though they are baked in a loaf pan, they are usually just sliced and eaten as they are with a cup of coffee, not buttered. Many recipes include raisins or currants but other types of fruit are uncommon.

The name *brúnkaka* literally means "brown cake" and these cakes are usually medium brown, although darker cakes are sometimes seen, due to a tablespoon or two of cocoa powder added to the batter.

Cinnamon, cloves, and ginger are the most popular spices and shops in Iceland sell a spice blend called *brúnkökukrydd* (brown cake spice), which usually includes these spices, and sometimes also allspice, nutmeg, or cardamom.

3 cups flour
1 teaspoon baking soda
1 teaspoon cloves
1 teaspoon cinnamon
1/2 teaspoon ground ginger
Grated zest of 1 lemon (optional)
1 cup butter, softened
1 1/4 cups packed dark brown sugar
2 eggs
1 cup buttermilk
1/2 cup dried currants

Preheat the oven to 325°F and butter a 9 x 5-inch loaf pan. Combine in a bowl flour, baking soda, spices, and lemon zest, if using. Cream butter and brown sugar and add the eggs, one at a time, whisking well after each addition. Gradually stir in the flour mixture, alternating with buttermilk, but do not stir the batter more than necessary. Mix in the currants. Spoon the batter into the prepared loaf pan and smooth the surface.

Bake for around 1 hour, or until a tester inserted in the center of the cake comes out clean. If the surface seems to darken too quickly, cover the pan with a sheet of foil. Let the cake cool in the pan for a few minutes, then turn it out and let it cool.

CHRISTMAS CAKE I

Jólakaka I
Makes 1 loaf cake

This cake still retains the name of its Danish ancestor, *julekage*, but the name is the only thing that connects it to Christmas these days—it would be hard to find a more everyday, down-to-earth cake. It is extremely common in Iceland and is served at all kinds of occasions. At elaborate coffee parties, where the tables are almost groaning with an overload of elaborate and eye-catching cakes and tortes, decorated with mounds of cream, canned fruit, meringues, chocolate, and other temptations, you will probably see some of the guests—especially older people—go straight to an unassuming plate carrying overlapping slices of *jólakaka*.

This is a simple cake, very easy to make, but despite that, there are many versions. The following is a fairly modern one.

1 cup butter or margarine, softened
1 cup sugar
2 eggs
1/2 teaspoon lemon extract, or grated zest of 1 lemon
3 cups flour
1 tablespoon baking powder
3/4 cup milk
1/2 to 1 cup raisins

Preheat the oven to 325°F and grease a 9 x 5-inch loaf pan. Cream the butter and sugar in a mixing bowl. Whisk in the eggs, one at a time, and add lemon extract or lemon zest. Mix flour and baking powder and stir it in, along with the milk. Mix only until just combined. Stir in the raisins.

Spoon the batter into the loaf pan, smooth the surface, and bake the cake for around 70 minutes, or until a tester inserted into the center of a cake comes out clean. Let the cake cool in the pan for 10 minutes or so, then invert it carefully onto a rack.

CHRISTMAS CAKE II

Jólakaka II
Makes 1 loaf cake

The following version at least retains some Christmas flavor with cardamom, candied peel, and raisins. Some older recipes for *jólakaka* call for or suggest "rhubarb raisins," small pieces of rhubarb stalk, drained of some of their juices, then mixed with sugar and bottled. This used to be a common substitute for raisins and other fruit.

Freshly ground cardamom is much better than the preground spice, which tends to lose its potency pretty quick, but the fact is that most Icelandic bakers buy the spice already ground, or use cardamom extract. I was never very fond of cardamom flavor until I began buying the pods whole; now I love it. Cardamom is less used for baked goods now than it used to be and many modern *jólakaka* recipes use lemon or vanilla flavoring instead of cardamom.

3 cups flour
2 1/2 tablespoons baking powder
1 teaspoon cardamom
1 cup butter or margarine, softened
1 cup sugar
2 eggs
1/2 cup milk
1 cup raisins
1/4 cup candied peel

Preheat the oven to 350°F and butter a 9 x 5-inch loaf pan. Mix flour, baking powder, and cardamom in a bowl. Cream the butter with the sugar, then add the eggs, one at a time, whisking well in between additions. Stir in the flour mixture in 2 or 3 batches, alternating with the milk, but do not overbeat. Stir in raisins and peel.

Spoon the batter into the prepared pan, smooth the surface, and bake for 60 to 70 minutes, or until a tester inserted in the center of the cake comes out clean.

Let cool for at least 10 minutes in the pan, then invert the cake onto a rack.

RHUBARB CAKE WITH ALMONDS

Rabarbarakaka með möndlum
Makes a 9-inch cake

In Iceland, spring is always very welcome after a long, dark winter, and one of the things to look forward to is the emergence of rhubarb shoots. My siblings and I would eat the new rhubarb stalks plain, despite their sourness, or peel them, dip them in sugar and nibble on them as a snack. And there were other treats to be savored. Most of the rhubarb was used for jam, compotes and such, but recipes for rhubarb cakes are found in Icelandic cookbooks from the nineteenth century onward.

1 pound red rhubarb stalks
2/3 cups butter, softened
1/2 cup sugar
3 eggs
1 cup flour
1 teaspoon baking powder
4 tablespoons finely chopped almonds

Preheat the oven to 350°F and boil some water. Chop the rhubarb stalks into 2-inch pieces, place them in a bowl, and cover with boiling water. Let stand for 1 minute, then drain well.

Cream the butter with the sugar and whisk in eggs, one at a time, with a couple of tablespoons of flour. Stir in the rest of the flour with the baking powder and almonds. Pour the batter into a buttered and floured 9-inch cake pan and smooth the surface. Arrange the rhubarb pieces in a pattern on top.

Bake in the center of the oven for 30 to 35 minutes, or until the cake is spongy and golden brown. Let cool in the pan for 10 minutes, then remove it and cool on a rack. Serve lukewarm (perhaps with whipped cream) or let cool completely.

DRIED FIG CAKE

Gráfíkjuterta
Makes an 8-inc, 2-layer cake

Until a few years ago, fresh figs had never been seen in Icelandic shops, but dried figs have been sold for centuries and used to be considered a real delicacy. In the nineteenth century, candy was virtually unknown in Iceland, but when farmers returned from their once-a-year trips to the coastal villages, they would bring home bags of dried figs, prunes, and raisins for the children. Children were usually allowed to keep any loose tufts of wool they found lying in the fields or caught in hedges, and these they collected in a bag, washed and dried them, and sent the wool to the market in the summer. These gatherings would often buy them quite a few figs or raisins to nibble.

Figs were also used for baking, and this old recipe is very much a favorite in my family, as the cake is easy to make and really quite good. The precooking can probably be omitted if partially dried figs are used.

1 1/2 cups roughly chopped dried figs
2 cups flour
1/2 teaspoon baking powder
1/2 teaspoon baking soda
1 cup butter, softened
2/3 cups granulated sugar
2 eggs
1 cup confectioners' sugar
1 teaspoon vanilla extract

Preheat the oven to 350°F and butter and flour two 8-inch cake pans. Place the chopped figs in a small saucepan, add 1/2 cup water, and cook the figs until almost all the liquid has disappeared. Let cool slightly.

Combine flour, baking powder, and baking soda in a bowl. In another bowl, cream 2/3 cup of the butter with the granulated sugar, then whisk in the eggs, one at a time. Gradually stir in the flour, alternating with the warm figs. Divide the mixture between the prepared pans, smooth the surface, and bake for around 20 minutes. Turn out on a rack and let the cakes cool completely.

Cream the remaining 1/3 cup butter with the confectioners' sugar and add vanilla extract to make a simple buttercream. Spread the buttercream on one of the cakes and sandwich them together.

I sometimes make a delicious variation of this cake by cooking the figs in apple or orange juice and adding a large apple, peeled, cored and roughly chopped, to the batter. Then I bake the cake in one 9-inch pan for around 35 minutes and serve it plain, without any icing.

TRAY CAKE

Skúffukaka
Makes a thin 9x13-inch cake

This is another very common everyday cake, for which there are innumerable recipes, as it is much loved by children and adults alike. The cake is usually baked in a large oven tray and is then only about 1 inch thick, or it may be baked in a smaller tray and can then be 2 to 2 1/2 inches thick. The recipe is fairly similar to some brownie recipes, except there are never any nuts in the cake and it is usually much drier than brownies.

The cooled cake is always frosted with a simple chocolate icing and usually sprinkled with some shredded coconut. It is never cut into bars or squares while warm; the cake is served whole on a large platter, or cut into long strips from which people would cut individual slices.

For a thicker version, just double the following recipe and bake for 30 minutes or so.

1/2 cup butter, softened
1/2 cup packed brown sugar
1/4 cup granulated sugar
2 eggs
1 1/2 cups flour
1 teaspoon baking powder
1 teaspoon baking soda
1/2 teaspoon salt
6 tablespoons cocoa powder
1/2 cup buttermilk
1/4 cup hot water
1 cup confectioners' sugar
2 to 3 tablespoons hot coffee or boiling water
2 to 3 tablespoons shredded coconut (optional)

Preheat the oven to 350°F. Cream butter, brown sugar, and granulated sugar in a mixing bowl. Add eggs, one at a time, whisking well between additions. Sift together flour, baking powder, baking soda, salt, and 4 tablespoons of the cocoa powder and add it gradually to the batter, alternating with buttermilk and hot water. Only stir the batter as much as needed to thoroughly combine the ingredients.

Spoon the batter into a well buttered and floured 9 x 13-inch rectangular pan and bake for 20 minutes (you can also use a round 12-inch pan, or use a square 9-inch pan and bake the cake longer). Remove it from the oven, let it cool slightly in the tray, then invert it onto a rack and let it cool completely.

Mix the remaining 2 tablespoons cocoa powder with the confectioners' sugar, gradually stir in hot coffee until the icing is fairly thin and absolutely smooth, and spread it on top of the cake with a spatula. Sprinkle with coconut, if desired, and let cool until the icing has hardened. Trim the edges of the cake and serve it.

WEDDED BLISS

Hjónabandssæla
Makes a 9-inch, single-layer cake

The Icelandic name for this very popular everyday tart, which is actually a distant relative to the famous Austrian Linzer Torte, is a bit of a mystery. The common explanation is that this version is so quick and easy that practically anyone can make it and it doesn't often fail, so it is the perfect cake for a young bride to bake when she wants to treat her husband to something special. It is also quite inexpensive.

The same recipe is also used for another tart where the dough is kneaded and rolled, a disc is cut out and placed in a tart pan, and dough strips are arranged in a lattice pattern on top of the jam, as when making Linzer Torte. This tart, properly named *furstakaka* (Prince's Cake) also sometimes goes by the name of *hjónabandssæla*, but that is hardly fitting, since this is a much more fiddly and time-consuming method and hardly the ideal cake for an inexperienced baker to make. Not if she wanted to ensure wedded bliss, anyway.

Rhubarb or prune jam is the traditional filling for this tart but any jam can be used. This recipe can easily be doubled and baked in a 9-inch pan.

1 cup rolled oats
1 cup flour
1/2 cup loosely packed brown sugar
1/2 teaspoon baking powder
1/4 teaspoon cinnamon
1/2 cup butter or margarine, softened
1/2 cup rhubarb jam

Preheat the oven to 375°F. Mix all the ingredients except the jam in a bowl. The mixture should be crumbly but soft. Reserve around 1/4 of it for the topping but put the rest into a 7-inch tart pan, preferably with a removable bottom, and press it firmly down and up against the sides. Spread the jam evenly on the bottom and crumble the reserved dough over it.

Bake for around 25 minutes, or until dark golden brown.

GRANNY'S CINNAMON ROLLS

Ömmusnúðar
Makes around 36 rolls

Two types of cinnamon rolls are common in Iceland; large rolls made of yeast dough, usually decorated with a thin white or chocolate icing, sometimes made at home but more often bought in bakeries; and this smaller type, made with baking powder. My mother used to bake huge mounds of them and there was a constant supply on the kitchen table. Her recipe was more economical, though, as it used no eggs, and she would spread the rolled-out dough with a thin layer of softened margarine before sprinkling the cinnamon sugar on it.

The baker's ammonia can be left out but this will change the texture of the rolls somewhat. They should be fairly hard but not dry.

3 cups flour
1 teaspoon baking powder
1/2 teaspoon baker's ammonia (optional)
1 cup sugar
1 cup plus 2 tablespoons cold butter or margarine
2 eggs
1 tablespoon cinnamon

Mix the flour with the baking powder and baker's ammonia in a bowl. Add 2/3 cup of the sugar and mix. Cut the cold butter or margarine in small cubes and crumble it thoroughly into the dry ingredients with your fingertips (or use a stand mixer), until the mixture resembles coarse bread crumbs. Make a well in the middle and break the eggs into it. Gradually stir in the flour mixture; if using a mixer, keep the speed low. Knead the dough until smooth. It should be fairly stiff but not dry. Wrap it in plastic and refrigerate for 15 to 20 minutes.

Preheat the oven to 350°F. Remove the dough from the refrigerator and roll it into a rectangle, around 10 x 18 inches. Trim the edges. Mix the remaining 1/3 cup sugar with the cinnamon and sprinkle over the dough (this may seem a rather excessive amount of cinnamon sugar and you can cut it by half if you like).

Roll up the rectangle, starting at one long edge. Cut the roll into fairly thin slices (slightly less than 1/2 inch thick is fine) and arrange them on a baking sheet lined with parchment paper.

Bake the rolls for 20 to 25 minutes, or until nicely browned and crisp.

OATMEAL COOKIES

Hafrakex
Makes 40-60 cookies

These easy, very popular cookies were probably the first thing I ever baked. I remember standing on a chair in the farmhouse kitchen, determinedly crumbling the semi-soft margarine into the coarse oat-flour mixture, and thinking this was far more fun than baking mud pies.

Oatmeal cookies were on the table almost every day during my childhood—and no wonder, since they are so versatile. They can be eaten plain, or they may be spread with either jam, for a sweet treat, or with butter and cheese and served as savory biscuits.

Curiously, this traditional recipe includes three different types of leavening agents, and each of them contributes to the texture. The baker's ammonia can easily be left out but the cookies will not be as crisp.

4 cups oats
2 cups flour
1 cup sugar
2 teaspoons baking powder
1/2 teaspoon baking soda
1/2 teaspoon baker's ammonia (optional)
1 cup butter or margarine, softened
1/4 cup milk

Preheat the oven to 400°F. Mix oats, flour, sugar, and leavenings on a work surface or in a mixer bowl. Work in the butter until the mixture resembles fine crumbs. Add milk, a tablespoon or so at a time, until the dough can be kneaded into a smooth ball.

Roll it out fairly thin on a lightly floured work surface. Cut out circles with a cookie cutter (2 1/2 to 3 inches in diameter) or cut the dough into squares with a pastry wheel, and arrange them on cookie sheets lined with parchment paper.

Bake towards the top of the oven for around 8 minutes, or until the cookies are pale golden. Let cool on a rack.

HONEY ROLL

Hunangsrúlluterta
Makes one 18-inch roll

A traditional Icelandic coffee party table usually features at least one type of roulade. A Swiss roll filled with jam is the most common type but chocolate rolls with buttercream are also popular, along with other types. The following spiced brown roll used to be my favorite cake. My mother got the recipe when she attended the homemaker's academy at Löngumýri in the late 1940s and always made it at least twice a year: For Christmas and for my birthday.

Honey was expensive and despite the name of the roll, the recipe made it clear that syrup could be substituted. My mother always used homemade syrup; I use golden syrup or honey. The cake will keep, well wrapped, for several days in a cool place.

1/2 cup mild-tasting honey
2 tablespoons sugar
2 large eggs
1 cup flour
1 teaspoon baking soda
1 teaspoon cinnamon
1 teaspoon ground ginger
1/4 teaspoon ground cloves
1/4 teaspoon salt
2 tablespoons buttermilk or yogurt
Simple buttercream (page 193)

Preheat the oven to 400°F. Whisk honey, sugar, and eggs in a bowl. Sift flour, baking soda, spices, and salt into the bowl, add buttermilk and stir until smooth. Pour the batter into a Swiss roll pan lined with parchment paper and bake on the second shelf from top for 8 to 10 minutes, or until the cake is spongy and just beginning to brown at the edges.

Remove it from the oven and invert the cake on a piece of parchment paper, which has been sprinkled with some sugar. Peel off the lining paper, then roll up the warm sponge with the sugared parchment paper. Leave to cool.

Unroll the cooled sponge, spread it with the buttercream, and roll it up again. Cool until the buttercream has stiffened, then serve whole or cut into slices.

MOTHER'S DREAM

Mömmudraumur
Makes an 8-inch, 2-layer cake

I'm not at all sure about the origins of the name of this cake but it is a school kitchen standard. It was the only chocolate cake in a home economics textbook that was in use for decades (originally called *The Young Girl and the Kitchen Tasks*, later changed to *The Young People and the Kitchen Tasks*), and consequently, it was the very first chocolate cake many youngsters learned to make. Some of them will without doubt have baked the cake at home to surprise their mother, but I don't know if the name is meant to reflect that.

The cake is often called *djöflaterta* (devils cake) but it is not as dark and moist as devil's food cake. The cake, and others like it, are very common in Iceland and most coffee houses and bakeries offer a version.

1/2 cup butter or margarine, softened
1/2 cup plus 2 tablespoons sugar
1/2 teaspoon vanilla extract
2 eggs
1 1/4 cups flour
3 tablespoons cocoa powder (or more)
2 teaspoons baking powder
Pinch of salt
1/2 cup milk
6 tablespoons rhubarb or strawberry jam
Chocolate buttercream (page 194)

Preheat the oven to 350°F and butter and flour two 8-inch cake pans. Cream butter and sugar until fluffy, add vanilla extract, and whisk in the eggs, one at a time, adding a tablespoon of flour with each egg. Sift the remaining flour with the cocoa powder, baking powder, and salt and gradually stir it into the cake batter, alternating with the milk.

Divide the batter between the prepared cake pans and bake for 18 to 20 minutes, or until spongy. Invert onto a rack and let cool.

Sandwich the cooled layers with the jam. Spread half the chocolate buttercream on the top and sides of the cake. Put the rest into an icing bag fitted with a star-shaped nozzle and pipe decorative patterns on the edges and top of the cake. Cool until the cream has stiffened.

CREAM LAYER CAKE

Rjómaterta
Makes an 8-inch, 2-layer cake

Until relatively few years ago, any festive occasion in Iceland meant a coffee party. And a coffee party meant a large assortment of cakes and tarts, including at least one *rjómaterta*—a one-, two-, or three-layered cream gateau, decorated with lots of whipped cream. The filling would usually be canned fruit, as in this version, but various types of custards and mousses could also be used, and if money was tight or the next store miles away, jam was a good substitute. The date filling described on page 196 is also very good.

Any type of sponge can be used for the cake layers but the one called for here is very popular because it is so simple and requires neither scales nor cups, just three glasses for measuring—extremely convenient for someone who is just beginning to cook on her own and has almost no kitchen equipment. This was the very first cake several of my friends learned to make and some of them have never tried any other sponge recipe, simply because this one is so easy.

The original recipe calls for potato starch but I've substituted cornstarch without problems.

3 eggs
Sugar
2 tablespoons potato starch (or cornstarch)
1 teaspoon baking powder
Flour
1 can fruit cocktail, or other canned fruit
2 cups whipping cream
1 teaspoon vanilla (optional)

Preheat the oven to 375°F and butter and flour two 8-inch cake pans. Arrange three identical glasses in a row. Break the eggs into one glass. Fill the next one with sugar, until level with the eggs. Into the third glass, put the potato starch or cornstarch, the baking powder, and as much flour as needed to fill the glass as high as the other two glasses.

Whisk the eggs and sugar in a bowl until light and frothy. Sift the flour mixture into the bowl and blend carefully with a spoon. Divide the batter equally between the pans. Place in the oven immediately and bake for 18 to 20 minutes, or until the cakes are spongy and spring back when touched. Let cool on a rack.

Drain the fruit (but do not discard the syrup) and reserve some pretty bits for decorating. Whip the cream until stiff, adding the vanilla and a couple of tablespoons of sugar, if desired.

Place one cake layer on a serving platter and moisten it with 3 to 4 tablespoons of syrup from the can. Spread most of the fruit evenly on the cake layers and cover with a third of the whipped cream. Place the second layer on top, moisten it, and spread it with some more cream.

Using a piping bag with a star-shaped nozzle, pipe the rest of the cream on the top and sides of the cake and decorate with the reserved fruit pieces.

RICE KRISPIES CAKE

Hrísterta
Makes a 9-inch, 2-layer cake

Many Icelanders do have a sweet tooth and when magazines and newspapers, in their pre-Christmas editions, ask people to provide a recipe for the family's favorite cake, quite a few variations of meringue layer cakes are bound to come up. Many of them include Rice Krispies or other similar cereal products. Chocolate-covered raisins and other goodies are sometimes added to the filling and used to decorate the cake.

These cakes are studded with calories, of course, but they are so rich and cloyingly sweet that it is usually difficult to eat more than a small slice, so they are hardly everyday treats.

5 egg whites
1 cup packed brown sugar
1 cup granulated sugar
1 tablespoon potato starch (or cornstarch)
2 cups Rice Krispies
2 cups whipping cream
2 tablespoons golden syrup (or corn syrup)
3 tablespoons butter
1 teaspoon vanilla extract

Preheat the oven to 275°F and prepare two 9-inch cake pans. Whisk the egg whites until they form soft peaks. Gradually whisk in 1/2 cup brown sugar and 1/2 cup granulated sugar and continue whisking until the meringue forms stiff peaks. Sift the potato starch or cornstarch over the meringue and gently fold it in with a spatula, along with the Rice Krispies. Divide between the prepared pans and smooth the surface. Bake for around 1 hour, or until stiff and dry.

Let the meringues cool in the pans for a while, then remove them and let them cool completely on racks.

Pour 1 cup of cream into a saucepan and add the syrup and the remaining 1/2 cup brown sugar and 1/2 cup granulated sugar. Stir to mix thoroughly, bring to a boil and cook gently until the caramel sauce thickens. Stir in butter and vanilla extract and let cool.

Whip the remaining 1 cup cream until stiff, spread it on one of the meringues and place the other one on top. Pour the lukewarm caramel sauce over the cake and refrigerate until stiff.

TRUFFLE CAKE

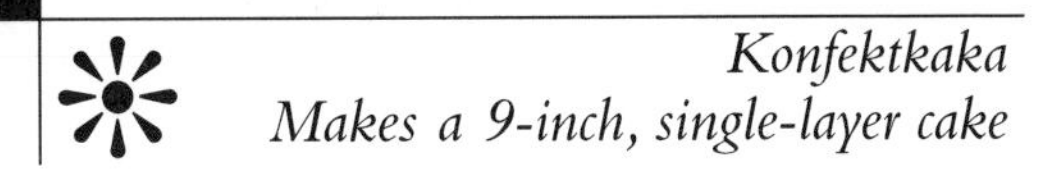

Konfektkaka
Makes a 9-inch, single-layer cake

This cake used to be very popular at children's birthday parties from the 1960s onward, and still is, in fact, when it is served, but these days most birthday parties seem to be pizza orgies. It is a very good party cake if you like coconut, rich but not cloyingly sweet as some similar cakes tend to be, and it is fairly easy to make. It is often decorated with chocolate truffles or other goodies; when served at children's parties, it is usually decorated with candy in colorful wrappings.

4 eggs, separated
1/2 cup granulated sugar
3/4 cup butter, softened
2 1/2 cups shredded unsweetened coconut
4 ounces bittersweet chocolate
1/2 cup confectioners' sugar
1/2 teaspoon vanilla extract

Preheat the oven to 450°F and butter a 9-inch cake pan. Whisk the egg whites until they form soft peaks. Gradually add 1/4 cup of the granulated sugar and continue to whisk until the meringue forms stiff peaks. Melt 5 tablespoons butter and stir into the meringue, along with the coconut and the remaining _ cup granulated sugar.

Spoon into the prepared pan, smooth the surface, and bake for 10 to 12 minutes, or until the cake has stiffened and is beginning to color. Let it cool on a rack.

Meanwhile, melt the chocolate in a bain-marie or microwave. Whisk the egg yolks with the confectioners' sugar for several minutes. Whisk in the remaining 7 tablespoons softened butter, the chocolate, and vanilla. Let cool until just beginning to stiffen.

Spread the topping evenly on top of the cooled cake but do not smooth with a spatula—it should look a little rough. Decorate with chocolates or candy if desired. Refrigerate until the topping has stiffened.

LENTEN BUNS

Bolludagsbollur
Makes around 16 buns

Icelandic Bun Day customs are described on page 11. Although yeast buns and choux buns are the most popular now, the following recipe and others like it were used much earlier for home-baking. They were the only buns I knew when I was growing up, since the nearest bakery was twenty miles away. My mother would make dozens of these buns, fill them with wonderfully fresh, thick cream from our own cows, and cover the top with a simple chocolate icing, and they would disappear almost immediately.

1/2 cup butter, softened
2/3 cup sugar
3 eggs
1/2 teaspoon ground cardamom, or grated zest of 1 lemon
2 1/2 cups flour
1 tablespoon baking powder
2 cups whipped cream
8 ounces chocolate, melted, or 1 cup chocolate icing

Preheat the oven to 375°F. Cream butter and sugar and whisk in the eggs, one at a time. Add cardamom or lemon zest. Sift the flour with the baking powder and stir until thoroughly blended but do not overmix.

Scoop up the dough with a tablespoon and make small mounds on a baking sheet covered with parchment paper—there should be around 16 buns in all. Bake in the center of the oven for 12 to 15 minutes, or until the buns begin to brown at the edge. They will spread out somewhat but should be around 1 inch thick in the middle.

Let them cool on a rack, then split each bun in half and pipe a generous dollop of cream on the bottom half. Dip the upper half in melted chocolate, or brush it with chocolate icing, and sandwich the bun together.

CHOUX BUNS

Vatnsdeigsbollur
Makes 12 to 16 buns

These melt-in-your-mouth delicacies are the most common homemade Bun Day buns now. The buns themselves are light and airy but they are always filled with whipped cream (often sweetened), pastry cream, chocolate mousse, or other rich and sweet filling, and usually covered with icing as well.

Sometimes the recipe is used for much smaller buns (around 1 inch in diameter), which are not split when they have cooled, but filled with a sweet or savory filling, using a piping bag fitted with a narrow tube-shaped nozzle which is inserted into the side of the buns. These small buns are then served as finger food at parties.

6 tablespoons butter
1 teaspoon sugar
Small pinch of salt
1 cup flour
3 large eggs
2 cups whipped cream
1 cup chocolate icing

Preheat the oven to 375°F. Place the butter in a saucepan, add 1 cup cold water (or a mixture of 1/2 cup water, 1/2 cup milk), sugar, and salt. Heat gently until the butter is melted. Bring to a boil, add the flour all at once, and stir briskly with a wooden spoon until the dough is smooth and comes away from the sides of the pan.

Remove from the heat and add the eggs, one at a time, stirring vigorously between additions, so the eggs do not curdle. Some prefer to cool the dough before adding the eggs. When the eggs are completely incorporated, the dough should be glistening and golden, thick enough to hold its shape, but not stiff.

Pipe or spoon the dough into rosettes or mounds, 2 to 2 1/2 inches in diameter, onto a baking sheet covered with parchment paper. Bake for around 30 minutes, or until a test bun doesn't begin to sink as soon as it is removed from the oven.

Let them cool on a wire rack. When they have cooled completely, split each bun in half and pipe or spread whipped cream on the bottom half. Brush the upper half with chocolate icing, and sandwich the bun together.

PRUNE CRESCENTS

Hálfmánar með sveskjumauki
Makes around 50 cookies

These popular cookies have been made in Iceland since the late nineteenth century, although the earliest recipes are rather different and use a puff pastry. They are among the traditional Icelandic Christmas cookies and are still made in many homes, although other types of cookies have replaced them to some extent.

Rhubarb jam or other jam can be used instead of the prune filling, or the spices may be omitted from the filling. If no spice is used, the dough itself benefits from being flavored, perhaps with half a teaspoon of ground cardamom or cinnamon, or some vanilla extract.

2 cups flour
1 teaspoon baking powder
1/4 teaspoon baker's ammonia (optional)
1/2 cup butter
1/2 cup sugar
1 egg
1 to 2 tablespoons brandy
Prune filling (page 195)

Mix flour, baking powder, and baker's ammonia (if using) in a bowl and cut or crumble in the butter. Blend in the sugar. Make a well in the center and add the egg to that, along with the brandy. Gradually draw in the dry ingredients and knead the dough quickly into a ball, adding a little cold water if needed—the dough should be fairly soft but not sticky. Wrap in foil or plastic wrap and refrigerate for at least an hour.

Preheat the oven to 400°F. Roll out fairly thin and cut out circles, 2 1/2 to 3 inches in diameter, with a cookie cutter or a water glass. Place a generous teaspoon of prune filling on the center of each cookie, fold it in half, and press the edges together with the tines of a fork to seal in the filling.

Arrange the crescents on a cookie sheet covered with parchment paper and bake towards the top of the oven for 8 to 10 minutes, or until beginning to brown at the edges.

JEWISH COOKIES

Gyðingakökur
Makes 50 to 60 cookies

My Danish dictionary notes that these cookies were once baked and sold by Jews in Copenhagen, where they are known as *jødekager*. There were few if any Jews in Iceland but the recipe was brought here from Denmark in the nineteenth century and the name was translated into Icelandic. They are one of the traditional Icelandic Christmas cookies.

If baker's ammonia is unavailable, just leave it out and don't use a substitute. The cookies won't be as meltingly tender and crisp but they will be good nonetheless. There are also versions where the dough is shaped into a cylinder, around 2 inches in diameter, and cut into very thin slices instead of being rolled out.

Pearl sugar is a type of sugar used for decorating many Scandinavian cookies and baked goods. It consists of large sugar crystals that do not caramelize easily during baking. Coarse granulated sugar or crushed sugar cubes can be used instead.

1 1/2 cups flour
1/2 teaspoon baker's ammonia
1/2 cup cold butter
6 tablespoons sugar
1 egg
1 egg white
3 tablespoons chopped almonds
2 tablespoons pearl sugar

Sift the flour with the baker's ammonia on a work surface and cut or crumble in the cold butter. Mix in the sugar. Make a well in the middle, break the egg into it, and gradually work in the dry ingredients. Knead the dough until smooth. It should be fairly stiff. Add a little more flour if it is too wet, a little egg yolk if it is too dry. Shape it into a ball, wrap with foil or plastic wrap, and refrigerate for at least an hour.

Preheat the oven to 400°F. Roll the dough out thin on a floured work surface and cut out round cookies, 2 to 2 1/2 inches in diameter. Use a cookie cutter or a water glass.

Arrange the cookies on cookie sheets covered with parchment paper. Brush them with egg white and sprinkle a little chopped almond and pearl sugar on each cookie. Bake them towards the top of the oven for 6 to 8 minutes, or until golden.

COCONUT COOKIES

Kókoskökur
Makes about 60 cookies

I don't make all the cookies my mother used to make each Christmas but I will definitely make these crumbly cookies, as they used to be my favorites. It is an old recipe that my mother got from her aunt and people who taste them often say: "Oh yes, my grandmother used to make these, can I have the recipe?" And they are quite good with a glass of cold milk or a cup of coffee.

This version will flatten somewhat during baking. For a thicker, rounder version, use 1/2 teaspoon baker's ammonia instead of the baking powder, and refrigerate the dough for an hour or two before baking.

2 cups flour
2 cups shredded unsweetened coconut
1 cup sugar (plus more for dipping)
2 tablespoons cocoa powder
2 teaspoons baking powder
1 cup butter, softened
1/2 teaspoon vanilla extract
1 egg

Mix flour, coconut, sugar, cocoa powder, and baking powder in a bowl. Add the butter and cut or stir it into the dry ingredients. Mix the vanilla with the egg until thoroughly combined. The dough should be fairly soft but not sticky; add a little more flour if necessary.

Preheat the oven to 375°F. Pinch off walnut-sized lumps of dough and roll into balls. Dip one side of each ball into sugar, flattening it slightly, and arrange the cookies, sugared side up, on cookie sheets lined with parchment paper. Bake on the top shelf of the oven for 10 to 12 minutes. Cool on a rack.

PEPPER COOKIES

Piparkökur
Makes 50 to 250 cookies, depending on size

Pepper cookies, perhaps best known in America by their Swedish name, *pepparkakor*, do not have as long a tradition in Iceland as they do in the rest of Scandinavia. Nevertheless, these are the only cookies that many people now bake for Christmas, and they do it for their children or grandchildren, because pepper cookies are meant to be baked with children, and you should have fun while baking them.

The children help with making the dough, and especially with cutting out the cookies with variously shaped cookie cutters, and the Pepper Cookie Song usually gets sung at least a couple of times, to everyone's merriment. This is actually a Norwegian song, from a children's play by Thorbjörn Egner. The play was translated into Icelandic in the early 1960s and has been immensely popular ever since. Every Icelandic child knows most of the songs from the play by heart. In the Pepper Cookie Song, the baker is teaching his rather clueless apprentice to bake pepper cookies by singing the recipe, but of course the apprentice doesn't quite get it right and uses a kilo of pepper instead of a teaspoon, and everyone has a big sneezing fit.

There are innumerable recipes for *piparkökur* and they may produce rather different cookies, in taste and texture. The following recipe, which has been used in my family for many years, will produce fairly crisp and brittle cookies with a quite spicy bite. Others may prefer softer, milder-tasting cookies. Few pepper cookie recipes actually include any pepper these days but allspice is often used, as are ready-made spice blends.

1 cup butter, softened
2/3 cup sugar
1/4 cup golden syrup or corn syrup
1/2 cup buttermilk
2 teaspoons baking soda
1 tablespoon cinnamon
1 tablespoon ground ginger
2 teaspoons ground cloves
3 1/2 cups flour, or as needed

Cream the butter with sugar and syrup. Mix buttermilk and baking soda and stir into the butter/sugar mixture along with the spices. Gradually stir in flour until the dough is no longer sticky and can be kneaded into a smooth ball. Cover with foil or plastic wrap and refrigerate overnight, or at least for a couple of hours.

CONTINUED

Preheat the oven to 350°F. Cut a piece off the dough and roll it out on a lightly floured work surface to around 1/16-inch thickness. Cut out cookies, using cutters in every imaginable shape, and transfer them to a parchment-paper covered cookie sheet. Bake them towards the top of the oven for 5 to 8 minutes, depending on thickness. Keep a close eye on them—they burn fast. Cool the finished cookies on racks.

Meanwhile, collect the cut-off scraps and knead them with a fresh piece of dough, roll this out and cut more cookies. Continue until all the dough is used up. Store the cooled cookies in airtight containers; they will keep for months in a cool place.

CINNAMON COOKIES

Kanelkökur
Makes 50 to 70 cookies

This simple cookie recipe is adapted from a cookbook published in 1906, called *Stutt matreiðslubók fyrir sveitaheimili* (A Short Cookbook for Farmsteads). These thin, crisp cookies have a delightful cinnamon taste and are especially popular with children, who often prefer them to the similar but more spicy *piparkökur.* These cookies can be cut into all kinds of shapes and figures, using special molds, but they can also be made into round or square cookies.

3 cups flour, or as needed
1 cup sugar
1 tablespoon cinnamon
1 cup butter, softened
1 small egg

Mix most of the flour with sugar and cinnamon in a bowl and crumble the butter into it. Make a well in the center, break the egg into it and gradually draw in the dry ingredients. Knead in more flour as needed; the dough should be soft but not sticky. Knead until smooth, then shape into a ball and refrigerate for at least half an hour.

Preheat the oven to 400°F. Roll the dough out thin on a floured work surface. Using a cookie cutter, cut out round or square cookies, and arrange them on cookie sheets lined with parchment paper. Bake them towards the top of the oven for around 8 minutes. Let cool on a rack.

AIR BARS

Loftkökur
Makes 30 to 40 cookies

These brittle cookies are very popular with children, and no wonder—they are almost pure sugar. If made with a cookie press, they will stay regular in shape and only expand upward. If made with a piping bag and a star-shaped nozzle, they will probably expand in all directions but still retain their ridged appearance.

They are hollow in the middle and full of air, which is the reason for their name, and also for their nickname, *þingeyingar*—people from the northeastern region of Thingeyjarsysla have a reputation for being somewhat full of air. (Part of my own family comes from there.)

The cookies are probably Danish by origin, since similar cookies are baked in Denmark and are called *rutebiler*, "buses," because of their shape.

This is one cookie where baker's ammonia is essential and there is no substitute. The smell disappears while the cookies bake but it is pretty strong and if you happen to open the oven during the first half of the baking time, you will probably feel like a heroine in a Victorian novel, who has just been revived from a faint using smelling salts.

3 cups confectioners' sugar
2 tablespoons cocoa powder
1 teaspoon baker's ammonia
1 medium egg

Preheat oven to 325°F. Sift confectioners' sugar, cocoa powder, and baker's ammonia into a bowl and stir in the egg, mixing thoroughly—an electric mixer is a very definite asset. The mixture should be very stiff and able to hold its shape; add more confectioners' sugar if it is too thin.

The ideal tool to use is a cookie press attachment on a standing mixer but the next best thing is a manual cookie press. Use a serrated bar-shaped disc and make ribbons, 2 to 3 inches long. Arrange them on cookie sheets covered with parchment paper and allow for some expansion, especially if using a piping bag and a star-shaped nozzle. It will be hard work to pipe the cookies, though, because the cookie mixture is very stiff.

Bake the cookies toward the top of the oven for around 15 minutes, or until they have puffed up and are dry. Let them cool on a rack.

SIMPLE BUTTERCREAM

Einfalt smjörkrem
Makes 2 cups

This cream and the chocolate version in the following recipe are used for many types of Icelandic cakes: simple everyday cakes, elaborate layered cakes, jelly rolls, cookies, and so on.

1 1/2 cups confectioners' sugar
1/2 cup butter, softened
1/2 teaspoon vanilla extract
1 egg yolk (optional)

Sift the confectioners' sugar into a bowl, add the softened butter, and cream the mixture until smooth. Stir in the vanilla and the egg yolk, if using. Beat well.

CHOCOLATE BUTTERCREAM

Súkkulaðismjörkrem
Makes 2 cups

A darker version of this cream is often made using more cocoa powder. A little orange marmalade or strawberry jam may be added for a more interesting taste.

1 1/2 cups confectioners' sugar
2 tablespoons cocoa powder
1/2 cup butter or margarine, softened
1 egg yolk
1/2 teaspoon vanilla extract

Sift the confectioners' sugar and the cocoa into a bowl. Stir in the softened butter, the egg yolk, and the vanilla extract, and beat until smooth.

PRUNE FILLING

Sveskjumauk
Makes 2 cups

If a prune filling for *vínarterta* and other cakes and cookies is made at all in Iceland today, it is not usually spiced. The prunes are just stewed with sugar and water or apple juice until tender.

The original recipe calls for soaking the prunes overnight and cooking them until the stones slip out but it is more convenient to use pitted prunes that do not need soaking.

1 1/2 cups pitted prunes
1/2 cup sugar
1 tablespoon cinnamon
1/2 teaspoon ground cloves

Put prunes, sugar, and spices in a small saucepan and add 1 cup water. Bring to a boil and cook at medium heat, stirring often, until the prunes are soft and the syrup has thickened. You should be able to see the bottom of the pan for a second when you scrape it with a wooden spoon.

Let cool slightly, then pour the prune mixture into the bowl of a food processor and process until smooth. Spread the warm prune filling on each cake layer, except the top.

DATE FILLING FOR LAYER CAKES

Döðlukrem á rjómatertu
Makes 2 cups

This filling can be used to fill the cream layer cake on page 180, instead of caned fruit and cream. The top of the cake is then usually spread with whipped cream and decorated with canned fruit. Canned pears are especially popular and the syrup from the can is used for the filling.

1 1/2 cups pitted dates
1 cup syrup from a can of fruit

Chop the dates and place them in a saucepan with the fruit syrup. Simmer gently until the dates are very tender and the liquid has evaporated, adding more syrup or water if the evaporation is too quick. Stir briskly until the dates are completely mashed up. Let cool and spread on the bottom layer of the cake.

RHUBARB JAM

Rabarbarasulta
Makes around 8 cups

This is the one and only Icelandic jam, the jam that was used for practically everything—as a cake and cookie filling, on crepes and waffles, on bread, in all kinds of desserts, with roasted meat and meatballs, and so on. Rhubarb jam is still popular but too sweet for many modern tastes. Less sugar can be used but then the jam will not keep as well.

3 pounds rhubarb stalks, preferably red
4 cups sugar
Red food coloring (optional)

Wash and trim the rhubarb stalks and chop them into 1/2-inch pieces. Place them in a large nonreactive pot. Add the sugar, stir, and let stand for a few hours, or overnight.

Bring slowly to a boil and simmer gently until the jam has the desired thickness—that could take 1 1/2 to 2 hours. If green stalks were used, it might be desirable to add a little food coloring to perk up the color of the jam. Pour it into hot, sterilized jars, close with a tight lit and store in a cool place.

BREADS

It is understandable, perhaps, that a country whose whole culinary history has partly been shaped by lack of grains should not have much in the way of great bread recipes. Due to the high price of flour in earlier times, traditional breads tend to be thin flatbreads, some very thin indeed, such as the leaf bread. Before the late eighteenth century, leavened bread seems to have been practically unknown in Iceland.

Even in the first half of the twentieth century, when flour was no longer scarce and all but the poorest homes had an oven, no great bread culture developed, neither commercially nor in the home. Yeast breads were rarely made at home and yeast could be difficult to buy. Instead, people baked flatbreads, fried breads, steamed breads, and quickbreads leavened with baking powder, which could be good when absolutely fresh but always pretty dreary the next day.

What really stands out in the Icelandic bread tradition, besides leaf bread, are the rye breads—especially the rye flatbreads and the steamed rye breads. But there are a few others as well. It must be added that many Icelandic bakers have done a very good job in the last two decades in their efforts to develop a new Icelandic bread culture.

LEAF BREAD

Laufabrauð
Makes around 50

Laufabrauð, the traditional Icelandic Christmas flatbread, has sometimes been called "snowflake bread" in English because of the intricate cut-through patterns. It is first mentioned in writing in the early eighteenth century and more than 100 years ago, it had become the one and only Christmas bread of northern Iceland. Now it is made all over the island, especially by people of northern descent.

There are many traditional leaf bread patterns, some quite elaborate, others simple. A special cutting wheel is available but not necessary, although it does make the cutting a lot easier. Children sometimes just cut a face into their bread.

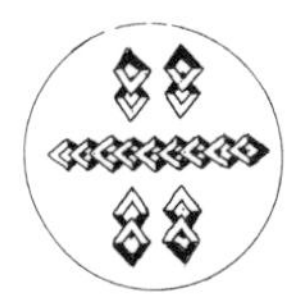    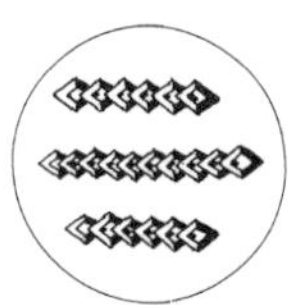 

Making *laufabrauð* is definitely not a job for one person, it is a family undertaking, and for many it is an essential part of the Christmas preparations. Dozens of family members or friends will often take a whole December afternoon or evening to knead, roll out, decorate, and fry the bread, which is then kept until Christmas Eve or Christmas Day, when it is eaten with the smoked lamb.

These *laufabrauð*-making gatherings were in many families, including my own, probably the only time of year when the men took any part in cooking—they either rolled out the dough (which takes considerable effort) or cut out patterns with their pocket knives. Even the smallest children usually got a cake or two to decorate for themselves, using a cutting wheel or a dull knife.

The following recipe has been used in my family for at least fifty years. It contains no salt and no one has ever complained but most recipes include a little salt. The dough should be stiff but still smooth and moist. It must not dry out and has to be kept wrapped at all times—each time a slice has been cut off, be sure to wrap the dough again. When rolling out the dough, use as little extra flour as possible. It is quite an effort to roll the dough as thinly as needed and a heavy marble rolling pin might be of help, although others will work, too.

Many people want the cakes to be very flat and free of air bubbles, so they prick them with a fork before frying and press them flat with a plate for a second or two while still hot, but this is never done in my family and we are quite happy with our *laufabrauð*.

3 1/2 cups flour
1 tablespoon sugar
1 teaspoon baking powder
4 tablespoons butter or margarine
1 cup lukewarm milk
Shortening or Crisco for frying

Mix flour, sugar, and baking powder and cut or crumble in the butter. Make a well in the middle, pour in the lukewarm milk and gradually draw in the dry ingredients. Knead the dough thoroughly, adding a little more flour or milk if needed.

When the dough is absolutely smooth, divide it into 2 rolls, around 2 inches in diameter, and wrap each roll in plastic film but do not refrigerate. Cut a thin slice off one roll and roll it out in a circle as thinly as possible on a very lightly floured work surface. It is often said that you should be able to read a newspaper through the dough—at least the headlines. Cut out a circle, 7 to 8 inches in diameter, and hand it over to someone for decorating.

Continue until all the dough has been used up and all the bread has been decorated. Any piece that is not decorated at once must be kept covered with parchment paper, plastic wrap, or a kitchen towel, so it doesn't dry out. Decorated bread must also be kept covered until it can be fried.

Melt the fat in a suitable heavy pan—an electric deep fryer will not work here. The fat should be at least 2 inches deep and it should be hot, 390 to 400°F. Carefully lower a bread into the fat, decorated side first. Fry until pale golden. It really takes only a few seconds, and note that the bread will darken slightly when it cools.

Lift the bread up from the fat, using 2 forks, let the fat drip off for a second or two, and place the bread on absorbent paper to cool. Stack them up when they have cooled, wrap them in plastic, and keep cool. They will keep for weeks, or even months.

At serving time, a stack of leaf bread is placed on the table, along with butter. It is a matter of opinion if the butter should be cold or soft—some prefer to spread their bread with butter, others want to cut off small pieces of cold butter and eat it with the bread rather than spread it—and some do not want any butter at all.

The scraps or cut-offs should not be kneaded back into the dough and reused. Instead, they are kept separate until all the bread has been fried. Then they are fried in the hot fat and eaten warm as a snack.

RYE FLATBREAD

Flatkökur (flatbrauð)
Makes 8 to 10

Thin flatbread, baked directly on hot embers, was probably the only bread most Icelanders knew up until the late eighteenth century. Leaveners seem not to have been used, not even sourdough. The bread was thin, because flour was expensive, and lack of fuel meant that fuel-intensive ovens were not built; all baking was done on embers, or on stone or iron plates placed over or by an open fire.

The flatbread was probably baked from barley in Viking times but in the eighteenth century, rye flour was being used. Today, a mixture of rye and whole wheat is often used for the bread, now made commercially and available in any store, and sometimes the rye is even completely omitted.

My mother learned to bake flatbread on embers, which often meant that you had to scrape off some ashes before the bread could be eaten. When electricity arrived, the bread was usually baked directly on the hotplate, but a heavy flat-bottomed pan can be used as well. Some versions use hot milk, or a mixture of milk and water, instead of just water, and some sugar may also be added.

Rye flatbread with butter and thin slices of smoked lamb is a very traditional Icelandic treat which is often found at grand feasts and banquets as well as in simple coffee-shops or at the midday coffee table in a farmhouse. Cheese is another popular topping, or you might try to wrap flatbread around some slices of herb-flavored barbecued or roasted lamb at an outdoor picnic.

2 cups rye flour
1 cup whole wheat flour
1/2 teaspoon baking powder (optional)
1/2 teaspoon salt

Mix the ingredients in a bowl, preferably using a stand mixer. Gradually stir in around 1 cup near-boiling water—you may need a little more or less, but the dough should be very stiff but not dry. Knead it well.

Take a piece of the dough and roll it out thinly on a floured work surface. Using a 7- or 8-inch plate as a template, cut out a circle and set aside. Knead the cut-off scraps back into the dough, then take another piece and roll it out. Continue until all the dough is used up. Prick the cakes with a fork.

Heat a heavy frying pan. When it is well heated through, place one of the cakes on it and cook until black flecks begin to appear on the bottom side. Turn it and cook the other side.

Stack the cakes on a plate and cover them with a moist towel as soon as they are baked, or they will dry out and harden as soon as they cool. Some dip the cakes quickly into lukewarm water as soon as they come out of the pan.

For *fjallagrasaflatbrauð* (rye flatbread with lichen), just add a fistful of Iceland moss. Soak it in hot water until soft, then drain it, chop it fine and mix it into the dry ingredients before adding water.

BAKED RYE BREAD

Ofnbakað rúgbrauð
Makes 1 large loaf

This is an old Icelandic recipe that uses rye flour, whole wheat flour and all-purpose or bread flour. The bread is fairly light but has a full-bodied rye flavor and is delicious with cheese.

My mother used to make her own syrup to use for baking breads and cakes: she boiled sugar and water until dark golden brown and thick. Others used sugar and whey to boil syrup. Golden syrup or corn syrup can be substituted, perhaps with a tablespoon of molasses added.

2 1/2 cups milk or skim milk
1/2 cup syrup
2 tablespoons dried yeast
1 1/2 teaspoons salt
3 cups rye flour
1 cup whole wheat flour
1 1/2 cups bread flour, or as needed

Warm the milk with the syrup. Pour 1/2 cup lukewarm milk into a bowl and stir in the yeast. Let stand until frothy.

Add the remaining milk and mix in the salt, rye flour, whole wheat flour, and half the bread flour. Mix until smooth, adding flour as needed, until the dough is stiff but still workable and moist. Knead well (a stand mixer is an immense help here). Shape the dough into a ball, place it in a large bowl, and sprinkle a little rye flour over it. Cover loosely and let it rise in a warm place for 1 1/2 hours, or until doubled.

Punch the dough down. Knead it lightly, then shape it into a loaf, around 1 foot long, place it on a baking sheet lined with parchment paper, cover loosely, and let it rise again for 30 minutes.

Preheat the oven to 400°F. With a sharp knife, cut a few diagonal slashes into the top of the loaf, then brush it with water—slightly sweetened for better color.

Bake the bread for around 30 minutes, or until you hear a hollow sound when you tap the bottom with your knuckles. Let cool on a rack before cutting.

STEAMED RYE BREAD

Seytt rúgbrauð
Makes one 2-pound loaf

Raised breads became common during the late eighteenth century—mostly sourdough rye breads, baked overnight in embers, covered by an inverted cooking pot, which gave them their name, *pottbrauð* or "pot bread." Those lucky enough to live in geothermal areas could use another method, though: They kneaded their dough and placed it in buckets, pots, or other containers, covered them tightly and buried the bread in hot earth, or partly lowered it into a small hot spring. The bread was left until next day. Then it was fully cooked, steamed in its own moisture rather than baked.

This is still done and *hverabrauð*, hot spring bread, can be bought in stores, but similar bread is also frequently baked at home. The bread container is either placed in a tall stockpot with some water, which is then simmered very slowly for many hours, or the dough is placed in a well sealed can or other suitable container (a paperboard milk carton is frequently used in Iceland) and baked in a very slow oven overnight. Both methods produce dark, moist, and tasty bread.

4 cups rye flour
1 tablespoon baking powder
1/2 teaspoon salt
1/2 cup packed brown sugar
2 tablespoons treacle or 1 tablespoon molasses
1 cup warm water
1 tablespoon butter

Preheat the oven to 200°F. Mix rye flour, baking powder, salt, brown sugar, and treacle in a bowl. Gradually stir in the warm water and knead the dough thoroughly. It should be fairly stiff but neither dry nor sticky; add a little more water if needed.

Butter a 1-quart coffee can or other suitable container generously and place the dough in it but take care not to fill it completely. It should not be more than 3/4 full.

Close the container tightly. Place it in the oven and bake for anywhere from 12 to 24 hours, depending on the size of the container and your own patience. The bread will be ready after 12 hours but many feel it gets better if you bake it longer.

In some recipes, the bread is placed in a cold oven, which is then heated to 100°F or so, and the bread is left to rise for up to an hour. Then the temperature is raised to 200°F and the bread is baked as usual.

ICELAND MOSS AND DULSE BREAD

Fjallagrasa- og sölvabrauð
Makes 2 loaves

This is not an old recipe but both Iceland moss and dulse were often added to bread in earlier times and enterprising Icelandic home bakers sometimes still experiment with these. The Iceland moss does not have much taste when used in this way and it is mainly added for nutrition reasons, as the lichen has many health-giving properties. No salt should be needed since the dulse is salty.

2 tablespoons dry yeast
1 teaspoon sugar
2 cups lukewarm water
1 cup whole wheat flour
1 cup soaked, packed Iceland moss
1/2 cup chopped dulse
3 tablespoons butter
3 cups bread flour, or as needed

Dissolve yeast and sugar in the lukewarm water and let stand until frothy. Stir in the whole wheat flour, cover, and let the sponge rise in a warm place for 15 minutes or so.

Meanwhile, finely chop the Iceland moss and the dulse. The Iceland moss can be chopped in a food processor but the dulse preferably should be cut with scissors.

Melt the butter and let it cool slightly, then mix it along with the lichen and the dulse into the sponge. Gradually stir in enough bread flour to make a soft but workable dough. Knead it thoroughly, then shape it into a ball, place it in a bowl, cover loosely, and let rise at room temperature for an hour or so, or until doubled.

Punch the dough down, knead it lightly, and shape it into 2 loaves. Let them rise on a buttered and floured baking sheet for 25 to 30 minutes.

Preheat the oven to 400°F. With a sharp knife, make diagonal slashes at 1-inch intervals on the surface of each loaf. Brush them with cold water and bake for around 30 minutes, or until they are golden and a hollow sound is heard when the bottom is tapped. Let cool completely before cutting.

BREAD CROISSANTS

Franskbrauðshorn
Makes 16 croissants

These small croissant-shaped buns are often served with soups, or split and buttered and eaten with slices of cheese. They are quick and easy to make and do not get stale as fast as quickbreads made from a similar dough.

3 1/2 cups flour
2 tablespoons sugar
1 tablespoon baking powder
1/4 teaspoon salt
6 tablespoons butter
1 cup milk

Preheat oven to 400°F. Mix flour, sugar, baking powder, and salt in a mixing bowl and cut or crumble in the butter until the mixture resembles bread crumbs. Gradually mix in the milk. The dough should be fairly stiff but not dry; add a little more flour if needed. Knead until smooth and silky.

Divide the dough in two and roll one half out on a floured work surface into a thin square, around 12 x 12 inches. Trim the edges and cut into 16 squares. Roll each square up, beginning at one corner, and bend the roll into a horseshoe shape.

Arrange the croissants on a baking sheet lined with parchment paper and repeat with the second half of the dough. Brush with a little milk or egg and bake in the center of the oven for 12 to 15 minutes, or until golden. Let cool on a rack.

FRIED PIECES

Steiktir partar
Makes around 20

These fried wheatcakes are called *partar* if the dough is cut into squares, but if plate-size rounds are made from it, they may be called *steikt brauð* (fried bread) or *soðið brauð* (boiled bread—boiled in fat, that is). They used to be common all over Iceland. The wheatcakes were usually fried in tallow but other types of fat, such as lard or vegetable shortening, are often used these days.

This is my mother's recipe, but what she actually makes is *steikt brauð*. I give the *partar* version because that is probably more widely known. Half a teaspoon or so of caraway seeds is sometimes added to the dough.

3 1/2 cups flour
2 teaspoons baking powder
1 teaspoon baking soda
1/2 teaspoon salt
3 tablespoons butter
1 cup buttermilk
Milk as needed
Shortening or Crisco for frying

Mix flour, baking powder, baking soda, and salt in a bowl. Cut or crumble the butter into the mixture, until it resembles bread crumbs. Make a well in the center, pour the buttermilk into it and gradually draw in the dry ingredients. Add milk as needed; the dough should be fairly soft but not sticky. Knead until smooth and silky.

On a floured work surface, roll out the dough to around 1/6-inch thickness. Cut it into squares, 3 1/2 to 4 inches on each side. Prick them with a fork.

Heat the fat to around 375°F. Fry the pieces, a few at a time, until golden brown, turning once. Remove with a slotted spoon and drain on absorbent paper. Let cool, then serve the pieces with butter and cheese, meat slices, or other toppings.

ROE WAFFLES

Hrognavöfflur
Makes 8 to 10 waffles

Roe waffles or pancakes are an old Icelandic way of using cod's roe. These waffles can be served warm as a starter, perhaps with a green salad and maybe a couple of slices of smoked salmon. They can also be served as a snack, spread with butter and cheese, or maybe a flavored cheese spread.

1/2 pound uncooked or cooked cod's roe
1 cup flour
1 teaspoon baking powder
1 teaspoon sugar (optional)
1/2 teaspoon salt
Pinch of freshly ground pepper
1 cup buttermilk
1 egg
Zest of 1 lemon, or a pinch of thyme
3 tablespoons butter or margarine, and more as needed

Remove membranes and break up the roe with a fork. Mix flour, baking powder, sugar, salt, and pepper in a bowl. Lightly whisk buttermilk, eggs, and lemon zest or thyme in another bowl, then combine with the flour mixture and stir until smooth. Add the roe and stir until well blended.

Heat the waffle iron, melt the butter and stir it into the batter. Cook the waffles at medium heat until golden brown, buttering the waffle iron as needed.

ICELANDIC SCONES

Skonsur
Makes 4 to 5 scones

Icelandic scones are really thick, large pancakes, but they are never eaten with syrup or jam. They are spread with butter and topped with cheese or meat slices, smoked salmon, cheese or meat spreads, or other savory toppings. They are often made into sandwiches, or stacked up with various fillings between layers and cut into slices as a cake. They can be eaten with a sweet topping, too, it just isn't traditional.

A good scone should be light and airy, full of holes, and at least 1/2 inch thick. It is best on the day it is made. Commercially made scones are usually drier and more compact. The egg whites in the recipe can be substituted with another whole egg but then an extra tablespoon or two of milk should be added.

1 1/2 cups flour
1 1/2 tablespoons baking powder
1/2 teaspoon salt
1 tablespoon sugar
1 whole egg
2 egg whites
1 cup milk
3 tablespoons butter or margarine

Mix flour with baking powder, salt, and sugar in a bowl. Whisk the egg and egg whites with the milk and add to the dry ingredients. Stir until smooth.

Melt the butter in a crepe pan or a small frying pan and stir it into the batter. Pour a ladle of batter (around 2/3 cup) into the pan and cook the scone at a very low heat until holes made by the bubbles that rise to the top side begin to stay open instead of closing almost immediately.

Turn the scone over (the best method is to slide it onto a plate, then invert it back to the pan) and cook it for a minute or so on the other side. Remove it to a plate and continue until all the batter is used up.

PARTY SANDWICH LOAF

Brauðterta
Makes one 4-layer loaf

A sandwich loaf (or literally, sandwich torte) is a standard feature on an elaborate Icelandic coffee table—at confirmation and birthday celebrations, for instance, or it may be served at a sewing club gathering (page 15). It can be described as a giant many-layered sandwich, dressed up to look like a cake. It is often a welcome alternative to the sweet meringues and cream layer cakes that tend to dominate the coffee table.

Some versions have only one type of filling but most have a separate filling for each layer. These fillings can be virtually anything you would use in a regular sandwich but they should neither be too wet nor too dry. In addition to the fillings in the recipe given here, some of the more popular versions are: peas or other cooked vegetables, usually canned; chopped smoked lamb; chopped smoked salmon; canned tuna fish; and cooked asparagus (usually mixed with ham). The layers can be as many as 5. Sometimes a round bread base is used, and a sandwich torte can also be made using scones (page 209).

The following recipe is one I've used for many years, with slight variations, and served at almost every birthday party and other family gatherings.

1 cup whipping cream
2 1/2 cups mayonnaise
Freshly ground pepper
Salt
6 hard-boiled eggs
1 teaspoon Dijon mustard
1 teaspoon paprika
1/2 pound cooked and peeled shrimp, roughly chopped
2 canned pineapple slices, chopped
6 ounces cooked ham, chopped fine or shredded
1 cup chopped parsley
4 long slices of white or
whole wheat sandwich bread (sliced lengthwise)
Cucumber slices
Tomato wedges

Whip the cream in a bowl until stiff, stir in the mayonnaise, and season with a little pepper and salt. Take 3 additional bowls and divide the mixture into 4 even portions. Reserve one portion for decoration (cover the bowl with plastic wrap and refrigerate).

Slice the hard-boiled eggs crosswise and reserve 2 to 3 nice center slices from each egg but chop the rest. Flavor one mayonnaise portion with Dijon mustard and stir in the chopped eggs. Flavor another portion with paprika and stir in shrimps and pineapple pieces. Mix the ham and 2 to 3 tablespoons parsley into the third portion.

Take 4 long slices of bread and cut off the crusts. Place one slice on a large chopping board or work surface and spread it evenly with one of the fillings. Place another slice on top and press down, firmly but not too hard. Spread another filling on top, then add a third bread slice, spread it with the contents of the third bowl and place the final slice on top. Press down evenly, trim edges, wrap in foil or plastic wrap, and refrigerate for several hours.

Unwrap the loaf and place it on a tray or wooden cutting board. Spread the top and sides evenly with the reserved mayonnaise. Sprinkle the remaining chopped parsley evenly on the sides and decorate the top with the reserved egg slices, thin cucumber slices or twists, and tomato wedges.

Some alternative decorations for the loaf: Ham slices rolled into cylinders, or finely chopped ham arranged in rows; pineapple pieces or canned peach wedges; halved grapes; kiwi fruit slices; cooked shrimps, arranged in neat rows; piped mayonnaise rosettes; chopped herbs—anything is possible, really, if you take care that the decoration doesn't clash too much with the fillings.

A FEW OLD RECIPES

I've added a small selection of recipes that do not really fit in elsewhere but I felt should be included in the book, although I'm not at all sure some of them will actually be much used outside Iceland. In several cases, a vital ingredient may prove too hard to find; in other cases, the dish may not sound very tempting—or even quite repulsive—to some people.

It has to be said that there are many local delicacies that you probably have to know from childhood to like. Icelanders often amuse themselves by shocking people of other nationalities with stories about some of our traditional food. Some additional delicacies are mentioned in the Thorrablót description (page 9) but things like dried fish, fermented shark and whey-preserved lamb's testicles are never made at home any more.

Most or all of the following dishes are still eaten and enjoyed by many Icelanders, although they are not made at home as often as they used to be. No one makes whey cheese or skyr, for instance; both are very time consuming and not worth the bother, when you can easily buy them in any supermarket. But many still make their blood pudding and liver sausage every October, and *rúllupylsa* is made in many homes.

BLOOD PUDDING WITH ICELAND MOSS

Fjallagrasablóðmör
Makes 12-15 puddings

The traditional blood pudding or blood sausage is usually rather plain and includes just blood, oats, rye flour, suet, and salt, but there are some variations and this is one of the more interesting ones. Iceland moss was one of the main ingredients in blood pudding in earlier times—in fact, much of the flour was frequently replaced with chopped Iceland moss.

Raisins are often a part of the pudding mixture, and some spices are occasionally added, such as cinnamon, cloves, ginger, allspice, and thyme.

2 to 3 lamb's stomachs
2 cups packed Iceland moss
4 cups lamb's blood
1 tablespoon coarse salt
2 cups rolled oats
6 cups rye flour, or as needed
1 pound lamb suet, chopped

Begin by laying each washed and cleaned stomach flat on a cutting board and cutting it in 5 to 6 double pieces. Sew the side edges of the pieces together, using a big, sharp needle and a strong cotton thread, but leave one end open. Keep the sacks soaked in cold water while making the pudding.

Wash the Iceland moss and soak it for a few minutes in cold water. Squeeze out the moisture and chop coarsely (a food processor may be used). Strain the blood, dilute it with 1 cup cold water, and add salt. Stir in the oats and the Iceland moss and mix thoroughly. Stir in the rye flour and finally the chopped suet. The mixture should be thick. If you plant a wooden spoon upright in the middle of the bowl, it should almost stand unsupported and only begin to lean slowly to one side.

Stuff the sacks with the mixture but take care to fill them only two thirds or a little less, as pudding will expand when it begins to cook. Sew the sacks shut or use pins to close them.

Heat plenty of salted water in a large and preferably wide pan. Add the stuffed sacks when the water boils and prick them vigorously with a knitting needle or fork as they rise to the surface.

Cover and simmer for 2 1/2 to 3 hours, depending on size. Turn the puddings occasionally to make them cook more evenly. Remove them with a slotted spoon and serve them hot or let them cool.

The puddings can be frozen uncooked and placed unthawed in boiling water. They will need somewhat longer cooking and must be pricked gradually, as they thaw and rise to the surface.

The cooked, cooled pudding can be cut in slices and fried in butter or margarine. It is then usually sprinkled with sugar and served with boiled or mashed potatoes and mashed rutabagas. It is also good with pan-fried apple wedges, although that is not traditional.

LIVER SAUSAGE

Lifrarpylsa
Makes 12 to 15 sausages

Blood pudding and liver sausage are so closely connected in the minds of most Icelanders that they don't realize that while blood puddings in some form have been made for many hundreds of years, perhaps ever since the Settlement, liver sausage is a relatively new invention. It probably wasn't made until the mid-nineteenth century, at least not widely. Lamb's kidneys are often minced with the livers, two kidneys for each liver.

Cold, cooked blood pudding and liver sausage can be bought in any Icelandic supermarket these days but many people still make them at home. Store-bought blood pudding is sliced and either pan-fried or eaten cold, for example with porridge or rice pudding. So is liver sausage, but it is never fried. Many like it best plain with a glass of cold milk.

2 to 3 lamb's stomachs
3 pounds lamb livers
4 cups milk or skim milk
1 tablespoon salt
3 cups rolled oats
1 cup whole wheat flour
4 cups rye flour, or as needed
1 1/2 pounds chopped lamb suet

Begin by making sacks from the lamb's stomachs (page 214). Clean the livers and remove veins and membranes. Cut them into pieces and mince them in a mincer, or use a food processor.

In a large bowl, mix liver, milk, and salt. Add oats and whole wheat flour. Gradually stir in rye flour, as much as needed to make a thick, porridge-like mixture. Stir in chopped suet. Follow the instructions in the blood pudding recipe to stuff and boil the sausage pouches.

Serve hot or cold, with mashed potatoes and mashed rutabagas.

ROLLED LAMB FLANK

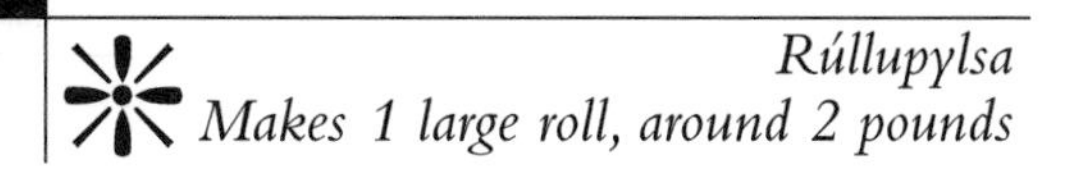

Rúllupylsa
Makes 1 large roll, around 2 pounds

The Icelandic name actually means "rolled sausage," but this isn't really a sausage. It is very popular and many Canadians and Americans of Icelandic descent will know it. The following version is rather spicy. In Iceland, special spice blends for *rúllupylsa* can be bought. Other spices and herbs may be used, such as garlic, thyme, rosemary, or grated fresh ginger.

1 large flank of lamb, or 2 small
2 tablespoons coarse salt
1/2 teaspoon nitrite (optional)
1 teaspoon sugar
1 teaspoon freshly ground pepper
1/2 teaspoon ground ginger
1/2 teaspoon ground allspice
1/4 teaspoon ground cloves
1 to 2 tablespoons chopped parsley (optional)
1 onion, finely chopped

Remove bones, if any, from the flank. Wash, pat dry, and cut off some excess fat if desired. Lay the flank on a work surface, skin side down. If it is in two pieces, overlap them to form a rectangle (or as close to one as possible). Trim the edges to make the rectangle more regular and place the cut-off strips on the meat. Mix the rest of the ingredients and sprinkle on the meat. Roll up tightly and sew or tie the roll with a cotton string.

Cook the roll fresh, simmering in a pot of water for 1 1/2 to 2 hours, or place it in a brine for up to two weeks before cooking. In either case, press or weigh down the roll while still hot. Special presses are available in Iceland but most people just press the roll between two cutting boards and place a weight on top.

When the roll is cold, it is taken from the press, cut into thin slices and served on bread, usually rye bread or flatbread.

The roll can also be placed in a brine for a couple of days and then smoked. In that case, the onion should be left out.

POTTED MUTTON

Kindakæfa
Makes around 4 pounds

One of the most common preservation methods for lamb and especially for old, tough mutton was to boil the meat until it fell apart. Then the bones were removed, and the meat was chopped and mashed into a pulp, mixed with melted or chopped mutton fat, and packed into jars or boxes and covered with melted fat. It could keep like this for months.

Kæfa is still popular but it is a lot less fatty than it used to be. Since it was so fat, it would be quite hard when it cooled and it was usually cut into slices and eaten with bread. Modern versions are often much softer and are spread on bread with a knife.

3 pounds mutton or lamb shoulder on the bone
1/2 pound chopped lamb fat (unless the meat is very fatty)
1 tablespoon salt
2 medium onions
1 teaspoon freshly ground pepper

Place the meat, fat, and salt in a saucepan, add water to barely cover, and simmer until the meat slips easily off the bone.

Grind the meat in a meat grinder with the onions. Skim the fat off the stock (or cool the stock until the fat sets) and add it to the meat mixture. Season with pepper and knead until well combined. Strain the stock and stir a little of it into the meat. The warm mixture should be thick but not dry. Spoon into molds and cool until set.

For a softer *kæfa* that can be used as a spread, boil the stock until heavily reduced and mix it into the ground meat.

SALTED LAMB

Saltkjöt
Makes 10 pounds

Salted lamb is probably very difficult to find, so here is a recipe, if anyone should care to try to make his own. A large part of the meat that was eaten during my childhood was heavily salted, or salted and smoked. This is not the most healthful food there is and the incidence of stomach cancer used to be very high in Iceland. That has changed now, and a little salted lamb now and then should not harm anyone, especially if the nitrite is left out, but it must be admitted that it makes the meat keep better and the color is much redder and nicer.

10 pounds lamb shoulder
4 pounds coarse salt
1 cup sugar
1 tablespoon nitrite (optional)

Cut the meat into fairly large pieces and trim excess fat. Wash it and pat it dry. Mix salt, sugar, and nitrite, if using, and cover the bottom of the barrel or bucket you are using with some of the salt.

Roll each piece of meat in the salt mixture and arrange them in the barrel. They should be crowded and all spaces between them should be filled with salt. Cover with the rest of the salt, place a plate or lid on top, and heavily weigh down. Let stand in a cool larder or other suitable place for at least two weeks.

When the meat is to be used, it should be rinsed in cold running water, placed in a pan with water to cover, and simmered for 45 to 60 minutes, or until tender.

If the meat is very salty (for instance, if it has been kept for a long time), it should be soaked in cold water before cooking.

SALTED LAMB WITH RYE DUMPLINGS

Saltkjöt með soðkökum
Serves 4

This is an old-fashioned way to serve salted lamb, which was once almost the only meat most people would eat for the greater part of the year. The rye dumplings are rarely seen anymore but there are those who still make them and love them. These dumplings can also be eaten cold with butter.

2 pounds salted lamb on the bone
2 cups rye flour
1 teaspoon salt
4 to 5 medium carrots
2 medium rutabagas

The meat—preferably from the shoulder—should be cut into fairly large chunks.

Begin with making the rye dumplings. Mix rye flour and salt in a bowl and gradually stir in some hot water, as much as needed to make the dough manageable—stiff but not dry. Knead it well and shape it into round cakes, 2 1/2 to 3 inches in diameter and 1 inch thick.

Place the meat in a large pan and add boiling water to cover by at least an inch. Skim well and add the dumplings. Simmer, partly covered, for around 40 minutes. Scrape or peel the carrots and peel the rutabagas. Cut both vegetables into pieces and add them to the pot.

Continue cooking for 20 to 25 minutes, or until tender. Remove the dumplings with a slotted spoon and drain them.

Pile the meat and vegetables on a platter, arrange the dumplings around them and serve with melted butter and boiled potatoes.

BOILED LAMB'S HEADS

Svið
Serves 4

Whole or halved sheep's heads are considered a delicacy in many European and Asian sheep-rearing countries and Iceland is no exception. The head is not skinned. Instead, the wool and hair used to be singed *(sviðin)* and scraped off the heads by an open flame; this is now usually done by chemical methods, which is no improvement at all and makes the skin, which is eaten with the meat, much less flavorful. The heads are cleaved lengthwise and the brain is removed. Then they are boiled until tender and served whole, either hot or cold, usually with mashed potatoes.

Every part of the head used to be eaten, including eyes, brain, and ears, except the ear tips, where markings were cut to indicate who the owner was. It was said that those who ate the markings would become sheep thieves. Nevertheless, the heads were always served with the ears intact, because anyone who cut off the ears before serving was automatically suspected of having stolen the sheep and removed the ears to hide his guilt. This tradition has continued almost to this day, even though there aren't many sheep thieves around, but a few years ago shops began to sell the heads without ears and not everyone was happy about that.

The brain is no longer sold with the head—it is thought unsafe to eat—but eyes are never cut out. Some will eat them with gusto, others won't touch them.

4 lamb's head halves, singed and cleaned
1 tablespoon salt

Place the lamb's heads in a large pan with the salt and add cold water to cover. Bring to a boil, skim, and simmer for 1 hour, or until tender. Remove with a slotted spoon and serve hot or cold with mashed potatoes and mashed rutabagas.

To make headcheese, boil the heads until the meat easily slips off the bone. Remove bones and gristle and chop the rest roughly. Pack tightly into a mold, pour a little of the cooking water over it, but not so that it reaches the surface of the meat, place a plate or lid on top and weigh it down, and refrigerate overnight.

Remove the headcheese from the mold and cut it into thick slices. It can be eaten fresh or soured in whey.

HUNG HADDOCK

Sigin ýsa
Serves 4

This partly dried fish dish is still popular with many in Iceland and, unlike many other traditional dishes, it is not tied to any particular season or feast day. This is an age-old method for adding a kick to the fish, which can be insipid, especially if it is served five or six days each week. In Scotland, they have a related dish called *rizzared haddies*. The haddocks are salted overnight, then left to hang, although for two or three days only, and then they are broiled.

The very best *sigin ýsa* is made from fish which is hung aboard a trawler or other fishing vessel.

1 haddock, cleaned and head removed, around 2 pounds
1 tablespoon salt

The haddock, which must be very fresh, is hung from the tail outdoors, in a sheltered but airy spot where the sun doesn't shine on it. The ideal weather for this is cool but not freezing.

Leave the fish hanging for at least 10 days; in good conditions, it can be left for up to 3 weeks, but then it may need some soaking before it is cooked.

The fish is usually skinned before cooking and cut into pieces. Place them in a saucepan, cover with water, and add salt. Bring to a boil and simmer for around 10 minutes, or until just cooked through. Serve with boiled potatoes, rutabagas, and/or carrots.

Melted sheep's tallow is a traditional accompaniment but butter can also be used.

BROWN WHEY CHEESE

Mysuostur
Makes 1/2 pound

Mysuostur is a sweet, brown cheese, made from whey that is simmered down for hours, until it thickens and begins to caramelize. It was the only cheese that was still made at home on the farm when my mother was growing up. She says that when factory-made whey cheese came on the market, it was thought to be much inferior to the homemade product, but that some of it was often bought and melted with some homemade cheese to stretch it further, as the cheese was bothersome and rather expensive to make.

The cheese, which is almost a kind of candy, is usually spread on rye bread or flatbread.

5 quarts whey
1/2 teaspoon salt
1/4 cup brown sugar
2 tablespoons butter
2 tablespoons cream (optional)

Pour the whey and salt into a wide pan, bring it to a boil and cook, uncovered, until it has reduced by at least two thirds.

Stir in brown sugar, butter, and cream. Continue cooking briskly and stir constantly, until the cheese thickens. Test it by placing a small teaspoonful on a plate; if it begins to set, the cheese is ready. Remove from heat and stir until cooled. Spoon into jars or a bowl.

The cheese should be golden brown, rather than dark brown.

BEESTINGS

Ábrystir
Serves 6

Beestings—no, not the stings of bees, but milk from the first, second, and third milking of a cow after it has given birth—is or was prized in some countries and used for certain recipes, but thrown out in others, or given to the calves, which is, after all, what it is meant for. Beestings (colostrum) can be very hard to get unless you milk your own cows, but in Reykjavík it can be bought frozen at the indoor flea market.

There is only one traditional recipe, a very simple one. I once did a comparison of several recipes from the British Isles; it turned out that recipes from the Shetland Islands were very similar, Scottish recipes slightly more elaborate, and this continued southward; beestings recipes from Devonshire were for fairly complicated puddings.

The dessert is traditionally cooked in a water bath but a microwave oven is the ideal tool to use. In fact, this is just about the only thing I ever use my microwave for.

4 cups beestings (cow colostrum)
Milk to dilute
1/2 teaspoon salt
Cinnamon sugar

The colostrum should be diluted if it comes from the first or second milking after the cow has given birth but not if it comes from the third milking. It is best to mix a little colostrum with milk in a cup (perhaps 2 parts colostrum to 1 part milk to begin with) and simmer in a water bath, or cook in a microwave. If the mixture coagulates fairly quickly but doesn't become too stiff and tough, the proportions are about right.

Pour colostrum, milk, and salt into a heatproof bowl and place it in a saucepan half filled with hot water. Simmer below boiling point until the mixture coagulates. It is impossible to estimate a cooking time—just keep checking. Serve hot or cold with cinnamon sugar.

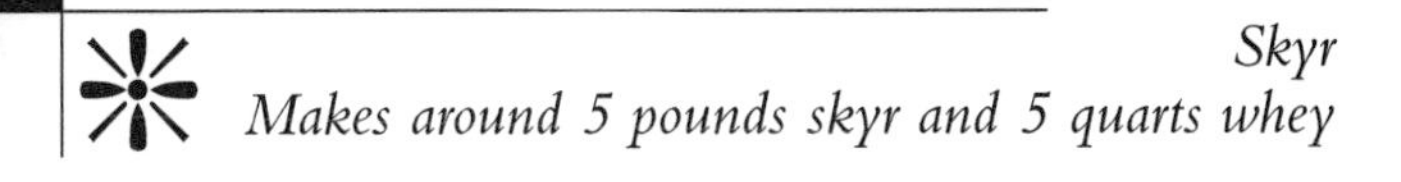

Skyr

Makes around 5 pounds skyr and 5 quarts whey

Skyr has been made in Iceland since the Settlement, but the skyr of those times was probably much thinner than it is today. Skyr was also made in Scandinavia and variations of it are still known there, but in Iceland it was extremely popular and most of the milk that was gathered from cows and ewes during the summer was used for making skyr.

Skyr is traditionally made with unpasteurized fresh skim milk, but buttermilk may also be used. Ideally, you should use a little skyr as a starter for the new batch but since anyone who tries to make skyr on his own is probably doing so because skyr is unavailable, sour cream will usually have to do. It won't be true skyr, of course, but it should be near enough for most uses.

10 quarts skim milk, or
8 quarts skim milk and 2 quarts buttermilk
2 heaped tablespoons skyr or sour cream
Rennet (see package for instructions on how much to use)

Warm the milk to 190°F and hold it at this temperature for 10 minutes, taking care that the milk doesn't scorch or come to a boil. Use a candy thermometer to be safe. Pour the milk into a large bowl or bucket and cool it quickly down to 100°F. If the room where you are working is very cold, the temperature should be a few degrees higher, but it must not be too high. Gradually dilute the starter with warm milk, until it has become so thin that it will mix easily with the milk in the bowl. Add the rennet (dissolved, unless it is in liquid form) and stir well.

At this stage, the milk should cool down very slowly. Place a lid on the container and cover it with towels to retain the warmth. After 3 hours, check the milk. It should have coagulated by now, enough to make a cut that doesn't close immediately. With a sharp knife that reaches to the bottom of the container, cut a double cross into it, all the way through. Cover again and let stand for 2 to 3 hours more. Check if the skyr and remove the lid if it is well coagulated, else keep it covered a little longer. Refrigerate overnight.

Spread a cheesecloth over a large colander and place it over a bowl. Pour or spoon the skyr into the colander. Tie the corners of the cheesecloth together, hang it over a bowl and let the skyr drain for 8 to 12 hours, until fairly firm.

The final stage used to be to weigh the skyr down for a few hours to drain it even further but that is rarely done now.

When the skyr is to be served, it is whipped until smooth and diluted with milk if it is very thick. Some sugar is usually added and it is served with more sugar and milk or a mixture of milk and cream. Berries or fruit are a good accompaniment.

CONTINUED

Most Icelanders eat skyr as a dessert or as a sweet breakfast or lunch dish but it was formerly used in other ways, too (stirred into soups, for instance), and imaginative cooks have been finding new ways to use it in later years. It can for instance be mixed with garlic, herbs, and spices and used as a dip (try making Greek *tzatziki* with skyr, for instance). It can be used in breads and cakes and skyr-cakes, similar to cheesecakes, are delicious.

INDEX

A

Age of Enlightenment, 4
Akureyri, 5, 58
Almond macaroons, 5, 14
Almonds, 1, 6, 172
Ammonium carbonate, see Baker's ammonia
Appetizers, see Starters and appetizers
Apples, 6, 7
  Apple Salad, 136
Arctic char, 3, 17-18, 23, 25, 45, 86, 88
  Grilled Rosemary-Flavored Char, 88
  Smoked char, 55
Ash Wednesday, 11

B

Baker's ammonia, 17, 176, 177, 187, 188, 192
Barley, 1, 3, 4, 12, 13, 139, 202
Beef, 2, 7, 15, 95, 106
  Boneless Birds, 106
Beer, 4
Beestings, 162, 224 (recipe)
Beginning of Lent, 11-12
Bell peppers, 36, 48
Berries, wild, 1, 3, 5, 17, 81
Bilberries, 17, 18, 102, 148
  Bilberry Ice Cream, 157
  Bilberry Soup, 148
  Fillet of Lamb with Bilberry Sauce, 102-103
  Skyr with Berries, 140
Björnsson, Árni, 1
Blood puddings and sausages, 2, 10, 18, 131, 213, 214-215, 216
  Blood Pudding with Iceland Moss, 214-215
Blueberries, 17, 18, 140, 157
Bog bilberries, 17, 148, 149
Boneless Birds, 106
Boxing Day, 15
Brandade de morue, 89
Bread, 2, 3, 8, 19, 199-211
  Baked Rye Bread, 203
  Bread Croissants, 206
  Fried Pieces, 206
  Icelandic Scones, 209
  Iceland Moss and Dulse Bread, 205
  Leaf Bread, 200-201
  Party Sandwich Loaf, 210-211
  Roe Waffles, 208
  Steamed Rye Bread, 204
Briem, Elín, 5
British Isles, 1, 224
Brown cake spice, 169
Brünnich's guillemot, 19
Bun Day, 11, 184, 185
Buns, 11
  Bread Croissants, 206
  Choux Buns, 185
  Lenten Buns, 184
  Yeast buns, 184
Bursting Day, 11, 40
Butter, paid as rent, 4
Buttercream, 168, 193-194

C

Cabbage, 6, 7, 33, 133, 134
  Cabbage and Apple Slaw, 134
  Glazed Cabbage, 133
Cake fillings and jams, 193-197
  Chocolate Buttercream, 194
  Date Filling for Layer Cakes, 196
  Prune Filling, 195
  Rhubarb Jam, 197
  Simple Buttercream, 193
Cakes, 166-175, 178-183
  Brown Striped Cake, 168
  Christmas Cake I, 170
  Christmas Cake II, 171

Cream Layer Cake, 180-181
Devils cake, 179
Dried Fig Cake, 173
Honey Roll, 178
Mother's Dream, 179
Rhubarb Cake with Almonds, 172
Rice Krispies Cake, 182
Spice Cake with Currants, 169
Tray Cake, 174
Truffle Cake, 183
Vinarterta, 166-167
Wedded Bliss, 175
Caramelized potatoes, see Potatoes
Cardamom, 162, 166, 171
Carrots, 6, 7, 15, 99, 118
Carrot and Raisin Salad, 135
Celtic influences, 1
Char, see Arctic Char
Cheeks and tongues, 18, 75-77
Breaded Cod Cheeks, 75
Cheeks in Pepper Cream Sauce, 76
Garlicky Cod Tongue Gratin, 77
Cheese, 24
blue, 118
Brown Whey Cheese, 25, 118, 223 (recipe)
cream cheese, 55
in fish cookery, 69, 70
Chicken, 2, 3, 117
Chocolate cookies, 14
Chocolate velvet pudding, 143
Christianity, conversion to, 20
Christmas, 4, 6, 9, 13-15, 41, 52, 53, 107, 118, 128, 132, 134, 146, 152, 153, 154, 156, 159, 170, 171, 200
Christmas baking, 12, 14, 178, 182, 186-190
Christmas beverage, 15
Christmas cookies, 186-190
Christmas Day, 15, 130, 200
Christmas Eve, 9, 13, 14-15, 21, 38, 118, 154, 200
Cinnamon rolls, 176
Climate, 2, 4, 107, 117
Cocktail Sauce, 7, 58 (recipe)
Coconut macaroons, 14
Cod, 64, 70, 71, 93, 112
Mashed Fish, 89
Pan-Fried Salt Cod with Tomato Sauce, 74
Salt Cod with Vegetables, 73
Cod cheeks, see cheeks and tongues
Cod liver, 49, 64
Cod roe, see Roe
Cod tongues, see cheeks and tongues
Coffee parties, 8, 12, 13, 15-16, 170, 180, 210
Colostrum, see Beestings
Cones (cookies), 5
Cookbooks and books on food history, 1, 3, 4-5, 27
160 fiskréttir, 73
A Plain Cookery Book for the Working Classes, 32
Danish cookbooks, 4
Earliest cookbook manuscript in Icelandic *(Libellus de arte coquinaria)*, 3
Einfalt matreiðsluvasakver fyrir heldri manna húsfreyjur (1800), 4-5, 35, 144, 162
German cookbooks, 166
Home economics cookbook, 67, 179
Íslensk matarhefð, 1
Kvennafræðarinn, 5
Matarást, 27
Matreiðslubók fyrir fátæka og ríka, 6, 106, 139
Matur og drykkur, 6, 44, 110, 113, 135
Norwegian cookbooks, 4
Saga daganna, 1
Stutt matreiðslubók fyrir sveitaheimili, 191
Cookies, 176-177, 186-192
Air Bars, 192
Cinnamon Cookies, 191
Coconut Cookies, 188
Granny's Cinnamon Rolls, 176
Jewish Cookies, 187

Oatmeal Cookies, 177
Pepper Cookies, 189-190
Prune Crescents, 186
Copenhagen, 5, 187
Cormorant, 117
Crepes, 5, 12, 13, 159, 160 (recipe), 162
Crescents, 5
Crowberries, 18, 140
Crullers, 5, 12, 13, 159, 162, 164 (recipe)
Cucumber Sauce, 61
Curry powder, 5, 37, 67, 80, 104

D

Danish influences on Icelandic cooking, 4-6, 11, 23, 33, 106, 128, 129, 133, 141, 143, 145, 152, 164, 170, 192
Danish pork roast, see pork
Desserts, 7, 8, 15, 139-157
Apricot Sauce, 155
Bilberry Ice Cream, 157
Bilberry Soup, 148
Butter pudding, 143
Christmas Ice Cream, 156
Cocoa Soup, 141
Egg Milk Soup, 145
Elbow Macaroni Soup, 144
Grandmother's Trifle, 152
Lemon Mousse, 153
Orange mousse, 153
Pineapple mousse, 153
Prune compote, 149
Rhubarb Compote, 149
Rhubarb soup, 149
Rice a'l Amande, 154
Rice Pudding, 146
Rye Bread Soup, 142
Sago Fruit Soup, 147
Skyr with Berries, 140
Spiced Fruit Soup, 151
Stewed Mixed Fruit Compote, 150
Velvet Pudding, 143
Devonshire, 224
Dips and sauces, 57-61
Cocktail Sauce, 58
Cucumber Sauce, 61
Dill-Mustard Sauce, 60
Honey-Mustard Sauce, 59
Shrimp Dip, 57
Drangey, 19
Dried fish, 2, 3, 4, 5, 10, 18, 213, 222
Dried fruit, 150, 151, 155, 173
Apricot Sauce, 155
Braised Wild Goose with Fruit Stuffing, 120
Dried Fig Cake, 173
Sago Fruit Soup, 147
Spiced Fruit Soup, 151
Stewed Mixed Fruit Compote, 150
Dried meat, 2
Dublin Bay prawn, see Langoustines
Ducks, 2, 117, 132
Dulse, 1, 3, 18, 205
Dumplings, 22, 220

E

Easter, 11, 12, 153
Eastern Fjords, 12
Egner, Thorbjörn, 189
Eldey Island, 22
Elliðaár River, 24
Epiphany, 9
Ewe's milk, 2
Eysteinsson, Úlfar, 49

F

Farmer's cookies, 14
Fattigmenn, 164
Figs, dried, 173
Finland, 21
First Day of Summer, 12-13
Fish, fish recipes, 63-91, see also Arctic char, Cheeks and tongues, Cod, Fishballs, Haddock, Halibut, Lumpfish, Monkfish, Ocean catfish, Ocean perch, Salmon, Salmon trout, Salt fish
Baked Fish with Vegetables I, 67
Baked Fish with Vegetables II, 68
Fried Fish with Onions, 66
Mashed Fish, 89

Fishballs, 90-91
Fishballs, 90
Fishballs with Brown Sauce, 91
Fish, dried, 2, 3, 4, 5, 10, 89
Fish heads, dried, 4
Fish tongues, see cheeks and tongues
Flatbreads, 3, 11, 19, 22, 199, 200, 202
Leaf Bread, 200-201
Rye Flatbread, 202
Food traditions, festive, 9-16
Francatelli, Charles Elmé, 32
Fried bread, cakes, and cookies, 159, 160-165, 200-201, 207-209
Crepes, 160
Crullers, 164
Deep-Fried Bows, 164
Fried Pieces, 207
Icelandic Scones, 209
Leaf Bread, 200-201
Love Balls, 165
Rice Pudding Pancakes, 161
Roe Waffles, 208
Waffles, 162
Fruit, 1, 6, 7, 149, 150, see also Dried fruit
Fruit compotes, 7, 139, 149-150
Rhubarb Compote, 149
Stewed Mixed Fruit Compote, 150
Stewed prune compote, 150
Fruit soups, 7, 130, 139
Bilberry Soup, 148
Sago Fruit Soup, 147
Spiced Fruit Soup, 151
Fulmar, 117

G

Game, 8, 21, 22, 25, 51, 53, 117-124, 136, see Game birds, Reindeer
Game birds, 117-124
Braised Wild Goose with Fruit Stuffing, 120
Christmas Ptarmigan, 118-119
Flamed Puffin Breasts, 124
Gravad Breast of Ptarmigan, 51
Guillemot in Brown Sauce, 123
Quick-Fried Wild Goose Breast, 121-122
Gannet, 117
Garlic, 8, 46, 74, 92
Gelatin-stiffened dishes, 7, 153, 154
Gestgjafinn, magazine, 15
Gísladóttir, Hallgerður, 1
Glazed potatoes, see Potatoes, glazed
Glögg, 14
Góa's Feast, 10
Goose, 2, 25, 42, 54, 117, 120-122
Braised Wild Goose with Fruit Stuffing, 120
Goose Soup with Raisins, 42
Quick-Fried Wild Goose Breast, 121-122
Roasted goose, 15, 132
Grain, lack of, 19, 117
Grain production, 1-5
Grandmother's Trifle, 152
Gratins, seafood, 47, 70, 77, 93
Gravlax, 43, 50, 59, 60
Gravy browning, 5, 19
Great auk, 22
Greenland, 22
Greylag goose, 25, 42, 117, 120
Grilling, 82, 84, 88, 92, 98
Grilled Langoustines, 92
Grilled Monkfish, 82
Grilled Rosemary-Flavored Char, 88
Grilled Salmon, 84
Pit-Roasted Leg of Lamb, 98
Ground meat, 7, 110, 111, see also Meatballs and patties
Guillemot, 8, 19, 22, 117
Guillemot in Brown Sauce, 123

H

Haddock, 7, 64-72, 93, 112
Baked Fish with Vegetables I, 67
Baked Fish with Vegetables II, 68
Breaded Pan-Fried Haddock, 65
Curried Haddock with Shrimp and

Pineapple, 69
Fish Gratin with Shrimp Sauce, 70
Hung haddock, 222
Mashed Fish, 89
Overnight-Salted Haddock, 71
Poached Haddock, 64
Salted Haddock in a Cream Sauce, 72
Shrimp Gratin with Mushrooms, 93
Halibut, 66, 67, 78, 79, 93
Halibut Soup, 35
Halibut with Leek and Mushrooms, 79
Poached Halibut with Lemon Butter Sauce, 78
Hartshorn, see Baker's ammonia
Harvest Celebration, 13
Headcheese, 2, 10, 221
Heart, lamb, 113
Stuffed Lamb Hearts, 113
Herbs, 6, 30, 38
Herring, 7, 11, 44
Herring with Sour Cream, 44
Holland, Henry, 85
Horsemeat, 19-20, 106, 112, 130
Hot spring bread, 204
Hung Haddock, 222
Hungarian goulash, 105
Húsavík, 83

I

Ice cream, 15, 155
Bilberry Ice Cream, 157
Christmas Ice Cream, 156
Iceland Journal of Henry Holland, 85
Iceland moss, 3, 19, 202
Blood Pudding with Iceland Moss, 214-215
Flatbread, 202
Iceland Moss and Dulse Bread, 205
Iceland moss jelly, 32
Iceland Moss Soup, 32
Icelandic Christmas cake, see Vinarterta
Icelandic Dairy Produce Marketing Association, 7, 70
Independence Day, 13
Ireland, 1

J

Jødekager, 187

K

Kale, 5, 6, 31
Potato Kale Soup, 31
Keflavík, 58
Kidneys, lamb, 113, 216

L

Lamb and mutton, 24, 95, 96-105, 112, 218, see also Salted meat, Smoked meat
Breaded Lamb Cutlets, 101
Brine-cured lamb, 97
Chops, 101
Cutlets, 7, 101
Fillet, 50, 52, 102-103
Fillet of Lamb with Bilberry Sauce, 102-103
Gravad Fillet of Lamb, 50
Icelandic Lamb Soup, 38
Lamb Curry, 104
Lamb Soup, 38
Leftovers, 56, 109
Pit-Roasted Leg of Lamb, 98
Potted Mutton, 218
Rolled Lamb Flank, 217
Saddle of lamb, 96
Shoulder, 100
Spiced Lamb Stew, 105
Stuffed Shoulder of Lamb, 100
Sunday Roast, 96
Langoustines, 7, 20, 46, 47, 92, 93
Curried Langoustine Soup, 37
Grilled Langoustines, 92
Langoustines with Garlic Butter, 46
Shellfish in White Wine Cream Sauce, 47
Látrabjarg, 22
Law texts, as culinary history sources, 3, 11, 18
Laxness, Halldór, 23, 159
Layer cakes, 6, 16, 166-168, 180, 182

Leaf Bread, 14, 15, 199, 200-201 (recipe)
Leftover rice pudding, 161
Rice Pudding Pancakes, 161
Leftovers, fish, 89
Mashed Fish, 89
Leftovers, meat, 56, 109, 112
Lamb Spread from Leftovers, 56
Meat Mash, 109
Salted Meat Patties with Fish, 112
Leg of lamb, 6, 7, 9, 12, 15, 95, 96-99
Pit-Roasted Leg of Lamb, 98
Salted and Slow-Roasted Leg of Lamb, 97
Smoked Leg of Lamb, 99
Sunday roast, 96 (recipe), 100, 132
Lemon Mousse, 6, 15, 153 (recipe)
Lent, 11
Lichens, 19, 32, 202, 205, see also Iceland moss
Ling, 67, 68
Linzer Torte, 175
Little Ice Age, 1
Liver, lamb, 113, 114, 216
Liver Patties, 114
Liver Sausage, 2, 10, 213, 216 (recipe)
Lobster, 20
Löngumýri Home Academy, 178
Lovage, 38
Love Balls, 11, 159, 165 (recipe)
Lumpfish, 20, 83
Poached Lumpfish, 83

M

Macaroni, 139, 144
Mallard, 117
Marrowfat peas, 7, 99
Maundy Thursday, 12
Mayonnaise, 7, 58, 59
Meat, see Beef, Dried meat, Ground meat, Horsemeat, Lamb and mutton, Pork, Salted meat, Smoked meat
Meat dishes, 95-114
Meatballs and patties, 6, 133
Meatballs in Brown Sauce, 110
Meat Patties with Onion Sauce, 111
Salted Meat Patties with Fish, 112
Mediterranean cooking, 74
Meringues, meringue cookies, 14, 182
Middle Ages, food, 3-4, 107
Milk puddings, 6
Butter pudding, 143
Rice Pudding, 146
Velvet Pudding, 143
Milk soups, 144, 145
Cocoa Soup, 141
Egg Milk Soup, 145
Elbow Macaroni Soup, 144
Icelandic Moss Soup, 32
Monkfish, 8, 20, 75, 82
Grilled Monkfish, 82
MSG, 25
Mushrooms, 6, 85, 93
Mustard, 6, 59, 60
Mutton, see Lamb and mutton

N

Newfoundland, 18
New Year, 9
Norway, 1, 2, 3, 4, 11, 22, 189
Norway lobster, see Langoustines

O

Oatmeal, 139
Ocean catfish, 66, 67, 93
Curried Ocean Catfish, 80
Ocean perch, 8
Ocean Perch in Mustard Cream Sauce, 81
Oeufs à la neige, 145
Offal, see organ meats
Oiseau sans tête, 106
ORA green beans, 7
Organ meats, 4, 113
Blood Pudding with Iceland Moss, 214-215
Boiled Lamb's Heads, 221
Liver Patties, 113
Liver Sausage, 216

Stuffed Lamb Hearts, 113
Overnight-salted fish, 71, 72

P

Pancakes, 5, 13, 159, 160, 161, 162
Rice Pudding Pancakes, 161
Parma ham, 52
Party Sandwich Loaf, 16, 210-211 (recipe)
Pasta, 7, 8, 139, 144
Pea soup, 40
Pearl sago, see Sago
Pearl sugar, 20-21, 187
Pentecost, 13
Pepparkakor, 189
Pepper Cookie Song, 189
Peppercorn mixtures, 21
Perdices de capellán, 106
Pickling, see Whey-preserving
Pigs, 2, 95, 107
Pineapple, canned, 6, 7, 69, 153
Pink-footed goose, 25, 42, 117, 120
Plaice, 93
Pork, 6, 7, 95, 132
Pork Roast with Cracklings, 9, 15, 107 (recipe)
Porridge, 2, 3, 5, 6, 12, 13, 19, 139
Portuguese cooking, 73
Potatoes, 5, 6, 31, 127, 128-130, 137
Glazed Potatoes, 7, 15, 96, 118, 128 (recipe)
Mashed Potatoes, 11, 109, 129 (recipe)
Potato Kale Soup, 31
Potato Salad, 137
Potatoes in a White Sauce, 99, 130 (recipe)
Potato starch, 21
Potted Mutton, 218
Prawns, see Shrimp
Preservation in skyr, 17
Prince's cake, 175
Provençe, 3, 89
Prunes, 173
Prune compote, 6, 150
Prune Crescents, 186
Prune Filling, 195
Prune filling, prune jam, 175, 186
Ptarmigan, 15, 21, 41, 51, 117
Christmas Ptarmigan, 118-119
Gravad Breast of Ptarmigan, 51
Ptarmigan Soup, 41
Puddings, 5, 6, 143, 146
Puffin, 8, 21, 54, 117
Flamed Puffin Breasts, 124
Puffin Spread, 54

Q

Queen Victoria, 32, 85

R

Rainbow cake, 167
Rainbow pepper, 21
Raw Smoked Lamb, 52
Razorbill, 19, 22, 123
Red cabbage, 15, 99, 118
Boiled Red Cabbage, 132
Red currant jelly, 118
Red Icelandic potatoes, 137
Reindeer, 22, 53, 108
Leg of Reindeer with Rosemary, 108
Reindeer Canapés, 53
Reykjavík, 5, 9, 13, 24, 49, 127, 152
Rhubarb, 5, 22, 35, 150
Rhubarb Cake with Almonds, 172
Rhubarb Compote, 149
Rhubarb Jam, 149, 152, 159, 160, 175, 186, 197 (recipe)
Rhubarb raisins, 171
Rhubarb soup, 149
Wedded Bliss, 175
Rice, 7, 8, 139
Rice à l'Amande, 154
Rice desserts, 146
Rice à l'Amande, 154
Rice porridge, 12, 13, 146
Rice Pudding, 15, 146 (recipe)
Rice Pudding Pancakes, 161
Ris à la Malta, 154
Ris a l'amande, 15, 146, 154, 155
Rice flour, 139

Rizzared haddies, 222
Rock ptarmigan, see ptarmigan
Roe, cod, 22, 49, 64
Cod Roe Salad, 49
Roe pancakes, 208
Roe Waffles, 208
Roe, lumpfish, 20, 83
Rolled Lamb Flank, 213, 217 (recipe)
Rutabagas, 5, 11, 23, 68, 73
Mashed Rutabagas, 131
Rutebiler, 192
Rye, 3, 202, 203
Rye bread, 56, 203-204
Baked Rye Bread, 203
Rye Bread Soup, 142
Rye Flatbread, 202
Steamed Rye Bread, 204
Rye Dumplings, 220

S

Sago, 23, 35, 139, 147
Saithe, 112
Salads, 7, 127, 134-137
Apple Salad, 136
Cabbage and Apple Slaw, 134
Carrot and Raisin Salad, 135
Cod Roe Salad, 49
Potato Salad, 137
Salmon, 3, 23-24, 34, 35, 45, 61, 84, 85
Grilled Salmon, 84
Salmon Soup with Whey, 34
Salmon Tartar Timbales, 45
Salmon with Wild Sorrel and Mushrooms, 85
Salmon, smoked, 43, 45, 55, 59
Smoked Salmon Spread, 55
Salmon trout, 3, 23, 25, 35, 61, 86, 87
Pan-Fried Trout, 87
Poached Trout, 86
smoked, 55
Salt cod, 23, 73, 74, 89, 131
Pan-Fried Salt Cod with Tomato Sauce, 74
Salt Cod with Vegetables, 73
Salt fish, 23, 71, 73, 89
Salt, lack of, 2, 18
Salted lamb, see Salted meat
Salted meat, 11, 12, 40, 109, 112, 130, 131
Meat Mash, 109
Salted and Slow-Roasted Leg of Lamb, 97
Salted Lamb, 219
Salted Lamb with Rye Dumplings, 220
Salted Meat Patties with Fish, 112
Split Pea and Salted Lamb Soup, 11, 40 (recipe)
Sandwich torte, see Party Sandwich Loaf
Sarah Bernhard cookies, 14
Sausages, 19, 113, 130, 133
Scallops, 8, 47, 48, 75, 93
Marinated Scallop and Pepper Salad, 48
Scampi, see Langoustines
Scones, 160, 209 (recipe), 210
Scotland, 1, 222, 224
Scurvy grass, 30
Seabirds, 54, 117, 123-124
Seal meat and flippers, 2, 10
Seamen's Day, 13
Serina cookies, 14
Settlement of Iceland, 1-3, 17, 18, 23, 24, 107, 216, 225
Sewing clubs, 15-16, 210
Shag, 117
Shark, fermented, 10, 213
Sheep's head, 2, 10, 131, 221
Boiled Lamb's Heads, 221
Shellfish dishes, 46, 47, 48, 92, 93
Grilled Langoustines, 92
Shrimp Gratin with Mushrooms, 93
Shetland Islands, 224
Shrimp, 7, 37, 47, 57, 69, 93
Fish Gratin with Shrimp Sauce, 70
Shrimp Dip, 57
Shrimp Gratin with Mushrooms, 93
Shrove Tuesday, 11, 40
Sigurðardóttir, Helga, 6, 44, 73, 110, 135
Sigurðardóttir , Jóninna, 6, 106, 139
Skagafjörður, 19

Skálholt, 13, 89
Skate, fermented, 13-14
Skyr, 2, 17, 18, 24, 25, 225-226 (recipe)
  Skyr with Berries, 140
Smoked and salted pork, 15
Smoked lamb, see Smoked meat
Smoked meat, 2, 5, 9, 10, 12, 14, 15, 24, 52, 130
  Raw Smoked Lamb, 52
  Smoked Leg of Lamb, 99
Smoked salmon see Salmon, smoked
Snowflake bread, see Leaf Bread
Sorrel, see Wild sorrel
Soup herbs, 38
Soups, savory, 29-42
  Chervil Soup, 30
  Curried Langoustine Soup, 37
  Fish Soup with Tomatoes and Peppers, 36
  Goose Soup with Raisins, 42
  Halibut Soup, 35
  Iceland Moss Soup, 32
  Icelandic Lamb Soup, 38
  Julienne Soup, 33
  Lamb Soup, 39
  Meat soup, see Icelandic Lamb Soup
  Potato Kale Soup, 31
  Ptarmigan Soup, 41
  Salmon Soup with Whey, 34
  Split Pea and Salted Lamb Soup, 11, 40 (recipe)
Soups, sweet, 7, 130, 139,
  Bilberry Soup, 148
  Cocoa Soup, 141
  Egg Milk Soup, 145
  Elbow Macaroni Soup, 144
  Rye Bread Soup, 142
  Sago Fruit Soup, 147
  Spiced Fruit Soup, 151
Sourdough, 202, 204
Spanking Day, 11
Species (cookies), 5
Spice cookies, 5, 14
Spices, 5-8
Spinach, 30, 85
Spreads, 54-56
  Lamb Spread from Leftovers, 56
  Puffin Spread, 54
  Smoked Salmon Spread, 55
St. Thorlak's Day, 13-14, 97
Starters and appetizers, 43-53
  Cod Roe Salad, 49
  Fishballs, 90
  Gravad Breast of Ptarmigan, 51
  Gravad Fillet of Lamb, 50
  Herring with Sour Cream, 44
  Langoustines with Garlic Butter, 46
  Marinated Scallop and Pepper Salad, 48
  Puffin Spread, 54
  Raw Smoked Lamb, 52
  Reindeer Canapés, 53
  Salmon Tartar Timbales, 45
  Shellfish in White Wine Cream Sauce, 47
  Smoked Salmon Spread, 55
Stone brambles, 18
Strawberries, wild, 18
String beans, 6, 33, 118
Sun Coffee, 12
Sunday Roast, see Leg of lamb
Sweden, 21, 154, 189
Sweet soup, see Fruit Soups
Syrup, homemade, 178, 203

T

Tallow, 14, 73
Teal, 117
Testicles, lamb's, 10, 213
Thingeyjarsýsla, 192
Thingvellir, 13
Third spice, 25
Thor, 9
Thorrablót, 9-10, 213
Thorri, 9-10
Thrír Frakkar hjá Úlfari (restaurant), 49
Tomato ketchup, 6, 67, 91
Tomatoes, 6, 36, 74
Trout, see Salmon trout
Turkey, 9, 15, 117, 136

V

Vanilla, 5, 6
Vanilla wreaths, 5, 14
Veal, 95, 106
  Boneless Birds, 106
Vegetables, 5, 6, 7, 23, 127, 128-133
Vinarterta, 5, 14, 166-167 (recipe), 168
  Prune Filling, 195

W

Waldorf salad, 15, 118, 136
Western Fjords, 12, 13, 19, 80
Westmann Islands, 19, 124, 167
Whale meat and blubber, 2, 10
Whey, 2, 25, 26, 223
  Fermented, 2, 25
  In modern cooking, 25, 34, 74
  Salmon Soup with Whey, 34
  Whey-preserved food, 2, 5, 10, 19, 22, 25, 113, 131
Whitsunday, 13
Whooper swan, 117
Wiener schnitzel, 7
Wiener Torte, 166
Wild sorrel, 25-26, 30, 85
Wild thyme, 26, 50, 111
Worm milk, 144

ICELANDIC INDEX

Icelandic terms, ingredients, and recipe titles (in italics).

A

Ábrystir, 224
Aðalbláber, 17
Aðalbláberjaís, 157
Álka, 22
Appelsín, 15
Apríkósusósa, 155
Áramót, 9
Ástarpungar, 11, 165
Ávaxtagrautur, 150

B

Bakaður fiskur með grænmeti, 67, 68
Beinlausir fuglar, 106
Berjaskyr, 140
Bláber, 17
Bláberjasúpa, 148
Bleikja, 17
Blóðberg, 26
Blóðmör, 10
Bolludagsbollur, 184
Bolludagur, 11
Bolluvöndur, 11
Brauðsúpa, 142
Brauðterta, 210
Brennivín, 11, 14
Bringukollur, 10
Brún randalín, 168
Brúnaðar kartöflur, 128
Brúnkaka með kúrennum, 169
Brúnkál, 133
Brúnkökukrydd, 169
Buff með lauk og brúnni sósu, 111

D

Dill-sinnepssósa, 60
Djöflaterta, 179
Drangeyjarfugl, 19
Döðlukrem á rjómatertu, 196

E

Eggjamjólk, 145
Einfalt smjörkrem, 193
Eldavél, 5
Eldsteiktar lundabringur, 124
Eplasalat, 136

F

Fiskbollur, 90
Fiskbollur í brúnni sósu, 91
Fiskgratín með rækjusósu, 70
Fiskisúpa með tómötum og papriku, 36
Fjallagrasa- og sölvabrauð, 205
Fjallagrasablóðmör, 214
Fjallagrasaflatbrauð, 202
Fjallagrasamjólk, 32
Fjallagrös, 19
Flatbrauð, 202
Flatkökur, 202
Flauelsgrautur, 143
Flengingardagur, 11
Föstuinngangur, 11
Franskbrauðshorn, 206
Furstakaka, 175
Fyllt lambahjörtu, 113
Fylltur lambaframpartur, 100

G

Gamlárskvöld, 9
Gellur, 18, 77
Glás, 105
Góugleði, 10
Gráfíkjuterta, 173
Grafinn lambahryggsvöðvi, 50
Graflaxsósa, 59

Grafnar rjúpnabringur, 51
Grágæs, 25
Grásleppa, 20, 83
Gratíneraðar hvítlauksgellur, 77
Grautarlummur, 161
Grillaður humar, 92
Grillaður lax, 84
Grillaður skötuselur, 82
Grilluð rósmarínkrydduð bleikja, 88
Gúllas, 105
Gulrófa, 23
Gulróta- og rúsínusalat, 135
Gúrkusósa, 61
Gyðingakökur, 187
Gæsasúpa með rúsínum, 42

H

Hafrakex, 177
Hákarl, 10
Hálfmánar með sveskjumauki, 186
Hamborgarhryggur, 107
Hamsatólg, 14
Hangikjöt, 10, 24
Hangilæri, 99
Harðfiskur, 10
Heiðagæs, 25
Heilagfiski, 78
Hjartarsalt, 17
Hjónabandssæla, 175
Hnoðmör, 14
Holugrillað lambalæri, 98
Hrásalat, 134
Hrátt hangikjöt, 52
Hreindýr, 22
Hrísgrjónagrautur, 146
Hrísterta, 182
Hrogn, 22
Hrognavöfflur, 208
Hrognkelsi, 20
Hrossakjöt, 19
Hrútspungar, 10
Humar, 20
Humar með hvítlaukssmjöri, 46
Hunangsrúlluterta, 178
Hundasúra, 25
Hverabrauð, 204
Hvítkálssalat með eplum, 134

J

Jól, 14
Jólaglögg, 14
Jólaís, 156
Jólakaka, 11, 170, 171
Jólarjúpa, 118
Júlíönusúpa, 33

K

Kakósúpa, 141
Kanelkökur, 191
Karfi í sinnepsrjómasósu, 81
Karrífiskur með rækjum og ananas, 69
Karríkrydduð humarsúpa, 37
Kartöflu-grænkálssúpa, 31
Kartöflumjöl, 21
Kartöflumús, 129
Kartöflusalat, 137
Kartöflustappa, 129
Kartöfluuppstúf, 130
Kerfilsúpa, 30
Kindakæfa, 218
Kinnar, 18
Kinnar í paprikurjómasósu, 76
Kjöt í karríi, 104
Kjöt í myrkri, 105
Kjötbollur í brúnni sósu, 110
Kjötkássa, 109
Kjötsúpa, 38
Kleinur, 164, 165
Kokkteilsósa, 58
Kókoskökur, 188
Konfektkaka, 183
Kryddlegið hörpudisks- og paprikusalat, 48
Kryddud sætsúpa, 151
Kryddud smásteik, 105
Krækiber, 18
Kæfa, 218
Kæst skata, 13

L
Lambahryggvöðvi með sveppa- og bláberjasósu, 102
Lambakjötssúpa, 39
Lambakótelettur í raspi, 101
Lambasmurkæfa, 56
Langvía, 19
Laufabrauð, 200
Lax, 23
Lax með hundasúru og sveppum, 85
Laxasmurostur, 55
Laxasúpa með mysu, 34
Laxatartartoppar, 45
Léttsaltað og steikt lambalæri, 97
Léttsteiktar villigæsabringur, 121
Leturhumar, 20
Lifrarbuff, 114
Lifrarpylsa, 10, 216
Loftkökur, 192
Lúða með blaðlauk og sveppum, 79
Lúðusúpa, 35
Lundabaggar, 10
Lundakæfa, 54
Lundi, 21

M
Magáll, 10
Makkarónusúpa, 144
Malt, 15
Mysa, 25
Mysuostur, 25, 223
Mömmudraumur, 179

N
Nýársdagur, 9
Nætursöltuð ýsa, 71
Nætursöltuð ýsa í rjómasósu, 72

O
Ofnbakað rúgbrauð, 203

P
Partar, 207
Páskar, 12
Perlusykur, 20
Piparkökur, 189
Plokkfiskur, 89
Pottbrauð, 204
Pottsteikt villigæs með ávaxtafyllingu, 120
Pönnukökur, 160
Pönnusteiktur saltfiskur með tómatsósu, 74
Pönnusteiktur urriði, 87

R
Rabarbaragrautur, 149
Rabarbarakaka með möndlum, 172
Rabarbarasulta, 197
Rabarbari, 22
Rauðmagi, 20, 83
Regnbogapipar, 21
Regnbogaterta, 167
Ris a l'amande, 154
Rjómaterta, 180
Rjúpa, 21, 118
Rjúpnasúpa, 41
Rófustappa, 131
Rósmarínkryddað hreindýralæri, 108
Rúllupylsa, 213, 217
Rækjugratín með sveppum, 93
Rækjusalat, 57

S
Sagógrjón, 23
Sagósúpa með ávöxtum, 147
Saltfiskur, 23
Saltfiskur með grænmeti, 73
Saltkjöt, 219
Saltkjöt með soðkökum, 220
Saltkjöt og baunir, 40
Saltkjötsbuff með fiski, 112
Saumaklúbbar, 15
Seytt rúgbrauð, 204
Sigin grásleppa, 83
Sigin ýsa, 222
Síld með sýrðum rjóma, 44
Silungur, 25
Sítrónubúðingur, 153
Sítrónufrómas, 153
Sjóbirtingur, 25

Sjóbleikja, 17, 88
Sjómannadagurinn, 13
Skelfiskur í hvítvínsrjómasósu, 47
Skonsur, 209
Skötuselur, 20
Skúffukaka, 174
Skyr, 2, 24, 225-226
Smjörgrautur, 143
Snittur með hreindýrakjöti, 53
Soðið brauð, 207
Soðið rauðkál, 132
Soðin lúða með sítrónusmjörsósu, 78
Soðin ýsa, 64
Soðinn rauðmagi, 83
Soðinn urriði, 86
Sólarkaffi, 12
Sósulitur, 19
Sprengidagur, 11, 40
Steikt brauð, 207
Steikt ýsa í raspi, 65
Steiktir partar, 207
Steiktur fiskur með lauk, 66
Steinbítur í karrísósu, 80
Súkkulaðismjörkrem, 194
Sumardagurinn fyrsti, 12
Sunnudagslærið, 96
Svartfugl, 19, 123
Svartfugl í brúnni sósu, 123
Sveskjumauk, 195
Svið, 10, 221
Sviðasulta, 10
Svínasteik með stökkri pöru, 107
Sýra, 4, 25
Sætsúpa, 151
Söl, 18

T

Töðugjöld, 13

U

Urriði, 25

V

Vatnsdeigsbollur, 185
Viðgrjón, 23
Villigæs, 25
Vínarterta, 5, 14, 166, 168, 195
Vöfflur, 162

Þ

Þingeyingar, 192
Þjóðhátíðardagurinn, 13
Þorláksmessa, 13
Þorrablót, 9
Þorri, 9
Þorskhrognasalat, 49
Þorskkinnar í raspi, 75
Þrettándinn, 9
Þriðja kryddið, 25

Ö

Ömmusnúðar, 176
Ömmutrifli, 152

Icelandic-interest titles from Hippocrene ...

Icelandic-English/English-Icelandic Concise Dictionary
Arnold R. Taylor

- over 10,000 entries in a concise and easy-to-use format
- alphabetical listings in both languages
- lists of English irregular plurals and irregular English verbs
- states gender of Icelandic nouns
- a rare and valuable resource
- perfect for students and travelers

5,000 entries ▪ 177 pages ▪ 4 x 6 ▪ ISBN 0-87052-801-7 ▪ $9.95pb ▪ (147)

Scandinavian-interest titles from Hippocrene ...

COOKBOOKS

Tastes & Tales of Norway
Siri Lise Doub

Siri Lise Doub welcomes you into her family's kitchen, sharing over 100 recipes for classic Norwegian dishes such as *Salmon Marinated in Hardanger Apple Cider, Herb-Cured Fillet of Elk, Fruit Soup, Norwegian Pancakes,* and *Cinnamon Wheels.* There is also a chapter on the famed *koldt bord* (cold buffet), typically laden with meats, cheeses, flatbreads, stewed potatoes with dill, open-face sandwiches, marinated herring, and other marvelous treats, as well as a chapter on "Holiday and Party Foods" with recipes for the best items on the Norwegian Christmas table.

Readers will be enchanted with the historical accounts, local customs, and excerpts from Norwegian folk songs, traditional blessings, poetry, and mythology that are also included in this treasury of Norwegian cuisine. Black and white photos complete this book, providing a unique perspective on Norway's rich history and cultural traditions.

288 pages ▪ black & white photos ▪ 6 x 9 ▪ ISBN 0-7818-0877-4 ▪ $24.95hc ▪ (341)

The Best of Scandinavian Cooking: Danish, Norwegian and Swedish
Shirley Sarvis & Barbara Scott O'Neil

This exciting collection of 100 recipes, each dish the favorite of a Scandinavian cook, spans the range of home cooking—appetizers, soups, omelets, pancakes, meats and pastries. Included are directions for making such tempting dishes as Norwegian Blueberry Omelet, Danish Butter Cake, Swedish Pancakes with Ligonberries—and a section entitled "A Smørrebrød Sampling," devoted to those openfaced Danish sandwiches. Each

recipe has been carefully tested with North American ingredients and measures.
142 pages ▪ 5 1/2 x 8 1/4 ▪ ISBN 0-7818-0547-3 ▪ $9.95pb ▪ (643)

Good Food from Sweden

Inga Norberg

This classic of Swedish cookery includes recipes for fish and meat dishes, vegetables, breads and sweets, including cookies, cakes candies and syrups. A large section is dedicated to the savory tidbits included in the traditional Swedish smorgasbord.
192 pages ▪ 5 1/2 x 8 1/4 ▪ ISBN 0-7818-0486-8 ▪ $10.95pb ▪ (544)

The Best of Smorgasbord Cooking

Gerda Simonson

Recipes for the traditional Swedish smorgasbord, including meat and game dishes, aspics and salads, fish, pastas and vegetables.
158 pages ▪ 5 1/2 x 8 1/4 ▪ ISBN 0-7818-0407-8 ▪ $14.95pb ▪ (207)

The Best of Finnish Cooking

Taimi Previdi

"Over 200 recipes are relatively easy to follow ... from meat pies and beef stews to puddings and casseroles."

—*The Midwest Book Review*

"The book is divided clearly into sections of different menu items and the directions are detailed ... *The Best of Finnish Cooking* is a good and practical cookbook. It makes a wonderful Christmas gift for people interested in cooking or things Finnish."

—*Amerikan Uutiset*

The Finnish-born author has compiled a delicious array of recipes for every occasion:
- Authentic Finnish recipes, adapted for the American kitchen.
- Traditional recipes for main courses, soups, salads, appetizers, sandwiches and desserts.
- Delicious baking recipes for breads (both sweet and savory), cakes and cookies.
- Menus for special holidays, such as Easter, Midsummer and Christmas.
- Finnish names for recipes and an index in Finnish and English.

242 pages ▪ 5 1/2 x 8 1/2 ▪ ISBN 0-7818-0493-0 ▪ $12.95pb ▪ (601)

Poetry and Folklore

Treasury of Finnish Love Poems, Quotations & Proverbs In Finnish and English

Börje Vähämäki, editor and translator

128 pages ▪ 5 x 7 ▪ ISBN 0-7818-0397-7 ▪ $11.95hc ▪ (118)

Norse Stories

Retold by Hamilton Wright Mabie

Illustrated by George Wright

"These ancient books, which a brave and noble race carried in its heart through all its wide wanderings and conquests, take one back to the beginning of the worlds and the coming of the gods to rule over them ..."

Thus begins the first story, "The Making of the World," in this unique illustrated collection of Norse myths and stories. Originally published in 1901, this rare volume of 17 stories has been brought back into print by Hippocrene Books one hundred years later. Stories of brave warriors, fierce gods, and exciting adventures included in such tales as "Odin's Search for Wisdom," "Thor Goes a Fishing," "How Thor Fought the Giant Hrungner" and "The Twilight of the Gods" will enchant children and adults alike.

250 pages ▪ 5 1/2 x 8 1/4 ▪ illustrations ▪ ISBN 0-7818-0770-0 ▪ $14.95hc ▪ (357)

Swedish Fairy Tales

Translated by H. L. Braekstad

A unique blend of enchantment, adventure, comedy, and romance make this collection of Swedish fairy tales a must-have for any library. With 18 different, classic Swedish fairy tales and 21 beautiful black-and-white illustrations, this is an ideal gift for children and adults alike.

190 pages ▪ 5 1/2 x 8 1/4 ▪ 21 b/w illustrations ▪ ISBN 0-7818-0717-4 ▪ $12.50hc ▪ (787)

The Little Mermaid and Other Tales

Hans Christian Andersen

This beautiful collection of 27 stories from the Danish master of fairy tales, Hans Christian Andersen, whisks the reader to magical lands, fantastic voyages, romantic encounters and adventures. Children and adults alike will enjoy timeless favorites including "The Little Mermaid," "The Emperor's New Clothes," "The Little Matchgirl," and "The Ugly Duckling." Stunningly illustrated throughout, this is a near replica of the first American edition of the collection.

508 pages ▪ 6 1/8 x 9 1/4 ▪ illustrations throughout ▪ ISBN 0-7818-0720-4 ▪ $19.95hc ▪ (791)

SCANDINAVIAN LANGUAGES

Hippocrene Children's Illustrated Swedish Dictionary English-Swedish/Swedish-English

- for ages 5 and up
- 500 entries with color pictures
- commonsense pronunciation for each Swedish word
- Swedish-English index

Hardcover: 94 pages ▪ 8 1/2 x 11 ▪ ISBN 0-7818-0822-7 ▪ $14.95hc ▪ (57)

Paperback: 94 pages ▪ 8 1/2 x 11 ▪ ISBN 0-7818-0850-2 ▪ $11.95pb ▪ (665)

Swedish-English/English-Swedish Dictionary and Phrasebook
Julie Hansen and Dick Nilsson
This dictionary and phrasebook is an essential resource for visitors to the land of Ingmar Bergman, Ikea, ABBA, the Nobel Prizes, Absolut Vodka, and Pippi Longstocking. A pronunciation guide and a grammar section ensure that users understand the structure of Swedish, while important contextual information will help travelers avoid embarrassing moments! The two-way dictionary totals 3,000 entries, and the phrasebook contains more than 20 sections ranging from introductions to shopping to weights & measures (with conversion chart).
3,000 entries ▪ 152 pages ▪ 3 3/4 x 7 1/2 ▪ ISBN 0-7818-0903-7 ▪ $11.95pb ▪ (228)

Swedish-English/English-Swedish Standard Dictionary
70,000 entries ▪ 804 pages ▪ 5 1/2 x 8 1/2 ▪ ISBN 0-7818-0379-9 ▪ $19.95pb ▪ (242)

Hippocrene Children's Illustrated Norwegian Dictionary English-Norwegian/Norwegian-English
- for ages 5 and up
- 500 entries with color pictures
- commonsense pronunciation for each Norwegian word
- Norwegian-English index

94 pages ▪ 8 x 11 1/2 ▪ ISBN 0-7818-0887-1 ▪ $11.95pb ▪ (165)

Norwegian-English/English-Norwegian Concise Dictionary
10,000 entries ▪ 599 pages ▪ 4 x 6 ▪ ISBN 0-7818-0199-0 ▪ $14.95pb ▪ (202)

Mastering Norwegian
Erik Friis
183 pages ▪ 5 1/2 x 8 1/2 ▪ ISBN 0-7818-0320-9 ▪ $14.95pb ▪ (472)

Finnish-English/English-Finnish Concise Dictionary
12,000 entries ▪ 411 pages ▪ 3 1/2 x 4 3/4 ▪ ISBN 0-87052-813-0 ▪ $11.95pb ▪ (142)

Danish-English/English-Danish Practical Dictionary
32,000 entries ▪ 601 pages ▪ 4 3/8 x 7 ▪ ISBN 0-87052-823-8 ▪ $16.95pb ▪ (198)

All prices subject to change without prior notice. **To purchase Hippocrene Books** contact your local bookstore, call (718) 454-2366, or write to: HIPPOCRENE BOOKS, 171 Madison Avenue, New York, NY 10016. Please enclose check or money order, adding $5.00 shipping (UPS) for the first book and $.50 for each additional book.